Cover Picture:
Hokah, Minnesota from the top of Mt. Tom
Circa 1940

Treadmill to Eternity:

An Engineer's Trudge Through Seventy
Years of the Twentieth Century

Richard J. Reilly

Copyright © 2018 Richard J. Reilly
All rights reserved.
ISBN13: 9781545197905
ISBN10: 1545197903

Other books by the author

Tell Me A Story:
46 Short stories from five continents

The Hush House Affair:
The chronology of a $49 million government contract

Marketing To The Government:
College course textbook with Keith Aakre

CONTENTS

Chapter		Page
1	In The Beginning: Genealogy and Such	1
2	Growing Up In A Small Town	15
3	College And University Years	39
4	Breakfast Cereal and Big Balloons	56
5	California Living	75
6	Northrop Aircraft	82
7	Back To Minnesota	106
8	Honeywell Aeronautical Division	112
9	Honeywell Military Products Research	124
10	The Lecture Circuit	142
11	Fired (Well, Sort Of)	164
12	Cytec Development Inc.	169
13	ADC Magnetic Controls	184
14	Dark Days And Saviors	191
15	Hush House	208
16	Cuyuna Corporation	221
17	NASA Contract	224
18	Lake Aircraft	235
19	Tsunami	241

CONTENTS 2

Chapter		Page
20	Grumman X29	245
21	Seabird Aviation Australia	248
22	Thrust Measurement	257
23	Kavouras Inc.	273

LIST OF FIGURES

	Page
Parents Marriage Certificate	2
Mother's College Graduation	3
Grandmother Olson Holding Me	5
Olson Family Homestead	6
Homestead Barn	6
Hokah Store	9
Postmaster's Convention 1940	10
Family Home, Hokah	11
Map of Ireland And Claremorris Region	12
Grandparents Marriage Certificate	13
Dad Watering 1912 Ford	14
Hokah, Minnesota With the Lake Intact	16
First Home	17
Squirrel Hunting With Jack	22
17 Pound Catfish	24
Reilly Homestead	32

FIGURES 2

	Page
Skyhook Launching	58
Scientific Load On Parachute	60
Pillow Balloon Launch	63
Grab Bag Double Tow String	65
Grab Bag Landing Site	66
First Home (California)	76
Flowers On Nutwood Street	77
Easter Dinner	78
A Little Bureaucratic Abuse	79
RJR and Tim, Inglewood 1956	81
NASA Ames 12 ft. Pressure Tunnel	85
9:1 Body In NASA Ames 12' Tunnel	86
Boundary Layer Transition Made Visible	87
Wing/Body Intersection Model	88
Lockheed F94 Fitted With Glove	93
Tim and Herman, Brooklyn Center	107

FIGURES 3

	Page
Vacant Lot 1759 Venus	108
The start of excavation	108
The basement is in	108
The sticks begin to go up	108
Building The Wall	110
The Red Hat	110
Satellite Supersonic Control Thruster	113
Pressure Ratio Transducer	114
Space Simulator Model	117
Space Cabin Interior	117
Earth Path Indicator Model	120
The Specification Globe	122
Mercury Capsule Instrument Panel	123
Bi-stable Fluid Amplifier	125
Induction Fluid Amplifier	126
Vortex Angular Rate Sensor	128

FIGURES 4

	Page
Jet Attachment To Round Cylinder	131
VDT Airfoil Patent	131
VDT Installed On Beechcraft M18	132
Stable Flight VDT To Trim Dead Engine	133
Early Fluidic Logic	135
Modular Construction	136
Munition Plugged Primer Sensing	137
Page From Brochure	138
Pipeline Magazine Cover	140
Shutdown Annunciator	140
Gas Turbine Startup/Shutdown Annunciator	141
Villa Monastero	145
Fermi Room (Old Chapel	145
Main Entrance of Villa Monestero	146
Tempelhof Air Terminal	153
New Church	156

FIGURES 5

	Page
New Church Interior	156
Heliot and Author	162
Aerotrain Prototype	170
La Defense Grande Arche	180
Vec Drive/Control Chain	180
Data Logging Patent	181
Data Card Embossing Device	183
Von Karman Vortex Street	195
Multiple Karman Streets	196
Barge After Launching	198
Barge Launch	198
Coal Gasification	201
Phil Klass Windshear Article	206
Individual Muffler	213
Hush House	213
High Temperature Probe C	234

FIGURES 6

	Page
Wing Root Flow	236
Intersection Flow	237
Plot Of Speed vs Power	237
Tsunami	242
Tsunami Airborne	242
New Inlet	243
Grumman Bearcat	243
Northrop F-5	246
Grumman X-29	246
X-29 Crew	247
Sentinel Original Inlet	249
Tuft-Testing	250
New Wing / Pod Fairing	251
With A Little Paint	252
Seeker At Work	253
David Eyre & The Author	254

Figures 7

	Page
New Iraqi Air Force	255
Statistical Normal Distribution	262
Business Card Array	277
Mobile X-band Radar	280
Six-Foot Portable Radar	280
14 foot Radar Yoke Design	281
10 and 14 Foot Radar Yokes	282
Experimental Power Supply	283
Radar Tower Placement	284
Setting On Concrete Ballast	285
Catwalk Placement	285
Radar Dish In Place	286
Radome Placement	286
Completed Radar Tower	287

ACKNOWLEDGMENT

I must express my appreciation to the late Richard Grantges whose years of encouragement finally led me to "write this stuff down."

PREFACE

I never anticipated writing an autobiography. Autobiographies are for royalty, politicians, celebrities or persons of notable accomplishment. For someone who just arose every morning to walk on life's treadmill, autobiography seemed a self aggrandizement.

About 25 years ago I met Richard Granges, a retired research engineer, who spent his professional life with Bell Laboratories. 'The Labs' were the lauded research arm of the telecommunications consortium, AT&T, before government edict broke it into discrete companies. Dick and I had many common interests: politics and technology to name two. We met over the internet, where he engaged in email political fisticuffs with a liberal adversary. Later, we began to exchange experiences in the research domain.

I visited his home in Northern Minnesota to attend a July fourth organ concert performed by a nationally-known organist, playing a large electronic organ that Dick designed and constructed as a centerpiece for his retirement home. The event was an annual gift for neighbors and friends.

During this time I was traveling extensively between Washington, DC, Edwards Air Force Base in California and Europe. My experiences mixed technology and politics, which fascinated Grantges. Often his closing line in an email exchange would be:

"Reilly, you've got to write this stuff down; your son and grandchildren will thank you someday." While I'm uncertain of lasting family interest, my meager knowledge of my parents' earlier lives left a void in mine, so I began to write small pieces on my life experiences: in airplanes, waiting in air terminals and evenings in hotels. What follows is not an organized autobiography but rather a chronological assembly of these past efforts.

Richard J Reilly
May 2019

INTRODUCTION

This compendium of an engineer's life in the last half of the 20th century is not intended as an autobiography but rather a recounting of mostly professional and business events lodged in memory during a 50-year engineering career. In the assessments of family and friends I have lived and unusual life. I didn't think it unusual at the time, and my employment diversity may portend the future for engineers, in some ways.

I began along the accepted path: education and engineering jobs with large companies, potentially leading to retirement and a 'gold-atch' lunch with friends and colleagues. After about 18 years in an orderly apprenticeship with General Mills Inc, Northrop Aircraft Company and Honeywell, Inc., I drifted into a consulting role with many clients ranging across five continents and 16 countries.

My clients were governmental:
    NASA Dryden Flight Research Center
    AGARD, a technical division of NATO

Major Companies such as:
    Computing Devices Canada
    Yamatake-Honeywell Japan
    United Technologies Research
    Fairchild Camera and Instrument

Smaller companies:
    Aero Systems Engineering
    Brown-Minneapolis Tank
    Casey Copters, Canada
    Seabird Aviation Australia
    Kavouras Inc.

Some of these relationships were short – weeks to months – while several lasted many years and ran concurrently:
    Aero Systems Engineering 5 years

Computing Devices Canada 9 years
Seabird Aviation 15 years
NATO 4 years
Kavouras Inc. 18 years

The latter evolved into an unusual relationship. Eventually I was provided an office with all the amenities such as a receptionist and telephone answering service for contact, wherever I might be. There was no charge for these courtesies, only an admonition to:

"Make some time available for us from time-to-time."

These 'times' were well received and were often accompanied with a package of business cards carrying the title of Vice President of whatever function was appropriate for the current assignment.

But not all was a wonderful life. During my corporate employment I was fired twice: once a 'sort-of' and the other a genuine '*we no longer require your services.*' In the first, an assignment began to take on an odor of fraud. When I sought relief from these duties, I was offered a promotion in another, geographically-distant division. The East Coast was never my favorite region.

In the second, the company's chief financial officer called me into his office to tell me how pleased he was with the year-end financial data due to changes I made in the product line. Three hours later the company President called to tell me my services were no longer required. Both incidents are covered in detail in what follows.

My somewhat chaotic professional life was made possible by the advent of the jet airplane and in later years, the personal computer. An early morning departure from a Minnesota base made it possible to meet with people on the east, west or gulf coasts and return home the same day. Two or three day trips to Europe became routine, but I managed to be home almost every weekend. My wife, Betty, made all this possible with her self-sufficiency in handling the problems of life around home.

DEDICATION

I dedicate this volume to my wife, Betty, whose support and competent self-sufficiency made my professional life possible

Treadmill to Eternity

1

In The Beginning

Life sometimes seems to be a series of random events. Time, people, places and events intersect in wondrous ways to construct a life ... there must be a plan.

* * *

I almost didn't get here. Mother and Dad married in 1925, when she was 39 and he 44. I had a sister, stillborn several years before me. Her death was attributed to Mother's having fibroid, uterine tumors. At the time the standard treatment for fibroid tumors was a hysterectomy; however, Mother insisted she was going to succeed with a live birth. My parents consulted an old Norwegian doctor, Gunner Gunderson, who was regarded as some what of a local miracle-man. Gunderson ran a clinic bearing his name in La Crosse, Wisconsin. He claimed – despite general opinion of 'Doubting Thomases' – to have once removed fibroid tumors from a woman who later conceived and bore several children. The operation was regarded as bearing significant risk, but my Mother insisted on giving it a try, so I arrived in 1930 and have lived without much in the way of physical problems for 89 years.

Mother

Mother, Julia Olson, was born in 1886 the daughter of O.U. (Ole) Olson and Hannah Breitenfield. Chronologically, she was near the middle of a group of nine brothers and sisters. She attended college, a so-called 'Normal School,' the approximate equivalent of today's teacher's college. She and my Dad met when she became Principal of the Hokah Public Schools, and taught the elementary grades.

My ParentsMarriage Csertificate

After she married my Dad she suffered much, but I wasn't aware of it. She was not well accepted in a closed family of traditional Irish culture. Dad's two maiden sisters, Mary and Nell, exerted an iron-fisted force in this regard. As a family, we were never invited to the old family homestead near the church and school, in the lower part of town. I didn't think this unusual because Mother never complained. I was the only child from a family of nine on my father's side of the family. I was treated dotingly and too young to be attuned to family friction.

Mother had more than a little talent for art. I recall her as an avid reader and a stickler for the English language. I still rail at the television newsreaders who talk about 'wite' snow and the second month of the year as 'Febuary.' Mother insisted I pronounce the 'h' in white, February contained two 'r-s.' and pumpkin two 'p-s.' She also did a bit of writing now and then.

College Graduation

About once a year, Mother was enlisted by the 'locals' to put on what were called 'home talent plays' she wrote in entirety, cast with local talent and produced either in the parish hall of St. Peter's Church, or later in the city auditorium. The latter was built during the depression by the WPA (Works Projects Administration), a government funded program that offset the 25% unemployment of 'The Great Depression.' I remember spending many long nights napping on a pile of winter coats, while practice sessions and rehearsals went on late into the night.

In the 1930s, the great depression limited available entertainment in a small town to radio and a rare movie. My Dad and I seldom missed the weekly programs of Fred Allen, Bob Hope, Amos 'n Andy and Red Skelton (Skeleton, as I called him). The home talent plays were a welcome diversion and drew packed houses for two weekend evenings.

There were always many books around the house, and I remember my Mother's reading and writing reviews for a 'study club,' as book clubs were then known. My favorite spot in the house was in front of a heat outlet in our dining room. It also contained a bookshelf packed with the volumes of the "Standard American Encyclopedia."

From a young age I perused it's maps and pictures. Later, when I was able to read, I became fascinated with the many maps these books contained. At an early age I had a pretty good concept of the world and its political divisions. I developed a gut-level fascination with maps, which persists today, the result of traveling much of the world.

A few years ago, while visiting a realtor's open house, I brushed brush back a tear when I saw a few of those dark blue, "Standard American" volumes, with their decorative gold lettering, being used as library props. They may have been garage sale bargains or worse, rescued from a dumpster; *sic transit gloria mundi*.

In late summer 1942, Mother became seriously ill with colon cancer. Dad insisted she be treated at the Mayo clinic in Rochester, Minnesota. There followed a series of trips to Rochester, where the surgery was performed, and Mother was hospitalized for a week or more. Dad and I stayed in a rooming house across the street from St. Mary's Hospital, so we could visit frequently. Motels were not the common traveler's abode they are now, and Rochester residents, who lived near Mayo Clinic facilities and hospitals, rented rooms for welcome cash. The depression was ending, but the recovery induced by mobilization for World War II just begun.

Mother came home with a colostomy, and just after Christmas of 1942 she returned to Mayo to have her colon reconnected to the large intestine. Dr. Charles Mayo, the son of the Clinic's founder, did all the surgeries. Nevertheless, Mother's health continued to deteriorate and she joined the 'innumerable caravan' on May 19, 1943 at age 57.

Mother's last months gave the Reilly family a chance to redeem the difficult times they visited on her. Soon after she returned from her second surgery in Rochester, we all moved into the family homestead 'in town' as opposed to our own home 'across the lake.' In a turnabout of monumental proportions, my Aunt Mary, a matriarch of sorts and almost eighty, nursed my mother day and night to the end. The family homestead became our home through my teenage years until I departed for college.

Mother's Roots

Although genealogy is not one of my intensive interests, someone who follows me may be inclined to explore his/her lineage. For those I'll present a brief discussion of my grandparents, recalling what little I've been told about them – I knew only my maternal grandmother – to give someone interested in familial roots a place to start.

Mother was born to Ole U. Olson Jr. and Hannah Breitenfield. I know little about Hannah – I knew her as 'Grandma' – although she lived with us for several years prior to her death in about 1933 or 34. She immigrated from Germany, and I believe she was 84 when she passed on. I recall Hannah fondly as a friendly, caring old woman who was my great defender in time of trouble.

Grandmother Olson Holding Me

When my Dad would threaten to spank me for some transgression, she would always have some ready excuse. I still recall one of these incidents when her well of excuses ran dry, and the best she could come up with was:

"Butch, (Dad's nickname) it's Sunday."

Ole Jr. was the son of Ole Olson Oppsal, who immigrated to the United States in 1845. The 'Oppsal' was long a family question mark until my cousin, Carol Olson Wiley and her husband, Robert, retained a professional searcher to explore the family background. He explained so many Ole Olsons immigrated to the U.S. in the mid-1800s that many were assigned a surname based on the village of origin in Norway, in his case Oppsal, southwest of Oslo in southern Telemark province. What little I know of Ole Olson comes from

Olson Homestead

memories of the old farm near Cashton, Wisconsin and from one of Mother's cousins, who was a collector of family lore. He recalled Ole as a rather tall, imposing figure and bore a neighborhood/regional reputation for wisdom and authority. Neighborly disputes were sometimes settled by calling Ole Olson to adjudicate. Further, he was also of independent nature and even shunned insurance for his property saying,

"If they can take the risk, I can take the risk."

Mother was born and grew up in the old Olson homestead, a modest house on sloping rural setting near Cashton, Wisconsin. The entrance from the porch opened to a large kitchen with a dining room beyond. In my time, the barn, down-slope from the house, was a much more imposing structure, and I enjoyed playing in the haymow as a child.

Homestead Barn

Dad

Dad was born in 1881 and as was Mother, into a family of nine. His father and mother, Edmund and Maria and their first child, John, emigrated from Ireland in 1867 during the economic chaos following the Potato Famine of 1846 – 1850. The famine killed an estimated 1.5 million Irish and left the country devastated for decades. Arriving in America in 1867, two years after the Civil War ended, they passed through Ellis Island in New York and settled in Minnesota, where he found work on a railroad section gang earning 50 cents per day.

Dad was next to the youngest of the family. I know little of his younger years except for his telling me he didn't much care for school. When he began 'playing hooky,' (skipping school) his father terminated his education in the fourth grade. He was then assigned to working on the family farm with his older brothers Ed and Mike. There were no buildings on the farm except a small shack for shelter and sleeping. It was located about five miles out of the town of Hokah in a region known as 'up on The Ridge,' a hilly area west of town. As I recall, the size of the plot of ground was 80 acres and the remains of the shack were weathering away in my time. The brothers worked the land, stayed in the shack during the week and returned to the family homestead in town for the weekend. In my time, Dad rented the land to an adjacent farmer, and I sometimes used the wooded portion for squirrel hunting.

Dad was no dumbbell, despite his aversion to school and early termination of his formal education. During his younger years he moved to northwestern Iowa, where he managed grain elevators in small towns such as Fonda and Storm Lake. These facilities were owned by large, national 'commission companies,' and he evaluated and purchased grain and livestock from local farmers. Subsequently, he arranged to sell and transport these products to commercial centers in Chicago, Kansas City or St. Louis. In going through some old letters and papers, I found a letter from a large commission company offering Dad a new position in a small, western Iowa town in 1910.

In these days, when a job offer often paints a glowing attraction of a new community with its sports teams, arts and cultural amenities, I find the letter amusing: two roads crossing … hmm. It is framed, so it can't be copied easily, but I duplicated it below as well as possible, including the errors in grammar and punctuation and the strange formatting: a kind of 'stream of consciousness' flow. Dad would have been about 29 years old at the time of this writing.

* * *

Neola Elevator Company

GENERAL OFFICES: 205 LA SALLE STREET
ROOM 701
CHICAGO, ILL

Jefferson, Ia. 7/11/ 10.

Mr. P.R. Reilly
Hokah, Minn.
Dear Mr. Reilly,

Just got your letter this morning, have not been in Jefferson since the morning I sent the messages.the station I have in mind for you is our Herndon station.lumber grain and coal.and is kept open the year around.think you will like the place while it is not a very large place there is always some thing doing, as the two roads cross there.wish you could get on the ground as soon as possible.as the party which is there now has bought a house of his own and wants to get started.hope the eye is alright by this time.

Yours truly,

(Signed)

G.M. Delin

* * *

Hokah and the Store

As a result of his close associations with shipping and the railroads during about ten years of working in the grain business, Dad developed an intense interest in railroading, which never died. Railroading was a dangerous business around the turn of the 20th century, perhaps the equivalent of the airline business in the 1930s and 40s. A career with the railroads was discouraged by the family, so Dad never pursued his dream. He succumbed to family pressure around 1913 and returned to Hokah to run the family grocery store, Reilly & Reilly, along with his sister Nell. I think his disappointment over railroading was a major factor in his later acquiescence to my endeavors in the aviation industry, neither encouraged nor discouraged.

The photograph below shows the old store building in about 1935. Note the post in the foreground with rings for tying horses. My uncle, Mike Reilly, is at the left wearing a straw hat, Dad is at the left

Uncle Mike, Dad, H. Houser Aunt Nell About 1937,
(note curbside post for tying horses)

on the step along with Howard Houser, a family friend visiting from Dayton, Ohio and my Aunt Nell. The time is approximate; Houser's visit and the move of Post Office into the store building occurred about 1935. I don't recall hearing how the family entered the grocery business.

The US Postal Service

About 1934, the job of Postmaster opened in Hokah. Dad took the required Civil Service Exam and qualified; he was appointed to

Postmaster's Convention 1940

the job, which he held until his 70th birthday in 1951.

Physically, the Post Office was incorporated into the store building, when Dad became Postmaster, and the relocation was the beginning demise of the grocery business. Serving the postal customers came first, and the grocery business dwindled to a few old reliable customers, who persisted to the end (1951).

Despite the relaxed vision of running a post office in a small, sleepy town, it was a rather demanding business. Dad arrived at the office at 7:00 AM every day including Saturday, after a half-mile walk from home. During winter months he would start a fire in a big, round, iron stove that heated the building. Soon, a carrier who brought the mail from the railroad depot, arrived with the morning's load. Locked bags were opened, the contents sorted and delivered to individual, combination-locked boxes, rented by postal patrons. All to be ready for opening the business day at 8:00 AM.

Closing time was 6:00 PM except for Saturday, when he closed at 1:00 PM, theoretically. However, a farmer in town for weekend shopping would be served on request, since the store remained open until 9:00 on Saturday night. Early mornings and late nights were the pattern of business in mid-century. Dad would rotate in his grave if he could see what has become of his beloved postal service. 'Service' real meaning to him.

Some Family Odds 'n Ends

After reading a bit about the Irish Potato Famine and the destitute condition of the Irish immigrants to the U.S., it appears the family had done well by the turn of the century. The old house, on main street northeast of town (Dad's notation), was set on a plot of ground about a half acre in size. There was a barn northwest of the house that housed horses and a cow or two, and they also kept a few chickens, judging from old pictures.

Family Home, Hokah

In my time, a large garden was still planted in the spring. We had abundant produce for the summer and root crops stored for winter, a longstanding family tradition. The family owned the farmland by 1891, when Dad was banished from school to work on the farm. So, from nothing in 1867, Grandfather Reilly, in about 24 years, was quite well established considering they raised a family of nine children.

Whatever was accumulated in the way of worldly goods must have been the result of frugal living. While my Grandfather started out as a laborer at 50 cents per day, he advanced to the position of Section Boss for the railroad maintenance section encompassed by the Hokah region. It is improbable that even the supervisory position would allow for any grand life style.

As with many of the Irish immigrants, he had no special skills. Below is replication of a hand written letter of recommendation written by his parish priest at the time he left Ireland. It speaks of his limited skills. Note the varied spelling of both the surname and the given name.

* * *

I know bearer Edmund Riley a native of the parish of Kilcommon, Co. Mayo ... well He is a remarkably well conducted young man. He is a Roman Catholic & the son of a Roman Catholic. He is married for the last 12 months. I feel much pleasure in recommending him to the attention of any person who may require an honest hard-working laborer –

Claremorris

Thomas MacDonagh Co. Mayo

R. C. C April 16 1867

* *

Map of Ireland And Claremorris Region

In The Beginning: Genealogy And Such 13

I have done some superficial explorations of County Mayo, specifically Kilcommon and Claremorris, the two proper names in the note of recommendation of Father Mac Donagh. Searches of the internet regarding Kilcommon, write it as 'Kilcommon (Erris),' an arcane barony in the northwest portion of County Mayo. However, Fr. Mac Donagh gives his parish location as Claremorris, which is in the south central part of the county. The map above is an enlargement of the small green block on the inset map of Ireland. Arrows point to the towns of Claremorris and Hollymount.

The district of Hollymount is listed on the marriage certificate of my paternal grandparents (following page). This document was discovered by Joe Cummins, a distant relative connected to the Reillys, through the family of Maria Solon, my maternal grandmother. Cummins mentions the Kilcommon associated with our families, no longer exists but was located just north of Hollymount, so this is the probable location of the Kilcommon mentioned in Fr. Mac Donagh's letter of recommendation.

Grandparent's Marriage Certificate

Loose Ends

Despite meager beginnings, it appears the family had some fancy horses in addition to the horses used to work the farm. Dad would reminisce with pride about having "a couple of nice Buck-skins", or a "beautiful pair of Sorrels," to pull a buggy, or cutter in the winter. By about 1912, they had a car; sometimes two cars appear in pic-tures, but I don't know whether both belonged to the family.

H. Houser, Dad, Uncle Ed: about 1910 based on Houser's age

In his late 80s, when the time came for the passing of the torch, Dad was reviewing the family finances with me, trying to decide what to do with the old family homestead. He disconnected from the immediate conversation for a moment, gazed off into the near-distance and said,

"Yes, we might have done quite well if it hadn't been for having to keep Ed out of jail." I didn't pursue the point; the pain was evident. His brother, Ed, ran the bank in Hokah for a time and perhaps the bank encountered financial difficulties during the Great Depression of the 1930s. As a result, Ed may have encountered some sort of legal jeopardy; we'll never know what happened and just as well perhaps.

2

Growing Up In a Small Town, 1930 1940

It was the time of the Great Depression. Unemployment rode the range unfettered in small-town America. It was a hardscrabble existence for many, but I was too young to understand life was tough.

* * *

We had them all in Hokah: a spectrum of 'normal' people spiced a millionaire inventor who devised the first hydraulically controlled accessory implements for farm tractors and sold the patents to Ford Motor Co., the village drunk and an old widow living out her life on welfare.

My memory of her is vivid. Her home was an almost upgraded chicken coop with a dirt floor, but she was safe from the indignities of institutional living. I can still recall the clay dirt floor, polished smooth by years of footsteps, and the smell of the smoky wood fire as I delivered her groceries. My father would toss in a few extras into her order. It was the good part of the Depression: almost everyone shared with a neighbor.

The spectrum was filled out with a variety of normal people: barber, butcher, businessmen and the general run of folks we all know

Hokah, Minnesota With the Lake Intact

today. A few, regarded as a bit off-center, were tolerated and received benevolent assistance as the need arose; it was the bright side of living in a small town.

Then there was Sammy Kirk, homeless I guess, who scraped a living from doing odd jobs and hauling heavy items about town with his wagon and a single horse. He had an excellent tenor voice and as they drove up Main Street he entertained his horse to the strains of "You Are My Sunshine," a favorite melody. Two teenage pranksters hanged him one summer afternoon. They fashioned and fitted a noose, tied it to beam in an abandoned barn, kicked the stool from under his feet and watched as he struggled for life. His legendary demonstrations with feats of strength may have gone too far, but more about this later. I'm getting ahead of my story.

Early Memories

My first recollection was the talcum powder; it was in Dr. Gallagher's office, ten miles away in La Crosse, Wisconsin. He was almost a part of the family, always addressed as "Doc," and made house calls when we needed him, regardless of the distance. I suspect my problem was over-pronation, the flat feet that would trouble me somewhat for the rest of my days. I must have been fascinated by the mess Doc made by sprinkling powder across the floor of his office for me to make diagnostic tracks. I remember nothing else about it, just the powder and the tracks. From my memory of the tracks and the footprints, I was perhaps one and a half or two years old.

My first home was a small house 'across the lake,' about a mile from the town center. There was no lake in my time; the dam across Thompson Creek, which formed Lake Como, was washed out by a major flood somewhere about the time I was born. I have vague recollections of hearing motorboats as I was dozing-off for my afternoon naps.

The picture below shows our house in 1998 and isn't much changed in appearance from when we lived there 75+ years ago. The garage in the background didn't exist and there was no propane tank; a wood-burning furnace heated the house. In my time, we would be looking beneath a row of large elm trees defining the lot line from the immediate foreground, parallel to the long side of the house and disappearing off the left side of the picture.

We had neither running water nor a flush toilet. Water for washing was roof runoff, piped from the house to a concrete cistern with a manual pump – 'soft water' courtesy of nature. Dad brought drinking water from an artesian well. It flowed year-around from a pipe in the remaining wall of an old creamery along the road from town to home; I recall it as having a wonderful flavor, tinged with iron. The small pond created by the flowing well also provided a continuous supply of tasty watercress we enjoyed as fresh salad greens in season.

First Home

As I grew a bit older, one of my jobs was to carry drinking water from a well on the property of my uncle Ed, who owned a large house about 100 yards away. In summer I used my red wagon, in winter my sled. I fitted each with an arrangement to hold a five-gallon can of the sort farmers use to store milk. While none of this seemed unusual to me at the time, I now wonder if our modest house was related in any way to financial problems of my Uncle Ed. He ran the local bank and encountered some difficulty related to the Great Depression. The family rallied round to help him cope with his problems.

In about 1935, when my father became the town's Postmaster, finances may have eased a bit. During the summer of 1940, when I was ten, Mother and Dad decided I needed a study and work room, and we needed the luxuries of hot and cold running water in the house. The roof dormer in the photograph was added, and I recall the delight of having a place to set up my electric train and leave it in place, rather than have to take it down a few weeks after Christmas each year. However, the best-laid plans often go astray as I learned at a young age: On December 7, 1941 World War II began. Able-bodied workmen went off to war, materials were scarce and plans for a new well and running water came to a halt.

In the midsummer of 1942, mother was diagnosed with colon cancer, and when she passed away in May 1943 life changed for me. Dad and I moved into the old family homestead 'in town,' the life-long home of my two aunts, Mary and Nell.

The Growing Years

In the years prior to World War II, Hokah was a small town; a sign on the edge of town announced: 'Population 449.' Now it is somewhat larger. Life revolved around the general store that sold both groceries and dry goods. I recall at a young age accompanying my Dad on weekly trips to La Crosse to purchase stock for the store. He bought most supplies at Gateway Grocery, where an inside salesman, named 'Casey,' gave me candy for pronouncing 'Philadelphia' correctly. Before the post office days, there was the delivery of telephone-ordered groceries to individual homes, often daily. Dad had a Model A Ford panel truck that served both as a general hauler and our personal transportation.

The phone-in orders assured everyone in town knew what you were having for supper; it was supper then, not dinner. These were the days of telephone 'party lines.' There were several subscribers on most lines, and you identified your call by a coded ring, a combination of 'longs' and 'shorts.' I still hear in memory the two 'shorts' at the store and four 'shorts' at the house. The telephone from the house now resides in our basement.

Calls were directed by a plug-type switchboard, operated by Tootie Krunkenfeldt, who may have listened-in now and then and knew everything going on in town. She was an astonishing source of information – and information leakage.

I learned to drive at a very young age, sitting on my Dad's lap. Later, it was a big day when I learned to put the car in motion by slowly engaging the clutch. When I was seven, I was allowed to drive the Model A alone from home, 'across the lake,' to the store on Main Street for the first time. I can't remember why, but it was some sort of minor emergency or inconvenience being avoided. I remember the biggest challenge on this one-mile trip: the stop sign on the hill alongside Charlie Sauer's barber shop. I was too short to reach both the clutch and brake pedals simultaneously. Holding the Model A on the hill, engaging the clutch, dumping the brake and getting my right foot on the gas pedal, all without killing the engine, was difficult.

By age 10 or 11 I was doing the grocery delivery with the Model A, always being admonished to 'be careful.' This sort of thing would never be tolerated these days; however, the demands of the post office overwhelmed the grocery business, and the delivery task dwindled.

I recall the post office as being a consuming business. Dad's day started by 07:00. He distributed the morning mail brought from the railroad depot by Bill Fohl and his wife, Emma. Bill was known to take a sip of ripple now and then, and I think Emma, never out of sight, was along to keep him straight.

The ordinary mail came in great, gray canvas bags: the first class letters in a locked sack. Letters, separated from their individual bundles, were sorted into combination-lock boxes. – gold-colored doors with two black knobs and white numerals – rented on a quarterly basis by patrons. By 08:00 Dad opened the business windows: a small one for stamp sales and a larger one for money orders, parcels, etc. He closed at 6:00 and I recall napping on a pile of empty mailbags, waiting for closing time.

I have one vivid memory of the post office. On the day the local weekly newspaper, "The Hokah Chief" appeared, the teenage girls would rush in after school to get at their copy of the paper. It was a race to see who could set the combination on their mailbox most quickly. The object of all this: 'Pelie Garlie,' a two or three-liner appearing, as I recall, at the lower left-hand corner of the front page. It was often slightly naughty or racy, sometimes a double entendre. I never understood them, but they were a big deal with the high-school girls and set the place buzzing for a few minutes.

Christmas brought mailbags piled to the ceiling in the morning and even longer working hours. The whole family turned out to help handle the heavy volume. On Christmas Eve everyone collapsed, glad the rush was over. Betty doesn't understand why I don't make a big deal of Christmas. However, while growing up, Christmas Day was more of a relief than a day of celebration.

Being an only child I didn't have the spirited family life one may have in a family with several siblings. Betty, who had four siblings, will often say,

"Didn't you ever do this … or that?" I have to say,

"No," and she doesn't understand. There were neither board games nor sibling rivalries in my life. Being a sort of 'loner,' much of my life revolved around books, my dog, roaming the hills with my .22

rifle and set-line fishing in the Root River.

In my younger years, when we lived 'across the lake' or 'Brooklyn' as it was known by some, I had few playmates. Being separated from the main body of the town limited my contacts. I spent some play time with a neighbor, Don Walcker, although he was a couple of years younger than I. He lived next door to my uncle Ed's house.

The high point of many days came with an evening visit to the Louis Pilger home to get a gallon of fresh milk. I would often stay late, talking to Phillip Pilger, who, although much older than I, was also interested in airplanes. As I grew older, we built models and shared airplane books and magazines. My interest in airplanes became a career, and Phillip remained a good friend until he passed away a few years ago – about 2012.

I was also close to Louis Pilger, Phillip's father, who farmed a tract of land a mile or two from their house. Winter and summer he passed our house almost daily. I'd wait for him, and whenever I could I would join him on his horse-drawn wagon or sleigh. Looking back, I now regard him as some sort of saint; his patience was unlimited. He would let me ride to and from the fields on his wagon or sleigh, balance me on his knee while mowing hay and find a secure place for me on the seeder, corn planter or hay rake. I don't know how he made the time to accommodate a little kid, let alone why; he was a fine man.

When I was seven years old, my Dad bought me a gun, a bolt-action, .22 caliber, Winchester Model 67, single-shot rifle; I still have it. He taught me a few basics: 'always' and 'nevers.'

> Always carry it pointed toward the ground.
> Never point it a person, whether loaded or not.
> Never point it at anything you don't intend to shoot.
> Never trust the safety catch.
> Never lock the bolt until you're ready to fire.
> Always place the gun on the ground on the other side of a fence, before crossing yourself.

At about age eight, I was allowed to go alone into the wooded hills, overlooking our house, to hunt squirrels. My dog, Jack, and I spent much time in the hills after that. When I was lucky enough to get a squirrel, I was taught how to skin it out and prepare it for the table. I'm not sure everyone enjoyed the gamy meal, but it was a rule: if you kill it, you eat it.

This kind of gun training and experience gives me a different view of the current

Squirrel Hunting With Jack

controversy on guns. Unlike the shooting and shattering of aliens and 'bad guys,' as in video games, the killing of game was very real and final. There was no pushing 'RESET' and starting the game over for the squirrel; he wound up on my dinner plate. It was a real lesson in life ... and death and gun safety.

The Move 'To Town'

When 'home' became the old Reilly homestead, adjacent to St. Peter's School playground, the change in location also altered the pattern of my days. In summer, every morning began with leaping out of bed, getting dressed and going to the Root River to check my set-lines for what the night brought in the way of fish. Transportation was my bicycle, powered by my dog, Jack, a Collie /Shepherd mix of doubtful ancestry. I'd slide back on the rear fender of my bike, wind my fingers in the long hair of Jack's back, and we'd be off, barking all the way. Jack would pull me this way until he dropped. He was good for about 20 mph. for a while, then slowed to a fast walk after a mile or so, but the barking continued. He loved these runs.

I spent much of my time around the Root River. I did some conventional fishing, casting into the rapid current with artificial bait, but I don't recall catching much of anything. However, it set me up for life; I see little joy in fishing.

The real attraction in this part of town was the railroad depot, located adjacent to the riverbank. Ray Miller (Sr.), the Depot Agent, was the town telephone expert, clock repairer and just an all-around clever guy. He was knowledgeable in basic physics and was a patient teacher; he was an endless source elementary electrical lore. He taught physics by demonstration. For example, he illustrated how sound was transmitted in steel by placing an ear on the rail and listening to the rail-conducted 'clickety/clack' of a train miles away.

When the train came, you could put a penny on the rail and get it smashed into an oval. The noon train was a diesel-electric, consisting of a lightweight locomotive and a combination mail-car/passenger accommodation. It was not heavy enough to do a good job on the pennies. A satisfactory job required a visit to the depot in the evening, when the freight came in. It was powered by a steam engine, belching black smoke and trailing a tender loaded with coal and water. The combination, followed by a string of freight cars, would crush a penny to a thin, knife-edged oval.

In the spring of the year, running a dozen or more set-lines in the Root River was almost a job. The lines needed tending twice a day, and between visits there was digging worms for bait. We most often caught Red Suckers, which were good to eat when caught in spring, while the water was cold. The occasional catfish was an event, and I once caught one that weighed-in at 17 pounds; most were smaller. Cabby's Cafe would buy them from us for preparation and serving to the boarding guests at the hotel. As I recall, Cabby gave us 5 cents per pound for Suckers, and I think he paid a little more for catfish.

17 Pound Catfishg

Set-line fishing was (and probably still is) illegal for adults, so it was a continual game of wits between those of us – Ray Feuerhelm was a frequent companion – who worked the set-lines and Jim Parrish, the regional Game Warden. He lived in Houston, an adjacent town, so his visits to our part of the river were irregular and unpredictable. I never met 'Old Jim,' as we called him, but he was regarded as a formidable adversary, and we never wanted to meet him. The trick to avoidance was hiding the line by placing its holding stake below the water level, while being careful to remember the surroundings so it could be located later. After the lines were in the water a few days, the attempt to hide the line's location was rather futile, because the river bank became so patted down by bare feet it looked as well-traveled as Highway 16. 'Old Jim' would look for the paths, snare the line with a hooked sapling and cut it loose.

After one of Old Jim's sweeps, it was back to John Ender's hardware store to get another ball of 'chalk line' – the same as used by carpenters to snap straight lines – and more hooks. Phil Buehler would help me find the fishing supplies and take my money. It was a big cash deal running less than a quarter for the entire rig, hooks and all. However, it represented a significant overhead expense for a five-cents-per-pound business operation.

During winter, I often ran a trap line and caught muskrats for a little pocket-money. The flooded areas, above the falls on Thompson

Creek, were shallow, weedy and dotted with a many rat houses. Rat routes were visible through the ice before first snowfall, and we set traps in the trails below the ice. Once caught, I skinned the hides for stretching and drying. I sent them to Sears-Roebuck in Chicago, which ran a fur-buying operation – yes the same Sears that sells hardware and appliances today. In the early 1940s, a muskrat hide sold for $3.00-$3.50, depending on its quality; a large, excellent pelt brought $4.00. Recently (2005), I saw an article citing the demise of fur trapping and noting muskrat hides were then worth between $3.00 and $4.00. This gives some idea of what has happened to the fur industry in the last 70 years. I didn't catch that many muskrats, but relative to today $3 was real money – by a factor of ten or more – and unlike the fishing set-lines, trapping was legal.

The hardware store was an interesting place to go and browse, looking at all the neat tools and things. Again, as with Lou Pilger, great patience was displayed as I cruised about, handling everything at least twice and dropping it once. Here in the city these days, the proprietor would either run me out of the store or watch with a big mirror or television monitor, to guard against shoplifting. However, in my growing years stealing anything was unthinkable.

No trip to the hardware was complete without stopping to watch Ed Rudesille resole shoes and doing other leather work in a corner of the store. I liked to watch as he skillfully stitched horse harnesses with a huge sewing machine; it drove a needle almost the diameter of my little finger. I always came away with a piece of scrap leather, which was prized in my boyhood world. I can't recall why, unless it was the pleasant, new-leather odor.

For boys, much of the growing-up entertainment in Hokah revolved around the hardware/building supply operations. When we were young, a gang of us would descend on Oscar Bernsdorf's lumber storage building, across from the Ford Garage. The lumber racks were great for climbing and playing hide and seek. It was fine place on a rainy day, and I can still recall the wonderful smell of the newly kiln-dried lumber.

When we tired of the lumberyard, it was across the street to Ben Ender's and later Neil Feuerhelm's, Ford Garage to get the latest brochures on the new cars. It was there I first learned about engines by watching Gus Radtke assembling a Ford V-8 engine after overhaul. He explained the function of piston rings and the critical dimensional tolerances required. He also warned of the dangers of the carbide generator used to produce acetylene for the welding torch.

Once in a great while, when Herb Wheaton was in a more relaxed mood, he'd invite us into the office of "The Hokah Chief" to see how he assembled the paper. Of course, most of the paper was in Herb's head, so the visible action was Bill Becker, pounding away on the Linotype machine. For those of you who think printing is done with computers and word processors, the Linotype is a gigantic typewriter that melts lead bars on one end and casts out little, lead letter-slugs, organized into words and lines, on the other. The individual lettered slugs formed the lines that put Herb's words on paper. Letter by letter they were assembled into the frames, which went into the printing press. The press stood idle except for the night before the weekly paper came out. Having written many proposals against deadlines in my professional life, I don't know how Herb and Bill lived with a weekly deadline from which there was no relief.

I recall Herb as being a bit more formal than the other businessmen in town, always impeccably dressed with his starched shirt, bow tie and straw hat.

Few of these learning experiences are available to the youth of today. Not only are people too busy to show and explain what they're doing; in many instances lawyers, liabilities and lawsuits have made it too dangerous and sometimes too costly for those who would share their knowledge with interested youth.

The World Outside a Town of 400

Sometime around the early 1940s, I traveled alone on the train to

Chicago, where I visited my namesake Uncle Dick and his family. His wife, my Aunt Marie, always made me feel at home and their sons, Robert and Edward, taught me all kinds of new and interesting skills, often wrapped up in model building of one sort or another. Bob built small electric trains and cars. Cousin Carol and I played "Battleship" endlessly, which still may be played with a computer program. It involves placement of virtual ships on a grid and targeted by blindly calling out coordinates on the grid and hoping one of the opponent's capital ships would be hit. This was great fun for me, because there was little game playing in a family of one.

In retrospect, one of the most important aspects of these trips were the days spent at 'the store.' Uncle Dick and his brother, my Uncle Ed Olson, were in the retail clothing and shoe business. It was here I encountered my first experiences with nationality and race. Phil, the resident tailor, was of Italian descent and spoke his own brand of English. Sam Easter, a black man, was the store's handyman. Sam, a benevolent gentleman, took me under his wing and we enjoyed a great time playing practical jokes on one another. Mr. Sam, as I referred to him, shaped my attitude toward other races at an early age.

At least once during these visits someone, often my cousin Bob, would take me to a Chicago Cubs game at Wrigley Field. As I grew a bit older and more experienced, I began to go to these games on my own, negotiating the street rail system, the 'L,' short for 'elevated.' It was a great confidence builder and established a foundation that allowed me to travel the world in later years without trepidation. Bob was also a fan of 'midget racing' – small, Indianapolis-style cars powered by an Offenhauser or a small-block Ford V-8 engine. Most of my visits included a night at the races at 'Soldier Field.'

These were great experiences for a kid from a town of 400.

Ken Jackson and His Machine shop

For my first mechanical education I again relied on small-town life. When I was about 13 (the outcome of World War II was still uncertain), Kenneth Jackson came to town and opened a machine shop. He built an attachment to a gas station just west of Tony Tschumper's Pure Oil Station near the 'Y' of Highways 16 and 44. Always fascinated with machinery, I started hanging out there. Among his many other talents, Ken was a great teacher and possessed a colorful vocabulary. He taught me how to operate a lathe and milling machine and to do some gas and electric welding, skills that served me well throughout my professional career.

During the war and for a few years thereafter, repair parts for farm machinery were unobtainable. I helped make replacement parts, and Ken also manufactured complete, rubber-tired, farm wagons. While we could machine almost any metal parts, new tires had gone to war. We went to Max's Auto Wrecking, in La Crosse, Wisconsin, to pick through great piles of scrapped tires and find those still usable for farm wagons. I learned to scrounge, repair and make-do.

Ken knew much about metallurgy. He was not formally trained, but he learned from experience and possessed outstanding recall. People from miles around would bring in large, cast-iron sprocket wheels from grain binders and other farm machinery, for welding. These large parts were unobtainable during the war and considered unrepairable by most. Welding circular cast iron parts often results in their shattering into many pieces as they cool. Cast iron can be welded successfully if one understands the problem and knows the proper procedure to relieve the internal stresses induced by localized heating required to join the broken parts.

Ken would bevel-grind the joints for welding, then arrange them on a sand bed in the correct position. Together we would heat the entire part to a glowing red using two acetylene torches. This might take a half-hour or more. At the proper temperature, which he would gauge by color and experience, the torches were extinguished, and he would quickly electric arc-weld the parts. Then it was my job to reduce the temperature of the part to room temperature by moving a single torch around the part and turning down the flame, little-by-little, a job of more than an hour. It was Ken's way of imitating the usual way of stress relief: using an oven. We always did these jobs at night because Ken didn't want others know how he did 'the impossible.' Although he may not have known much theory, he knew metals and metal working to a higher standard than some of my university instructors in later years.

Ken Jackson's machine shop was one of the more valuable experiences of my life. It gave me a feel for what could be done with machine tools, when combined with basic knowledge, persistence and understanding. It enabled me to 'one up' on people who would try to tell me what 'can't be done.' Being able to 'turn the handles' on metal working machines myself also allowed me to pull an engineering client out of a tight spot, when no other help was available.

You can imagine the surprise when someone wearing a suit and tie takes his turn at the machines late on a Saturday night. As the British might say,

"It just isn't done!" It was a sad day for me when Ken Jackson left Hokah to return to 'high work,' erecting large, steel-framed buildings during the postwar labor boom in New Mexico. I owe him much.

Growing up in Hokah in the 1930s and 40s provided valuable experience for life.

My First Real Job

The summer Ken Jackson left town I was 15 years old, then the legal age for certain types of employment. I saw an advertisement for a photo finisher at Moen's Photo Service in La Crosse, Wisconsin. Interested in photography, I had a 'Brownie' camera, as did many people. I knew 'developing' a film involved some chemistry and fluid baths, but this was about the extent of my knowledge. 'Real' summer jobs were not easy to find; de-tasseling and picking corn bordered on slave labor, and picking berries was for girls. Working in the photo business was somewhat appealing.

With summer vacation beginning, I hitchhiked the 10 miles to La Crosse one Friday, went to Moen's Photo – the major photographic shop in the area – and purchased a beginner's photo development kit. Back home, I read the instruction manual. Saturday, I built a panel in the basement of the old house to shut out the minimal light from a lone window. Sunday, after warning everyone not to turn on the light in the basement, I went to work. I prepared the developer, stop bath, fixing solution and the intermediate washes. I arranged all the containers, so I could identify them by feel. I spent about $.95 for the developing kit – maybe it was $1.95 – however, I didn't want to splurge the additional $.75 for a red light bulb, which would have enabled me to see what I was doing. I went through the processing in the dark. When I finished and turned on the lights, it was like magic: I had a negative strip with eight good images. I finished some of them by contact printing and was quite satisfied with the results.

The following morning, I again hitchhiked to La Crosse and presented myself to Bob Moen, the son of the company's founder, as a candidate for the job. Since I now knew all the terminology, I recall it as being a rather easy sell; I was hired at once for the unheard of sum of $.40 per hour. The experience taught me one could do an intensive, 'quick-study' and become usefully knowledgeable in a narrow band of skill. I still do it.

I worked the job for three months, hitchhiking the 10 miles to La Crosse and return every day, rain or shine. Rides often terminated at the East End of the bridge across the Mississippi River, so there was an additional four or five-block walk to the job; it was not much fun on a rainy day.

Along about midsummer, I began to pick up a consistent ride with the same man, several times a week. He commuted from Caledonia to La Crosse (about 25 miles), and eventually he became a daily catch, which improved my scheduling considerably. Eventually, he began waiting for me if I wasn't at my usual place when he passed through town. His name was Kern Ferris, a kind soul and a real class act. The ride home in the afternoon was always a random catch at the east end of the Mississippi River Bridge.

At the end of the summer, Bob Moen asked me to return the next year if I needed a job. The following summer, I was hired again as a photo finisher along with a salary of $.50 per hour. The third year I received a raise to $.60 per hour as a film inspector. My job involved removing developed film strips, hanging from a drying-conveyor, inspecting them and setting aside those negatives needing special print processing. As I recall, the extra $.10 was incremental compensation for the working conditions; working under the hot air dryer was not pleasant in a non-air-conditioned building.

After the dryer job, it was off to college and the end of my photo finishing days. Kern Ferris provided me outbound transportation for most of the three years at no charge; he was a kind, helpful acquaintance who passed through my life, gone but not forgotten.

Education

My total formal education prior to college was attending St. Peter's Catholic grade school and high school. Contrary to today's much sought small class size, class sizes were large and three grades were housed in one room, except for combined-grades one and two. This was a very fortuitous option for me since the classes were taught alternately; I was able to listen-in on the next grade's classes after completing my own work. As a result, the following year's work was easy for me. After the completion of my first year, I was promoted into the third grade. Socially, this turned out to be an unfortunate idea; it made me some sort of community oddball, and as an old Japanese aphorism says,

"The nail that stands up must be pounded down." Among other things, small towns can be cruel.

The high school turned out to be better than I thought it was at the time. I was envious of my peers, who were bused to a consolidated high school in Houston, an adjacent town 12 miles west. They took interesting classes such as wood shop and auto mechanics, while at St. Peter's I was stuck with many classical subjects such as Ancient History and Latin. A Notre Dame Sister, Sister M. Borgia, taught me advanced mathematics and even helped me on weekends after I was in college.

I hated Latin at the time. However, my life's work has required much writing – technical proposals, technical papers, even ghost writing for executives – and the two years of high school Latin has served me well in this area. It's a great foundation for English. I've traveled extensively over the years, and I could always get along in France, Italy or Spain with an English-to-local dictionary and my basics in Latin. All-in-all it was a great education in disguise.

Reilly Homestead

Geographically, St. Peter's was the utmost in convenience. The family homestead's front yard adjoined the school grounds, so the trip to school was about a one-minute run in an emergency.

The house was old, more than 100 years according to hearsay. I also uncovered some verifying artifacts while I did major reconstruction work on it during the wartime years of the early 1940s. Folklore said it was once been a hotel, which appeared possible because of its location in the lower part of town. It was conveniently near the railroad depot on the Root River, which bounded the north side of the town. In the photograph above our son, Tim, plays in the snow outside 'Grandpa's house.' The year is about 1960.

For a time, I slept in a large bedroom above the small bay window in the photo. Later I took up residence in the front porch on the right of the picture. The original, open porch was enclosed with windows all around; it was delightfully cool sleeping in summer. In the winter, a huge, old, leather-upholstered couch, surrounded on three sides by heavy, oaken back and arms, was piled high with quilts. I think I fancied myself as some sort of 'iron man' as I slipped under the quilts on below-zero nights. In later years, anticipating a late night out, an unlocked window offered convenient access without waking the household by climbing a squeaky stairway.

Looking back from today's vantage point, I was socially retarded compared with the youth of today. I never 'dated' during my high school years. My spare time, when not working at Jackson's machine shop or Moen Photo, was spent building airplane models and reading historical aviation lore.

Social interaction in a small town was a bit unusual. There were not enough people in a given age group to constitute a homogeneous age-set. My entire graduating class numbered nine, and several of those lived on farms, leaving a tiny group of age-related peers. As a result, an evening's social grouping might encompass young folks with broad age differences.

One or two of the older members had cars, and an evening out often took the form of packing and outlandish number of people into a car – nine in a Model A Ford Coupe with a rumble seat – and driving around to nowhere in particular.

A typical trip during wartime years, might mean a run to La Crosse to drive about, draining the hoses of gasoline pumps. They were often 'locked' by turning off electric power to the pump. Each hose produced about a quart of gasoline, so a large station would yield a gallon or more, no small event when gasoline was rationed to three gallons per week. While these social groups would be composed of both sexes, there was little or no pairing off; it was just one happy group.

With some urging from my family, I did take a classmate to the Senior Prom and dated her several times afterward. However, she was more experienced than I, dated older boys and had an appetite for places where I didn't want to go.

Odds 'n Ends

From here it was off to college. Small-town life had its pluses and its minuses, but it provided a breadth of experience impossible in today's economic enclaves. Anonymity was unknown in a community of 400; everyone knew who you were and what you were doing before even you knew. The plus side of this was the discipline it brought; if I was up to something untoward, my Dad knew about it before I returned home, so I approached my disciplinary boundaries with caution. However, my Dad bridled under the yoke of community curiosity. His admonition to me, as I went off to school, was:

"Whatever you do, settle in a community large enough, so not everyone knows your business." Despite the privacy limitations, the small-town environment was a positive influence. I was exposed to both rich and poor, farmers and craftsmen, the town drunk and the person who was a bit strange – as one old German neighbor put it:

"He's not crazy ... zakly, chust not reklar in the het.".

I was able to see firsthand the many ways there are to extract a living from a day's toil, sometimes from little or nothing. These experiences are missing from life in today's homogeneous, suburban communities.

Sammy Kirk

Oh yes, Sammy Kirk: Today I suppose he'd be called 'homeless,' but he seemed to get on all right. His material possessions amounted to the clothes he wore, his bedroll, an aging horse and a wagon he used in a meager, odd-job, hauling business. I don't know where he spent winter, but in temperate months, 'home' was a place under cover for his bedroll and the comfortable mattress of a hay storage bin at Deb Lee's stockyard. Likely, it was compensation for occasional hauling jobs, and I suspect food for his horse was part of his deal with Deb. He had a mellow, tenor voice and I can almost hear him still, seated at the front of his wagon, driving up Main Street and singing "You Are My Sunshine" to his horse.

Sammy was well over six feet tall and weighed perhaps 300 pounds; however, his rotund figure housed a large, powerful frame honed and hardened by heavy work. He was proud of his strength and would brace himself against a storefront while we teenagers took turns punching him in the stomach as hard as we could. He thought this to be great fun. It may have taken a bit of Heileman's brew to get into shape for these episodes, which usually occurred on Saturday nights.

He regarded himself as such a tough human being he once convinced a couple of teenagers to hang him by his neck in Joe Schnedecker's empty barn, near the Root River, just outside town. Taking a lead from Harry Houdini, Sammy warned the boys not to help him; he would free himself. After some difficulty fitting the noose around his ample neck, they kicked the low, supporting stool from under him. Luckily, the short drop wasn't sufficient to break Sammy's neck, and they watched as he struggled, finally hanging motionless without perceptible breathing. Soon, his eyes took on the fixed stare of a dog whose day is done. Frightened and desperate, the boys cut the rope and his great hulk crumpled to the floor. Too heavy for them to effect any real assistance, they left him for dead and ran.

Overcome with worry and convinced they would be charged with murder, they decided to hop the evening freight train out of town and disappear into the hobo world. That evening, as they waited to jump aboard the train, Sammy appeared walking across the Root River Bridge near the tracks, happily whistling, "You Are My Sunshine."

He died a few years ago in a nursing home, fittingly located in Harmony, Minnesota. At age ninety-something, Sammy yielded his proud, personal invincibility to the inevitable cycle of nature and the burdens wrought by time.

Some Snippets Don't Fit Anywhere Else

As I look back, I find many little trivialities were the spice of life in growing up in a small town. They don't fit anywhere in the flow of the narrative but shouldn't be forgotten. A few of these follow in no particular order:

The occasional job in the local cheese factory, packing the metal 'rounds' with raw cheese curds and compressing them into smooth textured roundels.

Dorothy Leitzau putting a little extra chocolate on your sundae at Cabby's Cafe.

Bill Engstler leading 'Topsy,' a large black bear he kept in a cage back of his garage. Topsy was rescued as cub and nurtured by an interested family. When he became too large (and wild) for the household, Bill constructed a steel-barred 'facility' for the bear at the rear of his repair garage, fed him gleanings from Cabby's Café and cared for him daily. In retrospect it was a pitiable existence for Topsy; however, he seemed to enjoy his walks with Bill. He would put Topsy on a LONG chain , perhaps 25 ft. or more, and let Topsy lead *him* around downtown Main Street.

Watching the floating debris in the flood waters from the Root River Bridge: an almost annual occurrence.

'Hanging-out' at Bob and later Gene Bissen's Texaco station to talk about hunting ducks and raccoons. Occasionally, after dawn, I shot pigeons from their roosts on the fascia of Dad's store across Main street. I sat inside the station office to muffle the sound of my .22 rifle. The pigeons were a real nuisance and left an unwanted mess on the walk in front of the store/post office.

Watching the ice harvest in winter. A six-foot+ diameter saw blade driven by an automobile engine, cut the frozen surface of a Root River backwater into large blocks. The two by three-foot chunks were packed into a two-story ice-house at the rear of Cabby's Café. The ice was for cafe use and after breaking into smaller pieces was also sold to homes without refrigerators. Ice blocks were separated and insulated by layers of sawdust from John von Arx's sawmill adjacent to the Root River.

'Jump-shooting' Wood Ducks just after sunrise in the forest ponds along the Root River. At the time, I a Black Labrador-Chesapeake retriever, named Butch, (also my Dad's nickname) who somehow understood the need for quiet in jump-shooting. As I waded slowly, with water almost to the top of my hip-boots, he would swim 'at-heel' alongside me. If I stopped he would also stop and sink to the bottom, with several inches of water over his head. He'd bob up for air now and then but never disturbed the scene.

Watching Bill Engstler put a charged automobile condenser on the bar at Cabby's Cafe and waiting for some unsuspecting, curious soul to pick it up and throw it away in pain. Today, such a prank might produce a lawsuit for both Bill and Cabby.

Watching Alden Ender fix radios; I thought he was a magician.

The smell of the newly-made butter as Phillip Frey and later Elmer Hample dug it out of the churn. The creamery displayed some great machinery, with large, overhead, line-shafts and belts to drive the churn and the various pumps.

'Hanging-out' at the stockyards and weighing ourselves on Deb

Lee's truck scale.

Neil Feuerhelm taking me for a ride in an airplane, an open cockpit, ex-military trainer he and Vic Leidel owned. It was a Fairchild PT-19 and a big thrill for a kid who was fascinated with airplanes.

Watching the 'new' town hall being built as a WPA Project (Works Projects Administration) in the late 1930s. While the WPA was much derided by some, it provided honorable jobs and a historic building, which survives today. It was built from poured concrete, using slip-forms.

Getting a haircut for a quarter at Charlie Sauer's barber shop. In 1957 our son, Tim, walked for the first time from my Dad, who was sitting in the 'waiting-chairs,' to me in the barber chair getting my hair cut.

Hokah, in the days just prior to and during WW II, was a true microcosm. We had one of almost everyone and everything, and the opportunities to learn the realities of life were many. I learned at an early age that life could be either be rewarding or difficult and not always fair. I also learned my approach to life's challenges would play a large part in how it might all turn out for me. Living in the cultural enclaves of a major metropolitan area, our son and later our grandchildren, missed the vivid examples evident in the diverse lifestyles present in a small town.

3

College and University Years – Out of the cocoon and into the real world.

* * *

There was no Grand March to "Pomp and Circumstance," and no cap and gown. However, the small high school class size enabled me to graduate as Valedictorian, which carried with it a scholarship to my choice of the Minnesota Association of Colleges (MAC). This short-circuited my plan to attend the University of Minnesota to study Aeronautical Engineering. However, a year's free education was not to be ignored, and I think there was the usual, family trepidation about sending me off into the cold, cruel world. For a variety of reasons, I chose to go to St. Mary's College in Winona, Minnesota, a school run by the Christian Brothers. The school's religious orientation satisfied my family's concerns.

St Mary's College

In reality, St. Mary's exhibited both advantages and disadvantages. While there were many upstanding young men attending the school, some of its students were 'fed-in' from Christian Brother's high schools in major metropolitan areas: Chicago, Detroit and Minneapolis. Some from these institutions constituted a rough clique and were at St. Mary's because of advice given to their parents:

"Send 'em to Winona and let the Brothers straighten 'em out."

One of my classmates, who hailed from Chicago, spoke with a bit of the Italian edge of his ancestors and would often say,

"Hey boy, you want your arm [yo ahm] broke? Or,

"I [hava] Rocco stop-by and [talka] to you on his way home." While this was mostly in fun (sort of), I'm sure it was important conversational currency in the part of Chicago he came from.

Two cousins came from a wealthy family in Guadalajara, Mexico. One of them confided to me in the cafeteria line:

"Henry not come back next year. He [likesa] his women." So, St. Mary's, a men's school, was not a sheltered haven. As is always the case, without a solid code of conduct to fall back on, one can get in trouble anywhere in the world. One of my Mother's old adages was,

"Show me who your friends are, and I'll know who you are."

St. Mary's was a typical boarding school: dormitory living and cafeteria eating whatever was on the menu for the day, no choices. I was assigned a room alphabetically, 315 Heffron Hall; my roommate, Dan Reid, came from Detroit. We had little in common except my radio, which he took over every night to listen to WJR, a high power, clear-channel, AM station in Detroit. I suppose he was homesick. Sometimes, when the atmospherics were bad, I could listen to my radio. We got along well; he had his friends, and I had mine.

I enrolled in what was termed 'Pre-Engineering,' a course emphasizing mathematics and science. St. Mary's was a much larger pool of characters, and my days of coasting through academically were over. From my freshman year at St. Mary's to graduation from the University of Minnesota, life was a struggle that produced about a 'B' average. Mathematics became much tougher, and I hitchhiked home many weekends, where Sister Borgia, my old high school teacher, spent some of her spare time tutoring me.

The courses in English Literature and Writing exposed me to many writers I would never have encountered on my own. Brother Damian's recitation of "The Shooting of Dan McGrew" from memory hooked me for life on the works of Robert Service. I've owned a three-volume collection of Service's works for many years and emulated Brother Damien by committing to memory the poetry of Service, Rudyard Kipling and Banjo Patterson, an Australian and early Poet Laureate of the country.

In reality, the scholarship from the MAC was a marketing tool for the individual colleges and there was pressure to continue beyond the first year at St. Mary's through graduation. It was a basic liberal arts college with, as I recall, occupationally related degree programs only in Chemistry and Business; it was not a place I wanted to be. For my sophomore year, I enrolled at the University of Minnesota.

University of Minnesota

The University was, in popular parlance, a whole 'nother thing' for a kid from a town of 400. It was just after World War II and many of the students were veterans, serious folks who brooked no nonsense from faculty or fellow students. In those years, the University was a somewhat dysfunctional place. It's size approached that of today (three times its prewar size), and it turned out graduates at a rate similar to earlier years. This meant eliminating a high percentage of the entering students prior to graduation. There was no tutoring or individual help available; it was 'root hog or die.'

The Aeronautical Engineering Department did not have a long history in 1948. Established by John D. Ackerman sometime in the late 1930s, the uncertainty of its role in the University's spectrum was on display in the admonition in the University's Course Catalog:

"This is a professional engineering course and not a training course for airplane pilots."

My undergraduate years at the University are not the stuff of dreamy nostalgia. In my opinion, the major objective of the undergraduate engineering programs appeared to be the elimination of as many students as possible. Maximum use of teaching assistants minimized the need to hire additional, professional staff. It was a way to deal with the influx of students brought by the GI Bill.

I found the U of M environment intimidating. Merely getting registered for classes should have qualified one for a degree in something or other. There were not enough class slots to meet the demand and registration was by lottery number. Getting a 'low number,' was key to early registration and enhanced one's chances of assembling a class schedule with courses properly sequenced for timely graduation. Every academic quarter, getting a low number required standing in line for a day and a night and sometimes two nights. The lines snaked for blocks, and open fires eased the night's chill for winter quarter.

Although my adviser was of limited help in his named role, he 'approved' my program each quarter. After I endeavored to assemble a class schedule that made chronological sense toward a degree, he was seldom available to 'approve' my program. He was a fine gentleman, but he struggled with the 'fruit of the grape.' Time was critical; minutes were important lest an essential course section would fill before my name appeared on the roster. I learned to forge my adviser's signature: Survival of the fittest ruled program planning.

One of my colleagues marveled at my ability to assemble a class schedule and get it signed-off so expeditiously. After several quarters of acquaintance, I revealed to him my ability with the pen. He had a slight speech impediment: When excited, he would lockup on a word or phrase and repeat it over and over, until he could produce a synonym for the offending word. When he learned of my forging the adviser's signature, he said,

"Reilly, if they ever catch you at this, they'll hang you, hang you, hang you, hang you ... you'll get THE CHAIR!" He was right, of course, but I was never challenged and even after successfully registering, high possibility of academic elimination loomed.

Physics and Calculus were the weapons of the academic weeders. In three undergraduate years, only three of my classes were taught by Professors. Teaching Assistants (TA) were the workhorses of every department. The TA who taught Integral Calculus announced in his initial class: His objective was not to teach calculus but to eliminate

50% of the class. His class mostly consisted of his ballet at the chalkboard; I managed a 'D,' the only one I ever received. However, I survived, and he met his quota.

Physics, with its daily classes and weekly tests, was a delightful form of torture. Though unannounced, elimination was the objective there also. I arose every morning to do battle with Physics. I frequently lost. Every Friday I'd stare at the testing 'blue book,' write my name on the cover, scrawl a few hopeful equations and turn it in: baffled. On Monday, the blue-books were back with red scrawls, and on a good week a score in the teens … yes, teens out of 100. I passed the second quarter – entitled 'Electricity and Magnetism,' I'll never forget – with a score of '16,' which in this bizarre institution, brought a grade of 'B.' The top score in the class, if I recall correctly, was under '30' and the break between a 'D' and 'F' was '6.' In this asylum, appearing for the test brought the student a score of '5' for writing a name in an otherwise empty blue-book. Grades were all published in ignominy, on a public bulletin board every Monday, in a spirit of confidentiality, political correctness and a 'safe' academic environment. Not only was this bad physics, it was also indifferent statistics.

Strangely, in later life self-study of classical physics became almost an obsession and my professional lifeline on many occasions.

The Teaching Assistants were bright young people, often of foreign extraction and lacking a working knowledge of English. This should have been a prime requisite for employment, but 'Inclusively' and 'Diversity' were already making inroads into academia. As a result, some courses were sheer torture. Even the TAs who communicated reasonably well, lacked the experience and background to make the courses 'live.' In later years, while I was guest lecturing at a German University, a weathered Professor told me, not in jest,

"Formal classes are just a way of transcribing material from the professor's notebook to the student's notebook with minimum effort on the part of each." And so it was with the polyglot, TA environment in the Institute of Technology; even that minimal accomplishment failed. My undergraduate years at the University were a wretched experience. In 1951, I obtained a bachelor's degree certifying my completion of what was essentially an accredited course of self-study.

Graduate School

As an undergraduate, I made the acquaintance of Dr. Rudolph Hermann, one of the so-called 'Paper Clip' scientists who were brought to the United States from Germany after WW II. Dr. Hermann worked with Dr. Werner von Braun in the development of the V2, Hitler's "Vengeance Weapon," used against the British. Hermann was also a specialist in compressible fluid flow, high-speed aerodynamics and supersonic inlets, in addition to his experience with rockets. During my senior year, he took me under his wing, advised me to continue in graduate school and volunteered to act as my adviser. At the same time, I took full-time employment with General Mills Incorporated, Aeronautical Division. Juggling a job in conjunction with graduate school required some fast footwork. From my current energy level, I now wonder just how it was all accomplished.

Hermann's tutelage in compressible flow and supersonic inlets formed the basic core knowledge that sustained my professional career. I sometimes strayed far afield from my primary interest, aerodynamics, and relied on a continuing self-study of classical physics for a 'quick-study' of the requirements of a pending consulting job. I completed all the course work required for a master's degree, but after we moved to California, I never found a suitable study-problem for a thesis. Then, Dr. Hermann left the University of Minnesota and my MS degree died on the vine.

Life Outside Classes

I often hitchhiked home on Friday night and returned on Sunday afternoon, about 150 miles each way. When I didn't go home, I mailed my laundry home in a fiberboard mailing box sold for the purpose; laundromats were yet to arrive. At home, Saturdays meant visiting the wholesale grocery outlets in La Crosse, Wisconsin and hauling the week's stock for the family store. If the weather was inclement, Dad often insisted I take the Burlington Zephyr for the return to Minneapolis, but hitchhiking was my primary mode of transportation throughout my school years.

Dormitory life struck me as being a bit noisy and pricey, so I explored other living accommodations, which changed almost every quarter after the first year. A hometown University student, Maurice McCauley, graduated, thus opening a certified superior living arrangement fitting my needs. It was a room in an apartment whose prime landladies were two widowed sisters, Mrs. Runnels and Mrs. Monk. Its major disadvantage was the remote location from the campus, a twenty-minute streetcar ride with a transfer. It was a quiet and peaceful environment, and Mrs. Runnels provided breakfast each day. Lunch was a catch-as-catch-can near the campus, and for dinner I walked three blocks to a diner on Nicollet Avenue. Because of the location, I seldom participated in evening campus activities, and the looming Friday Physics tests assured I was well occupied. At the end of the calendar year, the younger of my two landladies retired from her job, and they both moved out-of-state, so I searched for a new living arrangement.

Ultimately, this turned into a continuous scramble over a couple of years. Following leads from Student Housing – 3x5 cards posted on a bulletin board – I found a room in the home of a Mrs. Getchell, scrupulously clean and a much shorter streetcar ride from the campus. A first look displayed the appearance of a comfortable place, but after I moved in things changed. The thermostat in the hallway remained set at 55 degrees; however, my rent was prepaid for the fall quarter, so there was no recourse. On bitterly cold days in December, Mrs. Getchell would sometimes greet me upon my return from classes wearing two heavy wool sweaters and overshoes. She would remark on what a wonderful day it was. I wore my long winter overcoat and overshoes while studying and didn't complain.

There were two other roomers, both older ex-GIs who often complained (and in four-letter words) about the lack of heat, but Mrs. Getchell stuck to her guns . . . and her sweaters. Somewhere about midterm we had a break: Mrs. Getchell embarked on a trip to visit one of her children. She left me with the key to the thermostat with strict instructions never to set it above 60. As soon as she was out the door, I set the thermostat for 72 and we lived it up for three weeks: survival of the fittest once again. When Mrs. Getchell returned she was furious; we used all the fuel oil she planned to last through the Spring Quarter. I moved out at the end of the quarter, and the search was on again.

A fellow student I met in class belonged to a fraternity. Short of pledges for the winter quarter, they were renting rooms discounted just for the revenue, no need to pledge the frat. So, I moved my meager belongings in and went home for Christmas vacation. I returned on a weekend to find I was assigned a room on the second floor of the fraternity house, above the living room. Instead of attending the weekend party, I spent the evening arranging my things. I tried to get some sleep, but the party just below was a pretty noisy affair. When I arose in the morning and went downstairs, I found a pledge cleaning up broken glass in the living room using a garden rake. I stopped to talk with him and listened to his complaint. He was growing weary of cleaning up after the regular, weekend soirees. This was not a place for an engineering student battling with Physics; the hunt was on again.

I saw a sign 'ROOMS,' on a big, old house on Washington Avenue, which had the advantage of being just one house away from Mrs. Erickson's coop eatery, where I took most of my meals. I inquired, signed-on and moved, all within an hour.

I drew an Indian roommate, Krishna Misra, a Hindu whose religious belief required an hour-long, private, ritual bath each day. This was not an easy exercise in a house with 17 roomers and one bathroom. Although Misra attempted to minimize conflict by bathing after midnight, the lock on the bathroom door was broken out of the door frame many times. When someone with an urgency put a shoulder to the door, over Misra's wailing protestation,

"I take 'baath,'" the response from outside was,

"I take s***;" the shoulder was applied, and the lock was gone again. When I lived there, the door lock had been relocated half a dozen times and was at about the five-foot level.

Misra owned a phonograph and some cultural, classic, Indian records he played incessantly. To my ear, the 'music' seemed to emanate from a single-stringed instrument. When plucked, a single, loud tone emerged and was allowed to die away while being modulated in a 'wow, wow, wow' manner. I learned a great deal about another culture, but it was not a totally satisfactory living arrangement.

Earlier in the year, I joined the University Flying Club, where I met Tom Croswell, who was having trouble concentrating on engineering studies while living in his fraternity house. We decided to seek a room together. We found a room in a great, almost a mansion, white house with a grand portico supported by fluted white pillars: 629 Washington Avenue SE. A sign in the yard proclaimed: 'Medical Placement Registry,' the landlady's primary business. The place was a zoo posing as a rooming house, and at one count 22 men crammed into this large house, again with one bathroom. However, it did have two China basins and two 'foot washers.' Its primary attraction was a tribute to the realtor's song:

"Location, location, location." It was a block from Main Engineering and only a bit farther to other technical buildings.

A Mrs. Kohner, who had a knack for turning every square inch of space into revenue, owned the house. Tom and I had a room on the third floor, essentially attic space, for which we each paid $13.33 per month to share a room with a sloping ceiling. Tom was 6 feet 5 inches and couldn't stand erect except at the center of the room. At one time, it was likely a $10 room that the OPA allowed Mrs. Kohner to re-price by 33%. During WW II and for some time thereafter, rents and many other items came under control of the OPA (Office of Price Administration).

On warm evenings we would exit onto the roof, through our one-window dormer, where we could study in relative comfort; air conditioning was generally uncommon. Vermin of one sort or another were present and any surplus food we placed in a bag and stapled to the ceiling, or it was gone by morning.

Guns weren't viewed with the unbridled terror persisting in the current environment, but one night I awoke to gun shots. From my bottom bunk, I could see Tom's legs dangling from above. He was sitting in his bunk with a flashlight in one hand and his Hi-Standard, automatic pistol in the other, firing BB-Caps (a low-powered .22 caliber round) at a mouse scurrying to escape along the length of the distant baseboard.

Lest I give the impression derelicts and ne'er-do-wells inhabited the place, I met Deke Slayton there. Deke was a WW II Air Force veteran who in later years became one of the original seven Astronauts. However, most people of substance occupied the first and second floor rooms at a higher price. Nevertheless, it was not a cushy place, and at times coordinating a full day's schedule around a single bathroom could be a nuisance.

As the year drew to a close, Tom and I sought better accommodations and committed to a room with an older couple, Bertha and Henry Gohr, for the following year. Hank and Bertha rented out one room in their apartment, near the old football stadium. The apartment was demolished to make space for the Hilton hotel, which now stands on Washington Avenue SE. In the middle of our senior year, Tom joined the Air Force, but I stayed on with Bertha and Henry, moving with them when they purchased a house at 2520 Como Ave. SE. I took all my meals with the Gohrs and Bertha packed a lunch for me every day. I paid them $25 per month for the room and food. I stayed with Henry and Bertha through graduate school and until Betty and I married. They remained lifelong friends.

College And University Years

Tom Croswell came from a wealthy family that owned three airplanes, and Tom often had both an airplane and a car at school. Some nights, when we finished studying, we would drive out to the old University Airport on Highway 8, crank up Tom's Globe Swift or Stinson Voyager and fly across town to the International Airport, Wold Chamberlain, where we would get a late-night hamburger. In those days, we could taxi to the passenger terminal, where we would park the small airplane in front of one of the passenger gates and walk into the restaurant.

The return flight was a bit trickier. University Airport was not lighted, but we had two, red, kerosene lanterns we placed at the ends of the runway, so we could land with some degree of accuracy. In later years, when I had my own airplane, I would return late at night from a weekend home. I landed there without any lighting whatsoever, except for the landing light on the airplane. A lighted sign in the FBO's office window served for establishing general location. It didn't seem dangerous at the time, but it was long ago; I was younger, and *'what could possibly go wrong anyway?'*

Ultimately, Tom was a great influence on my life: He was a rated flight instructor's and taught me to fly. I soloed on the 16th of December in 1950 and Tom's father, Roy, gave me one of the family's airplanes, a Piper PA-11, to take home for Christmas vacation. I sometimes flew three to four hours per day to complete the 40 hours time required to present myself for my Private Pilot's test. I passed on January 6th 1951. Flying has been a part of my life ever since, both as a hobby and engineering flight test, but more of that later.

Food

After my arrangement with Mrs. Runnels and Mrs. Monk terminated, eating became a haphazard affair. It meant a streetcar ride to the campus, where there were a number of commercial establishments catering to students and a cafeteria in Coffman Memorial Union. Depending on the timing of classes, I would often eat at a place called 'Steaks and Shakes.' Establishing a reputation as a 'regular' was a distinct advantage: When the week was longer than the finances, a familiar waiter would serve a bowl of hot water at no cost. An acceptable bowl of tomato soup could be prepared from countertop catsup and a dash of salt and pepper. Crackers were also available gratis, and nobody complained because you were a 'regular' and turned up for a paying meal later in the day. None of this was because I was deprived or destitute; Dad would have made sure I was sustained in much grander fashion. However, I was inexplicably driven to get things done on my own and mostly succeeded, except for an occasional $20 bill slipped to me on a weekend trip home.

During my second year at the University, my eating situation became a bit more settled: I ate at a cooperative run by a Mrs. Erickson. Cooperative meant 'Mrs. E' planned the menus, bought the food, prepared the meals and dedicated the entire ground floor of her home to the preparation and serving of food to students. Students did all the serving, cleanup and the general dog-work. The food was good, not fancy, and the price was right: $3.50 per week if you worked at the coop, $4.50 if you didn't. Beginners were assigned to the cleanup of pots and pans, which were many and large.

Mrs. E served about 100 people three times a day except for Sunday, which collapsed the menu to one major meal at noon. It was here I met Merv Jensen; he introduced me to Betty years later.

After working up through 'pots and pans' at the coop, better jobs became available. One of the more desirable jobs was preparing lunches for people who belonged to the coop but found themselves on the far side of the campus at noon, with an early afternoon class. In the balmy days of fall and spring, the lunch job was a breeze; everyone enjoyed the walk back to the coop for lunch. However, in the below zero chill of January, things were different and the lunch list grew. Merv and I found ourselves on the lunch-prep shift together and when the lunch list reached 50, we were getting up at 05:00 a.m. to meet the schedule. One sleepy, winter morning Merv exclaimed,

"D**n, we're going to put a stop to this."

The evening meal the night before included baked beans and there was a good supply of leftovers. Mrs. E devoted a large part of the basement of her house to a huge walk-in refrigerator. Merv disappeared into the refrigerator and came out with the remains of a three-gallon tin of mint jelly, a leftover from an earlier Easter dinner. We produced sandwiches of cold beans and mint jelly, which cut the lunch list by half the next day.

The coop was an adequate place to eat for several years until I started rooming with the Gohrs, where I became a part of the family. They were farmers from Southern Minnesota, who went bankrupt during the Great Depression of the 1930s and came to the big city in survival mode. I had a good life, eating farm food with people who really cared about me. It was my first taste of true stability away from home.

Social Life

Social life around a metropolitan university is pretty limited for one who doesn't have a car, or access to one. There was the Friday night 'mixer' at Coffman Union; however, being escorted home on the streetcar was not a young lady's idea of a big night out. I dated a girl from South St. Paul a few times. This involved about a 45-minute streetcar ride from the campus and was punctuated with three transfers. In 1949, after midnight, the streetcars ran once each hour. This meant, if I was unlucky, the return trip after a movie and a snack might run three hours of waiting plus 45 minutes riding. After returning to the big, white house with the pillars near daybreak a couple of times, my interest in the young lady waned.

Occasionally there was relief from the streetcar. Also, living at the Medical Placement Registry was John Herfurth, a friend of Merv Jensen. John owned a car, a tired, 1935 Plymouth with a bad crankshaft. This meant the connecting rod bearings would last only a few hundred miles before needing replacement. On a Thursday afternoon, John would sometimes burst into my attic room and yell,

"Hey Reilly, do you want to double-date with us tomorrow night?" His girlfriend could often supply and extra for me and if I replied,

"Yes," John would respond,

"OK then we have to go down to 'Western Auto' and buy some new rod inserts for the Plymouth." After another streetcar ride to 'Seven Corners', he'd buy the required parts and we would be off to work on his car, parked on the street near the big, white house.

Replacing the connecting rod bearings is no small job, especially lying in the street in the dead of winter. It involved draining the oil (frugally saved), jacking and blocking the car for working clearance, dropping the oil pan and removing the six connecting rod ends. We filed the new bearing inserts to assure proper fit and the entire process reversed for assembly.

In the cold, John and I had this job down to a little more than three or four hours by working until fingers were too stiff to manipulate small parts. We alternated warming in the house while the other worked. John and I learned to work together effectively, and he became a lifelong friend until his tragic death at age 27. When Betty and I lived in California, John and his girlfriend became a big part of our social life until we returned to Minnesota.

John's friend, Merv Jensen, knew an endless supply of girls looking for dates. Merv sold *Hope Chest Linens* to young working girls. It was almost a scam: First he sold them the chest, a nice piece of furniture. Then, with a succession of visits, he helped them fill the chest with sheets, blankets, towels and even a supply of expensive pots and pans. One night in the summer of 1951 he convinced me to accompany him to a house in North Minneapolis occupied by five working girls. Betty was one of them, and we all know how that evolved. Betty just finished her degree in Home Economics and had a teaching job secured for the following school year. She came to the 'big city' to seek work for the summer. By this time, employed at the

University's Rosemount Aeronautical Research Facility located twenty miles south of the city, I needed a car. No longer bound to the streetcar, Betty and I spent much time together for the summer.

Part-time Work

One of the students I met during my Sophomore year, Dick Eckholm, worked for the Dean of Admissions and Records. He graduated at the end of the fall quarter and asked me if I'd like the job, which I eagerly accepted. It was essentially a drafting job. I maintained the giant, tracing-cloth map, photographically reduced and displayed in the various course catalogs, pamphlets and other University publications. Each new building or walkway required a map modification accomplished by scraping off old lines, drawn in India Ink, and adding lines of the new construction. The job came with a semiprivate office. Not only was this a place to work but also a place to study, when the crowded living spaces and noise became unbearable. In addition, it enabled me to pay most of my way through the University, after my first year there – tuition for 20 credits: $33 per quarter. Text books new: $2 - $3.50 each)

While the job paid fairly well, about a dollar per hour, the main benefit was the office in 'Temporary North of Mines.' This was one of many little frame structures, erected between permanent buildings during WW II, to accommodate wartime activities on the campus. It also came with a 'Square-Root Frieden' mechanical calculator, a real asset to an engineering student. It is hard to convey the importance of this machine these days, when every high school student has the equivalent of an IBM industrial computer available in his back pack and for less than $25. In 1948, only God and the University had a '*Square-Root*' Frieden.

I also did sporadic jobs for the Dean of Admissions and Records, Dean Summers. 'The Dean' was a smallish man, nervously composed and a classic hypochondriac. He was never without his box of Kleenex, which he used to combat a pesky respiratory problem. He always deployed a tissue to isolate himself from door handles for sanitary entrance and exit to anywhere.

Working for 'The Dean' was a bit strange; the big campus map was an ongoing, semi-continuous assignment interwoven with hot jobs for The Dean. I saw little of him initially; his jobs were assigned to me through an office manager, Jean McCarthy. Jean managed a mostly female staff of perhaps 50 or more people; we developed a congenial relationship from the start.

The Dean's job seemed to me to be a selling job in part, searching for money from a variety of sources. He was a man of some note, often traveling and making presentations to others of his sort. He would glean data from the Records Archives and have me prepare charts and graphs to support his talks. I don't think The Dean was familiar with anything other than simple plots presenting one parameter against another in linear fashion. Ms. McCarthy once told me The Dean was making a pitch trying to impress the Board of Regents on the effect of the then-large enrollment. Instead of presenting a simple plot, I constructed a bar chart drawn with three-dimensional bars in an isometric presentation. This was just psychological trickery. While one bar might be twice the height of its neighbor, the three-dimensional effect gave the perception of eight times the bulk. The Dean was delighted. Thereafter, he would give me an outline or the text of his talk, and I would construct the graphic presentations accordingly: log charts to compress data and smooth variations, bar charts for the 'big' picture and what little I knew of statistics thrown in for good measure. I could have retained the job until the Dean might be discharged or eliminated by some mysterious malady decking him, because he forgot his box of Kleenex.

Another side benefit of the job: Ms. McCarthy found employment for Betty for several summers during her teaching years.

During my Senior year I was offered a part-time job with the University's Rosemount Aeronautical Laboratory. It was a chance to get experience in the professional application of my studies. The Lab was about 20 miles south of the city and required I have a car. Dad let me take his car each week, but I returned home most weekends to do the wholesale buying to keep the family store running. Although the business was winding down at that point, Dad kept it going to serve a few faithful old customers.

At Rosemount, I was assigned to work on a project doing detailed studies on cooling the exhaust gases from jet engines. I couldn't know at the time this experience would be invaluable in landing a major consulting contract some 35 years later. A further benefit of this job was my supervisor, Richard DeLeo, who was to be the best supervisor I worked for in my professional career. Dick was a patient teacher and an all-around gentleman. He taught me much about experimental methods and aerodynamic measuring techniques.

After graduation, I took a full-time job with General Mills Incorporated, Aeronautical Division and juggled it along with graduate school. How General Mills came to have an aeronautical division is a story in itself for the next chapter.

4

Breakfast Cereal and Big Balloons

What do breakfast cereals and aeronautical research have in common? Almost nothing, as one might expect, but enough to attract a major food manufacturer into high-altitude, atmospheric research. The connection is a story in itself, and this unlikely marriage produced some of the most vital scientific sleuthing of the 'Cold War' at the beginning of the 'Atomic Age.'

* * *

My professional engineering life ran the full gamut from aerostatics to supersonics and space flight, so it was fitting I started at the slow end of the spectrum. I can't recall how I found General Mills Aeronautical Division; two friends, Bill Foley and Jim Winker, worked there and perhaps induced me to apply for a job. At the outset, while in graduate school, I prepared myself to work in the field of supersonic aerodynamics and free-flying balloons didn't strike me as being exciting. However, the income accompanying full-time employment was an attractive adjunct to graduate school. I had some trepidation over how I was going to juggle the demands of a job with a significant course load, however, I chose to give it go and worry later.

Breakfast Cereal And Big Balloons

The folks with the breakfast cereals were in the ballooning business for about two decades, and this came about through an unlikely connection. Dr. Jean Piccard, under whom I studied "Physics of the Atmosphere," was a professor in the Aeronautical Engineering Department at the University of Minnesota. Jean and his twin brother Auguste, natives of Switzerland, devoted their adult lives to scientific research and education. Both were interested in the advancement of knowledge of the atmosphere and the means for humans to survive at high altitudes. Auguste developed a pressurized, spherical, balloon gondola in which he flew to a record altitude of 53,000 feet in 1932.

Jean Piccard moved to the US in 1926, and following his brother's work with balloons ascended to 58,000 feet in 1934 with his wife, Jeanette, piloting. During the flight he conducted scientific experiments leading to the liquid oxygen converter that paved the way for modern high altitude aircraft. Piccard realized balloons of the 1930s had reached their altitude limits because of the weight of the fabric – silk with gas-tight impregnation – used in the envelope. He began experimenting with balloons constructed of thin plastic films.

After coming to the University of Minnesota, Piccard conceived the idea General Mill's knowledge of fabricating thin-film cereal packages could be transferred to the construction of large, lightweight, gas-tight envelopes. By the time I started working in the field, scientific balloons 300 feet in diameter and evolved from smaller (20-40 feet in diameter) balloons used primarily for manned flight.

The 'Skyhooks'

The incentive for these large balloons was not only the exploration of the upper atmosphere but also the fact there was no other vehicle capable of lifting heavy loads to high altitudes, circa 1950. Airplanes were limited, 30,000 ft. machines, and while there were a few sounding rockets in use, they had barely progressed beyond the hobby stage. The large balloons were named 'Skyhooks' for their ability to hang loads above 100,000 feet for days at a time. Physicists flew and remotely photographed cloud chambers looking for the tracks of cosmic ray particles. Film packs were also a common scientific load with the same objective. General Mills' Skyhooks were the workhorses of the research community working in particle physics.

The photo below shows a 'Skyhook' just after launching. It has not yet picked up its load chain, strung out on the ground to the right.

Skyook Launching

The bubble of gas at the top of the envelope expands as the balloon rises, becoming over 100 times this volume at 100,000 ft. and almost 300 times as large at 130,000 ft. At full expansion its shape is a sphere with a tangent cone coming to a point at the bottom of the envelope.

In the photo, the balloon is beginning to pick up its load, located at bottom far right. The white object, just lifting from the ground, is a parachute rigged between the balloon and the scientific package. It is used to lower the experimental load to the ground at the end of the flight, when it is cut from the balloon with a with a radio controlled explosive squib.

The launching of such a flight, beyond preparation of the scientific experiment, is a matter of managing hundreds of square yards of plastic film perhaps only a half mil thick – 0.0005 inch not half a millimeter. Depending on the application, one to three mils was more common but still extremely fragile. For comparison, the average kitchen Ziploc bag is about three mils.

No-wind at launch time is preferred, but with a light breeze the load line is laid out along the direction of the wind with the balloon farthest upwind. Upon release of the gas bubble, the balloon drifts downwind – left to right in the picture – over the load to be picked up, in a smooth motion. However, upon release, the bubble's many yards of loose film spread and create a virtual, moving, aerodynamic center that tends to pull the load upwind toward the rising balloon. This problem is alleviated by having one or two men pick up the load and run upwind until the load is aligned under the rising balloon and then released. For heavy loads, some about 7,000 pounds, the running men are replaced by a truck and a skillful driver who maneuvers in reverse to get the load under the balloon at the correct moment.

It was essential to follow these flights with an airplane for several reasons. For long-term flights it was necessary to decide when to drop the scientific load to avoid its drifting out to sea, a judgment call based on the balloon's current position, speed and trajectory. I saw a large part of the United States east of the Twin Cities, while following these flights.

A secondary reason for flight following, was the need to be near the scientific load when the landing occurred. Curious farmers would unintentionally destroy valuable data while picking through equipment that landed on their property. In one such incident, a farmer returned the scientific package through the mail with a note explaining how he cleaned up the equipment he found. Specifically, he speculated there must have been a fire in the instrument package because he found a round disk with a smoky residue on it, which he cleaned.

We built our own inexpensive barographs by fitting a six-inch diameter aluminum disk onto the hour-shaft of a 'Big Ben,' eight-day alarm clock – a cheap, disposable time reference. An aneroid pressure capsule, whose output arm moved as a function of altitude, scribed a

Scientific Load On Parachute

line on the smoked, rotating disk. A simple reference graph allowed the reading the altitude of the flight as a function of time. The helpful farmer obliterated the record of the flight with his 'cleaning' exercise. Whenever possible, the tracking airplane landed in an open field near the parachute, to preclude such 'help.'

My beginning job at General Mills was designing minor equipment to support the Skyhook program. Assisting with late night and early morning rigging and launching of these flights became a normal part of the workday and fit well with my graduate school program. Occasionally, I was part of the aircraft flight crew following the flight to its conclusion.

Flying Saucers

Once filled out to their sphere/cone shape, these large, translucent bubbles were a spectacular sight. They were captivating after on-surface sunset, when they remained brilliantly sunlit at 100,000-130,000 feet against a black sky. We generated many UFO reports (Unidentified Flying Objects) and contributed to much of the UFO ('flying saucer') hysteria of the 1950s.

The Air Force program, *'Project Blue Book,'* investigated these reports because of the public interest in so-called 'flying saucers.' Below is one of these reports I recently (October 2006) ran across by accident while searching the internet for something unrelated. One of a sequence of search links contained a listing of many sightings

Breakfast Cereal And Big Balloons

of UFOSs dating back 50 years or more. While this report is a bit garbled, – we were flying a Piper Pacer airplane, not a balloon – it was one of many such generated by our organization, whose people spent many hours perusing the sky professionally. I am astounded this report is still around and indexed on The Web.

The incident Joe Kaliszewski and I generated, was of special significance to the Air Force, because we refused to put a size on the object: it could have been a dime hanging in front of the windshield or 100 ft across and 20 miles away. We had no size/distance reference. Two officers were sent from Wright Field to talk to us; I suspect if we estimated the size of the object in the report it would have been discarded as another unreliable report.

* * *

October 11, 1951 (either 6:30 or 8:30 a.m.) *Near Minneapolis, Minnesota and St. Croix, Wisconsin **[Project Blue Book unknown]* – In the second sighting the next day, Kaliszewski was riding in a balloon with pilot Dick Reilly north of Minneapolis. On the ground were aerologist Charles B. Moore and Doug Smith (also Richard Dorian and Zuckert) observing through theodolites. The flight crew saw two objects. The first object was brightly glowing with a dark underside and a halo around it. It "was moving from east to west at a high rate and very high." Using a reinforcing member of the windshield as a reference point, the men estimated it was moving at about 50 degrees per second. "The object arrived high and fast, then slowed and made slow climbing circles for about two minutes and finally sped away to the east. It crossed rapidly and then slowed down and started to climb in lazy circles slowly. The pattern it made was like a falling oak leaf inverted. It went through these gyrations for a couple minutes and then with a very rapid acceleration disappeared to the east." Total time the first object was seen was about 5 minutes. Soon afterward they saw another object shoot straight across the sky from west to east. Kaliszewski radioed observers at the University of Minnesota Airport who were tracking the object through a theodolite. Two of them (Smith and Dorian) got fleeting glimpses of what appeared to them to be a cigar-shaped object viewed through the theodolite, but they could not keep it in view due to its fast angular motion. Sighting of the second object lasted only a few seconds. While the Oct. 11 main sighting was officially categorized as "Unidentified," for some reason the Oct. 10 sighting was called an "Aircraft." Kaliszewski could not understand how such a distinction could be made, since in his opinion both objects matched no known aeronautical device.

[McDonald; Sparks; *NY <http://roswellproof.homestead.com/NYTimes_4_12_52.html>**/Times <http://roswellproof.homestead.com/NYTimes_4_12_52.html>/*.]

(In another strange coincidence I am writing this on October 11, 2006, 55 years later to the day.)

Radio Free Europe And Pillow Balloons

The early 1950s were tense times in international politics. The Russians had just consolidated many small Eastern European Countries into the Union of Soviet Socialist Republics. The Cold War was beginning, and Western Countries were endeavoring to create unrest among these recently oppressed, unruly countries now under Soviet control. The U.S. set up a powerful radio network in Europe, Radio Free Europe (RFE), broadcasting Western political philosophy, music, news and cultural programming. The USSR responded by setting up jamming transmitters to prevent the Western content from getting through to the newly consolidated republics. Electronically thwarted, RFE contracted with General Mills to communicate political content to Eastern Europe using 'Pillow Balloons,' so named because of their working shape. Basic construction consisted of two flat pieces of polyethylene sheeting, three or four feet wide and six to eight feet long. With edges heat-sealed, these balloons looked like empty pillow cases. They carried a small load of leaflets printed with the news and other Western oriented content. A corner cut from the pillow allowed insertion of the printed paper load.

These simple devices relied on a complex interaction between meteorology and the loading of the pillow to accomplish delivery of the load to a regionally predicted target. The relationship between surface meteorological conditions and wind direction at altitude was not as well understood as it is today. The program undertook a sig-

Breakfast Cereal And Big Balloons

Pillow Balloon Launch

nificant development program to establish relationships between balloon loading, desired altitude, inflation of the balloon and its leakage rate that were correlated with target distance and direction. We flew many balloons with different loads and inflation levels. The loads consisted of cards – return to sender – on which the finder would inscribe the time and location where it was found. It was an enormous record keeping process that correlated flight's end point with the meteorology at the time of the flight. A high percentage of the cards returned.

Once the basic work was done, pillow balloons were amazingly effective. The physics of this simple system resulted in a particularly spectacular delivery. As the balloons descended, the load of paper in the bottom corner would be first to touch the ground, and with the load thus supported, the balloon would then have enough excess lift to rise again, a few feet. Still too heavy sustain itself, it would return to the ground to repeat the process. The balloons would dance, drifting along in the wind for miles until found by the target population or confiscated by a government patrol. They drove the East German and Russian authorities to distraction, a welcome though unexpected consequence of simple weight and balance characteristics.

In retrospect, this was a dangerous research enterprise. Because Europe has no helium, the research work was done with hydrogen as the lifting gas. Valid research data required a large group of similarly loaded balloons be released simultaneously. This meant many pillows filled with hydrogen were restrained in a building until all of a batch were properly inflated and carefully loaded. An enclosing room, filled with these inflated pillows floating near the ceiling, contained sufficient hydrogen to destroy the building if ignited. The inflation process created a static charge that would lift one's hair when moving among the balloons. There was enough voltage to generate a huge spark under the proper circumstances. I don't know whether such a spark might have sufficient energy to set off an explosion; we never worried about it much; and no disaster occurred.

Project 'Grab Bag'

After the pillow balloons were flying in Europe, I was assigned to 'Project Grab Bag,' a highly classified program at the time and also related to the 'Cold War.' The exact purpose of the program was never disclosed nor discussed. However, given minimal analytical thought, the program's technical objectives began to unravel when coupled with the frequent newscasts of Russian atomic and hydrogen bomb experiments. Grab Bag's technique for bringing air samples from high altitudes had an obvious purpose: The air samples contained dust with the radioactive signature of the nuclear explosion inherent in the dust particulates.

The basic concept was a modified balloon whose conical appendix

Breakfast Cereal And Big Balloons

Grab-Bag Double TowString

was enlarged by a ten-foot diameter ring. The balloon was deflated and tied-off to prevent contamination of the sample with surface air. The whole arrangement was tied into the load line at the bottom of the parachute as described earlier in the Skyhook launching. It was flown to high altitude, and when cut loose with an explosive squib it descended on the parachute. It all sounded simple; however, the parachute descent rate was too rapid to collect a proper sample, so things became more complicated.

To slow the descent, the sampling balloon (black in the photo above) was linked to two smaller balloons for ascent. Once at high altitude, one balloon was cut away and the collection bag opened to fill while drifting slowly down on the remaining balloon. This created a logistic nightmare because the descending assembly continued to drift with the prevailing wind, and it's landing point was fraught with far more uncertainty than a simple, parachute descent.

At a programmed lower altitude, the collection bag was sealed using a small electric winch to tie the sample bag tightly. It was essential the ground crew be present at the landing site with an air compressor, ready to collect the air sample from the sampling bag.

Because of the fragility of the collection bag, we tried working the program from the shore of Lake Superior, hoping a water landing would eliminate damage to the sample bag. Before the logistic contingencies of tracking airplane, boat with compressor and a support flotilla could be coördinated, winter set in, and the entire program moved to Texas. A typical landing site appears in the picture, left. The circular ring of the collection bag is visible beneath the tow-balloon, which controlled its descent. As is evident from the terrain, an uncontaminated sample, not violated by damage to the collection bag, was difficult to accomplish. It required much wild, high-speed driving by the ground crews; ultimately, the operation was often successful.

Grab Bag Landing Site

Manned Flights

Other classified programs generated by the Cold War provided lively entertainment. For a while I was assigned to the design of equipment for manned flights of small balloons, approximately 30 ft. in diameter when fully inflated. Again, the exact purpose was never disclosed, but all the rigid components were made of wood; it was before the time of structural plastics. Added structural components of canvas and heavy cotton or nylon webbing were a distinct clue this contraption would not be visible on radar. Further, the final package consisted of hydrogen cylinders, so use outside the US was obvious. The assembly of gas cylinders, balloon and a man-carrying gondola, packed for parachute delivery, made it appear that injection/extraction of intelligence operatives might be a possible application for the finished product.

Breakfast Cereal And Big Balloons

As with pillow balloons, the interaction of meteorology and baloon systems were critical. Beyond designing equipment, we undertook a program to determine the reliability of being able to predict a specific destination from a set of meteorological data. In contrast to the pillow balloon system, the pilot of this system could vary his altitude and thus incrementally change his direction. Many flights and data established operational procedures and tested the equipment designs.

The secrecy requirement meant all such testing was done at night. Launching from a Minnesota location was a late afternoon exercise, and the landing would be made before dawn, often in mid-state Iowa, Illinois or Missouri. Upon landing, the pilot would gather his gear, go to the nearest farmhouse to determine his exact landing location and request the use of a telephone. A necessary part of the act was an attempt to impress on an improbable ally the need to suppress news of his arrival. A call to home base in St. Paul relayed his location and an airplane dispatched for pickup. The equipment was rolled up tightly and packed in the airplane, leaving no evidence for the farmer to validate any improbable story he might tell his neighbors. He would be left with one or two twenty-dollar bills to convince him this whole thing never happened.

This worked out well with one or two unwelcome exceptions. One inexperienced pilot from the sponsoring military agency insisted on 'testing the system' and managed to become entangled in electrical power lines near the Twin Cities. The use of an alias to avoid identification led to a series of news stories with headlines heralding "Nicolas Greene and His Flying Machine."

Another such incident had an even more frenetic outcome. The military sponsor, while satisfied with the success of the program, was skeptical that the system could ever be adapted to the next objective: long distance flight, purpose unknown. The company plan to prove such utility relied on rudimentary knowledge of the jet stream, just evolving with the aerologists of the time. During Midwest winters, the bottom of the jet stream, with its wind speeds of 100 miles per hour or more, could sometimes be found at altitudes of 10,000 to 15,000 feet: An idea was born!

A two-man gondola was built, calculations performed, and with all made ready, the wait for a favorable meteorological pattern began. After an interminable wait, it finally happened in late winter, as I best recall.

The trajectory analysis predicted an overnight flight from the Twin Cities might land in upstate New York or perhaps Southern New England. Two of the program's most experienced pilots were assigned to the flight and inflation of the balloon began. At the last minute, Charles Moore, an experienced balloonist and Vice President of the Aeronautical Division, decided he would substitute for one of the planned fliers. Sunrise would find the flight over upstate New York and Charlie, a native New Yorker, knew the geography well. After a last-minute decision, he donned the leather and sheepskin flying clothes over his business suit, and the flight took off.

Navigation of a balloon at night is a difficult undertaking. Balloons are never quite in altitude equilibrium and as they slowly drift up and down they also tend to rotate slowly. The balloon has no inherent directional stability, such as an airplane has, and any clump of lights in the distance may look like the last clump of lights solidly identified. Thus, the last solid landmark might be unknowingly be replaced by another clump of lights, a few degrees rotation off the previous fix. Sometime after midnight the crew's last solid landmark was Toledo, Ohio, easily identified because of its proximity to Lake Erie.

When the sun awakened, they had no firm idea where they were. In the distance they saw a large body of water that Charlie identified as Lake Champlain in the early morning haze. Looking about, the other crew member, Harold (Bud) Froelich, said,

"Charlie, if that's Lake Champlain what's the big tall building off to the northeast?" Panic struck immediately; the big building was the

Empire State Building. They were at high altitude over a suburb of Newark, New Jersey and headed for the Atlantic Ocean.

They began to dump helium at a rapid rate until the rate of descent approached a dangerous velocity. As they neared the ground they checked the descent by throwing ballast overboard, stabilizing at 'drag-rope' height, about 40 – 50 feet. To understand what happened next requires a short lesson in how a balloon landing is accomplished.

* * *

In a normal landing, at the mercy of the wind for direction of flight, the pilot watches the approaching terrain for a large, acceptable landing site ahead; an agricultural area is a good bet. The lifting gas is valved away, and the balloon descends slowly until the descent is stabilized at about 50 ft. altitude. Then a device called a drag-rope is dropped overboard; the drag rope is weighted to make it heavy. A length of garden hose filled with lead shot and attached to a rope is a common design.

When a portion of the drag-rope touches the ground, the balloon longer has to support its weight, so has a surplus of lift and begins to rise slowly. As the drag rope is picked up its weight is again carried by the balloon and equilibrium is restored. The drag rope has a smooth exterior and can drag through trees, over power lines and almost any obstacle.

The pilot can 'drag-rope-along' for miles until a suitable landing spot appears close by. Then, the drag rope is quickly pulled up, and the balloon descends the final few feet to a landing. When touchdown occurs, the pilot pulls a second rope attached to a section of the envelope near the top of the balloon. This panel, known as a 'rip panel,' is designed to be torn out of the balloon, dumping all the lifting gas quickly and assuring the craft stays on the ground.

* * *

We return to Charlie and Bud on their super-secret mission. They have reached a stable equilibrium on the drag-rope, low over a suburb of Newark rather than going out to sea. However, it's 'from the frying pan into the fire.'

The time is about 7:30 in the morning, and the streets are filled with children going to school. The wind, fortunately light, is almost directly out of the west. They are drifting along a row of suburban houses, each of which sports an external television antenna, as was common in the 1950s. Fragile things they are, and our pair on their secret mission is pulling a TV antenna off almost every house along the street. In addition, they accumulated a claque of children and barking dogs, which is increasing by the block; there is no friendly place to put the balloon down. Then, the kids' destination school appears ahead; its playground seems a welcome haven, but they miss the playground by less than a hundred feet. It begins to look as though the ocean is the next-best bet. Suddenly, a vacant lot appears in line with the direction of flight; as they pass over the empty lot Charlie pulls the rip panel out of the balloon, and they fall unceremoniously into their last possible landing area. They are uninjured, but it's a very rough landing, and now their troubles begin with a vengeance.

By this time a large cheering section has accumulated, accompanied by two police cruisers. As it evolved, the flight was traveling down the border between two suburban communities. They were tearing TV antennas out of one community and have landed in another, all in secret, of course. The two cops get into a heated argument over which of them is going to take these 'Men From Mars' into custody. Charlie, never at a loss for a quick decision, gathers all the scattered equipment and stuffs it into the trunk and back seat of one of the squad cars. He then goes to the two arguing cops, matches the name on the car with the officer's badge, taps him on the shoulder and says,

"Hey, I've loaded all the stuff, let's go."

On the way to the police station, Charlie somehow convinces the officer this is all part of a government secret program and the importance of its not getting into print, which is relayed to the

Breakfast Cereal And Big Balloons

Newark newspaper 3/6/53

Balloon Lands In Union Town

Staff Correspondent.

WINFIELD—An observation balloon with two men aboard, presumably Navy Department weather experts, landed in a lot in Seafoam avenue here at 6:45 A. M. today. The balloon, seen by scores of residents in this part of Union County, was rapidly dismantled by the two men, who, according to Winfield police, refused to give their names or any further information. Neither man was hurt.

A patrolman from nearby Clark said, however, that the men identified themselves as Charles Bachman Moore Jr. and Harold Edward Froehlich, both of Minneapolis. They said they were making a Naval instrument test for a classified study of the lower atmosphere and were bound for Newark Airport.

Patrolman Arthur Miskin of Clark, who attempted to follow the course of the balloon as it drifted toward Winfield, said the craft was a round balloon about 15 to 20 feet in diameter with a basket made apparently of nylon with a plyboard bottom underneath, in which the two men were ridign. He said the balloon had no motor.

Miskin said that the two men shook hands with pleased expressions and said, "Well, we made it." Miskin said that they seemed to think that their mission had been accomplished. But, Miskin asserted, the men refused to explain.

The men in the balloon deflated the gas-filled bag, which Miskin thought was made of plastic, and let spectators rip off pieces of it, Miskin added. Miskin said that the men folded the cloth basket with their instruments and supplies inside and took it with them.

Minneapolis STAR-TRIBUNE ~ 3/7/53

General Mills Balloon Sets N. J. on Ear

By VICTOR COHN
Minneapolis Tribune Staff Writer

A General Mills plastic balloon drifted out of the sky at Winfield, N. J., Friday and, as General Mills balloons do, kicked up a stir.

This one kicked up a little more stir because two men were in it.

THEY WERE C. B. Moore, Jr., engineer in charge of General Mills balloon operations at Minneapolis, and Harold E. Froehlich of the General Mills staff.

They climbed out of a nylon-and-plastic basket, the United Press reported, and shook hands as though pleased.

Moore

They deflated the expendable balloon, and let people rip off parts of it. Then they folded their basket, packed their instruments and supplies and left.

Moore and Froehlich told police they were making a study of the lower atmosphere. General Mills in Minneapolis said they were doing research for the office of naval research. The navy in New York said they had gone up in connection with "research and development of aerial flight techniques and instrumentation."

WHERE THEY came from, or how long they had been in the air, no one would tell. And everyone said details were "classified," that is, secret.

General Mills has been making high-altitude unmanned balloon flights and low-altitude manned flights for some time under navy auspices.

The main flight base has been at the University of Minnesota airport near Minneapolis, but other flight bases have been located from Greenland to the Caribbean.

precinct headquarters by radio. Arriving there, the precinct captain hides Charlie and Bud in the drunk-tank just as two television news crews arrive.

The precinct captain, now a partner in the deal, gives the TV crews the 'palms-up, who me, what men from Mars?' treatment and invites them to look around. Mixed in with the prior night's collection of drunks, Bud and Charlie, with flight suits off and appearing disheveled from the night's flight, look like the rest of the drunks and escape completely. After making insurance arrangements to repair the damage they've done, they are loaded into a squad car and whisked off to Kennedy Airport (then Idlewild) for a late-morning flight back to Minneapolis.

I don't know whether the company received a follow-on contract. The publicity was muted, but copies of clippings from Newark and Minneapolis papers appear on the prior page.

The balloon business, by the very unpredictability of both the weather and the vehicles themselves, were a great preparation for life. Technical improvisations to get a planned flight experiment off the ground were electro-mechanical in one way or another and accomplished under severe time pressure. Flight-following and recovery of the scientific experiment were excellent preparation for dealing with uncertainties and finding one's way about the world.

Serratia Marcescens

About this time, General Mills received a contract from the Army's bacterial warfare center to experimentally grind a pathogen, Serratia Marcesens and its supporting nutrient matrix, probably a starch of some sort, into a fine powder. This sounded like an appropriate bit of research for a milling company. Assigned to the program, I undertook a study of the aerodynamics of fine particles entrained in an air stream and the design a filter system that wouldn't allow any of this material to escape into the local environment.

Physicians have long used Serratia Marcescens (SM) as a biological marker for studying the transmission of microorganisms. Considered a harmless saprophyte in 1950s, Serratia Marcescens only became recognized as a human pathogen during the 1960s.

In the General Mills program, SM was used as a proxy for a biological warfare agent never revealed to us. It was a bacterial organism that could live on the same nutrient compound as the SM. In the beginning, while designing and constructing the laboratory, the entire scope of the program was never disclosed.

The objective of grinding the material to a specified fineness became clear as the work progressed. For a substance to be retained in the human lung, it is essential the particle size be in the range of 3 to 5 microns; smaller particles are inhaled and exhaled – think cigarette smoke. Most larger particles are filtered by nasal hair and mucous membranes before entering the lung, thus defining the narrow-range particle size for an effective, biological pathogen. This is an essential part of the process known as 'weaponizing.'

Dry grinding tends to heat the material being ground, and the SM was killed by elevated temperature as would the bacterial agent being weaponized. The multiple grinding steps to achieve a specific fineness are a compromise between producing the required size and killing the pathogen with the heat resulting from the grinding. When it became evident that the program could evolve into a mass killing program, I began to send out resumes. It was time for me to go. Perhaps someone must do the work of biological warfare, but after much contemplation I decided this technology could be left to others.

I prepared a resume and scattered it about the aircraft industry in California, where my friend John Herfurth moved the year before. He assured me life in California was wonderful. When I received responses from Lockheed, North American Aviation and Northrop Aircraft, I decided to make the move. John also arranged interviews with Douglas Aircraft, and I took a short vacation to explore these opportunities

The aircraft industry was booming with post World War II activity and my confidence level was high as I loaded my little airplane and embarked toward a new career horizon. I planned an intermediate stop along the way see my old mentor, Ken Jackson, now settled in Tucson, Arizona after leaving Hokah a decade before. Sadly, it would be the last time I would see him.

5

California

Fascinated with airplanes from boyhood, the aircraft industry, centered in California, had a strong attraction.

* * *

In late November 1953, I loaded my little airplane and set out for California, spending an evening along the way with my old mentor, Ken Jackson. I arrived two days later, with my interview appointments in-hand, and began interviewing with Lockheed Aircraft. My first interview went well, and the offer of a job buoyed my spirits. The next day it was Northrop, and it also ended with a job offer. The interview the following day at North American Aviation was less heartening.

The personnel man met me in the corporate lobby. I presented my resume, and we had a short discussion after which he disappeared into the bowels of the building, promising a quick return. I spun my wheels for several hours before he reappeared. He said he presented my capabilities to a number of people who were interested in interviewing me, but it was now lunch time and he would arrange interviews after lunch. I lunched on snacks from a vending machine.

The personnel man finally returned about 2:00 p.m. He said an extensive discussion with the Chief Engineer revealed 'serious interest,' but he was busy. He proposed arranging an interview with a section manager and disappeared again. It was nearing 4:00 when he returned again and asked me to come back the following day. He expressed hope things would go better. The entire day passed without anything significant happening. I was hungry and already had two job offers, so I asked him to give me my application, which I tore into small pieces and sprayed on the front of his suit and left. Ah, the impetuousness of youth!

I accepted a job with Northrop Aircraft Inc. The following day, I moved my airplane into temporary storage at Fullerton Airport and spent the remainder of the week with my old friend, John Herfurth. Then I flew home via airline to marry Betty on Jan 2, 1954. We returned to California by car in early January to begin a new life together that has extended 65 years as I write this.

First Home

First Home

After some looking about, we rented a furnished duplex at 730 E. Nutwood, in Inglewood. The best things about it were the flowers and the landlord, who lived in the larger house with the Pine tree in the front yard. The landlord and his wife, Tommy and Minnie Thompson, were great gardeners; they had flowers everywhere around both their house and the duplex we lived in.

Our home was within walking distance of downtown Inglewood and three or four miles from Hawthorne Airport, where Northrop was located and where we kept our airplane.

Flowers On Nutwood Street

It was a pretty humble place, but Betty made it more than tolerable with flowers, and a great meal greeted me in the dining room every night. We had no responsibilities. Evenings and weekends we enjoyed visiting the ocean, Hollywood, the Palos Verdes Peninsula and other sites we saw only in movies or heard about in newscasts. We were often joined by my old friend, John Herfurth and his girlfriend, Jo. The evenings often finished at our home or at a drive-in restaurant called 'The Clock.' Clocks served delicious, deep dish, Boysenberry pies with a scoop of ice cream as topping. There were no worries about weight control in those days.

For all of his painting skills, Tommy's eye for color was limited. Here Betty serves Easter dinner in our dining room with its dark green walls and dark blue carpets. However, as a landlord, he was great and didn't complain when Betty and I recovered the wings of the Cessna in our duplex. This required moving the furniture against the walls and setting up a shop passing through the archway between the living room and dining room.

Easter Dinner

(If you look closely, Betty didn't have all the apparent hair. Much of it is a shadow on the wall from the flash.)

We kept this small place during our entire California stay because we were always on a six-month contingency: a 1-A classification for induction into the Army to serve in the Korean War.

I was initially deferred from military service due to essential work in the aircraft industry, but looking forward to the semiannual news from the Draft Board back in Minnesota became burdensome. We decided to enlist in the Navy while we still controlled of our own destiny. I signed up, took the physical exam and was rejected due to my flat feet. The examining doctor, also named Reilly, submitted my application with recommendation for approval over the protestations of a medical corpsman who kept repeating,

"You can't do that Doc; look at his feet, they're like two little bags of sand." Several weeks later, the Navy's official rejection appeared.

*   *   *

California Living

Our California welcome wasn't all the stuff of sweet nostalgia. Soon after we settled on Nutwood Street, we received a postcard in the mail from Los Angeles County stating we owed back-taxes on our airplane for the year *prior* to our arrival. This was a 'use tax,' of which I was unaware. I wrote a letter of inquiry with documentation as to our arrival in the state. There was no answer, but about a week later a

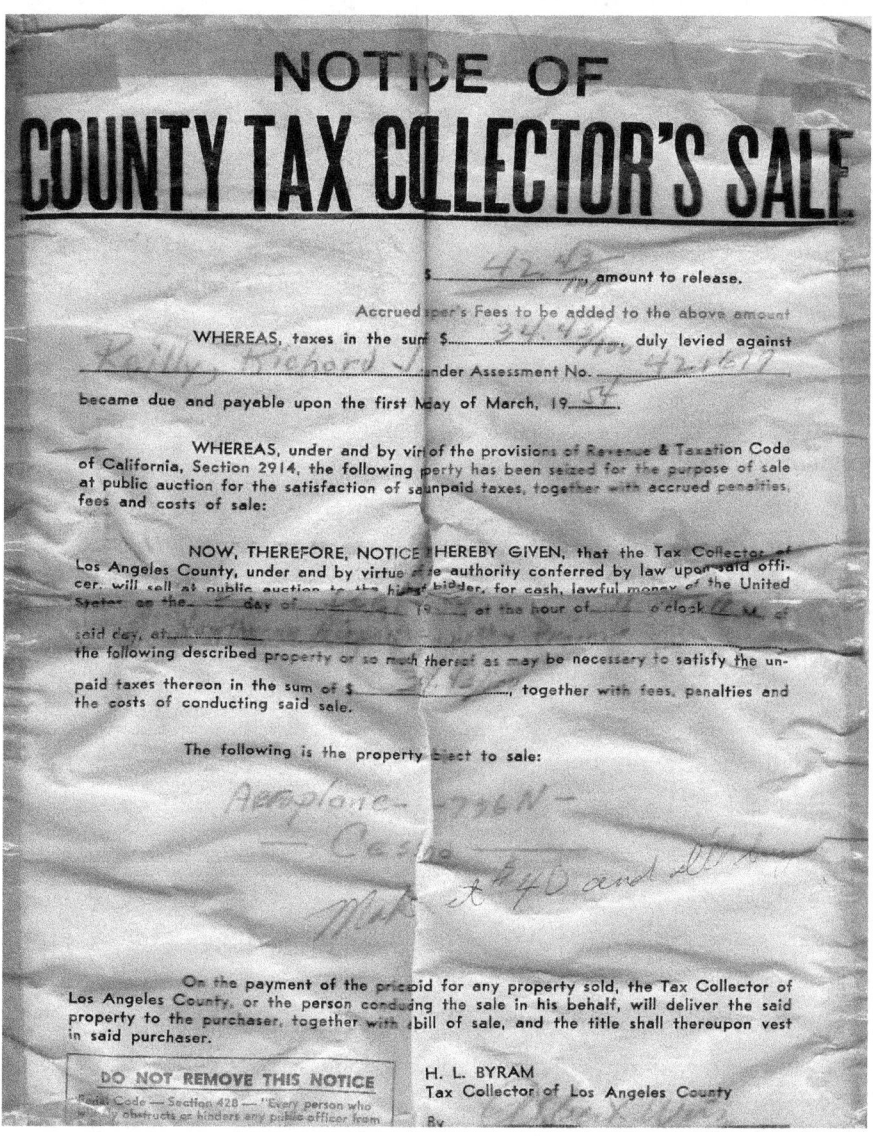

A Little Bureaucratic Abuse

big, burly man turned up at our front door while I was at work. When Betty answered the door, the man, without identifying himself, told her gruffly,

"You'd better start paying your bills kid, or you'll be in lot of trouble." She had the presence of mind to ask to see his identification. He refused and told her,

"The paper hanging on the airplane is proof enough I've got the right to do what I'm doing," then stalked off. When I came home, Betty was tearful, but neither of us understood the problem. How could we owe any tax when we were in the state less than a month?

We drove to Hawthorne Airport that evening and found the notice on the prior page taped to the door of the airplane. The amount demanded was a bit over $42, which doesn't sound like much today. However, inflation considerations would increase that tax by more than ten times what it was in 1954. Forty-two dollars wasn't chopped liver to a young couple just starting out in life. This was a serious problem because we were leaving imminently for the San Francisco Bay area on an extended trip for a test program at NASA's Ames Laboratory. With no time to do-battle; we swallowed hard and payed the bill.

After some difficulty, Betty became pregnant in mid 1955, and Tim was born on February 20, 1956. He was seven weeks premature; despite medical advice to rest, Betty walked to Daniel Freeman Hospital daily, nearly a mile each way, to visit Tim in his incubator. It was a difficult time; he wasn't expected to survive.

Tim arrived so early we hadn't made any of the usual preparations for a new baby. During his three weeks in the incubator it didn't appear we would need clothes or crib. Surprisingly, after nearly a month, within two days Tim improved. He was out of the incubator and we took him home to the duplex, where his first bed was a pillow in a built-in set of drawers in a hallway.

We had three difficult months. Feeding every four hours, day and night, minimized sleep. Betty managed the daytime hours, while I took the 6:00 and 10:00 p.m. feedings, allowing Betty to sleep. After the 10:00 p.m. feeding, often consuming over an hour, I would bed-down in a sleeping bag in the hallway trying not to interrupt Betty's sleep. She would take the 2:00 a.m. feeding, and I would shift to the bed if I happened to hear her step over me. She would then switch to the sleeping bag, so I could survive with enough energy to go to work.

We had no relatives to help us, but sometimes we received a bit of a boost from our landlady, Minnie Thomson. Warren and Alice Meyer, friends I acquired on the job, helped occasionally. However, they lived in Palos Verdes, about 15 miles away, so helping us wasn't easy for them. Eventually, we all survived, and as the schedule eased we found time to purchase baby clothes and a proper crib for Tim.

It was a difficult three months, but in general, life on Nutwood Street was a happy, carefree time of life for us.

RJR and Tim, Inglewood 1956

6

Northrop Aircraft

It was a bit of old Europe. The paternalism of 'The Doctor' rested heavily on my shoulders, but it was a great place to learn.

* * *

Initially, the job at Northrop, conducting basic research on laminar boundary layer flow, was a real joy. The head of the group was Dr. Werner Pfenninger, a scientist from the Swiss Federal Institute in Zurich. *'The Doctor,'* as he was reverently referred-to around the office, was about 50 years of age and had devoted his entire professional life to the study of laminar boundary layer flows. He had an international reputation in the field; for me it was an unparalleled learning opportunity.

We worked in a hangar-like building about 50 feet wide and 150 feet long with a circular-arc roof. It was located a long-block from the company's main facility and was split into two approximately equal sections. The front half was set up for offices and the rear housed a splendid model shop with first-class metal working machines. The office section housed a couple of corporate offices and a conference room, but it was largely an open space with desks and drafting tables for about 25 people, arranged side-by-side and row-upon-row. A real gentleman, with the improbable name of Jesse James, ran the shop staffed by about a dozen model makers.

Plucked from the Swiss Federal Institute by the U.S. Air Force, *The Doctor* joined Northrop to do basic work on long-range aircraft. This implied extensive, laminar, external flow. The Northrop organizational structure gave him the administrative support and physical facilities required to conduct basic research leading toward what could be a revolutionary aircraft.

His nominal Division Head, Roger Moore, was an experienced Northrop executive, administering the finances and maintaining liaison with the Northrop management structure. However, there was never any doubt as to who was running the show.

Roger was a rather sorry figure. He once held a top-level job in the Northrop hierarchy, and my guess is he was forgotten by the organization. He functioned as though he were hiding in this little research enclave, with a substantial salary and fearful of being rediscovered. Essentially, he had no job and spent his time wandering aimlessly from his office in the front of the building, through the desks and machine shop and returning to his office, only to repeat the process a few minutes later. He did this, perhaps a hundred times a day or more; he was a pathetic figure. I felt sorry for him.

The Doctor ran the group as a real, European subculture: paternalistic and autocratic. He reviewed all technical reports we received from the library in the main plant facility before allowing the rabble to read them. At the end of each day, he stood aside the front door to make sure we all took home appropriate reading material for home study. He studied under one of the eminent men in the aerodynamics field of the 1930s and 40s, Jacob Ackeret. *The Doctor*, who spoke in accented Swiss/German English, peppered his conversation with aphorisms beginning with:

"Ya, Ackeret always said … ." In this case *The Doctor* justified his insistence on daily home study with:

"Ya, Ackeret always said, 'one must be careful with what one does with one's spare time while one is young." At other times, he advised, "Ya, Ackeret always said 'one must be careful,'" without specification. It might be applied to almost any situation. (Jakob Ackeret was somewhat of an icon in the aerodynamics field prior to WW II and an associate of Ludwig Prandtl).

The Tube

I was assigned to 'the tube,' making fundamental, precise measurements of boundary layer development in a 40 foot long, two-inch diameter tube, housed underground in an old bomb shelter on a corner of Hawthorne Airport. Laminar boundary layers are extremely sensitive to temperature gradients. The underground shelter, heated continuously by infrared lamps, provided a very stable temperature environment. After a few day's indoctrination by an old hand, John Goldsmith, I worked alone underground for several months, reporting-in at the office and proceeding to my bomb shelter. I missed my old dog, Butch, left at home in Minnesota, but I adopted a small gray mouse who became tame enough to appear in my presence. Betty packed a lunch for him daily, along with mine.

I learned much about experimental methods because the tube was an extremely sensitive device and required meticulous care to get good data. The boundary layer in the tube was very sensitive to acoustic disturbances and would be tripped from laminar to turbulent flow by the engine sound-pressure waves from a passing truck on a nearby street. I could follow the engine speed of such a vehicle for several blocks because the right frequency tripped the tube to turbulence as the engine speed varied while shifting gears. *The Doctor* dropped in a couple of times a month to see how I was doing and look at my data. He would pick up my data sheets and stand scowling for some time before saying,

"Ya, it looks pretty goot." Upon departing he would often say, "Ya, Ackeret always said, 'one must be careful' .... "

I thought I was doing original work and gave it my all. When I completed the assigned task, I wrote a large report and turned it in to *The Doctor*. He accepted it without comment and reached into his file to retrieve several similar reports for comparison. It became evident that nearly everyone who was hired into the group did a stint on the tube as an indoctrination, and by comparing my results to others he could assess my experimental skills. The whole process was sort of a probationary test; I passed.

NASA Ames

NASA Ames 12 ft. Pressure Tunnel

Early on, I was assigned to the finishing and testing of a 9:1 fineness ratio, three-dimensional, elliptically-shaped body to be conducted in the old 'Twelve Foot Pressure Tunnel' at NASA Ames Laboratory, near San Francisco. Testing lasted about a month and Betty went along; we set up housekeeping in a motel in Mountain View. She took her sewing machine along to pass the dull days.

The old pressure tunnel was a magnificent facility. Built with thick steel walls, it could be pressurized to pressures greater than atmospheric or pumped down to a near vacuum to simulate flight at high altitude. For our 3D body tests, this capability allowed us achieve a wide range of Reynolds Numbers.

The pressure tunnel was expensive to operate due to characteristics not visible in the photo. Since the pressure could be varied, the circuit was tightly closed. Grinding a fixed mass of air around and around heats it significantly. Thus, the facility included a refrigeration system to cool the air and maintain a controlled temperature during a test. It is gone now, fallen to the budget ax and the Space Shuttle … sob. As far as I know, there is no other facility like it anywhere in the world, and I was privileged to work with it.

Dr. Eric Groth was also a part of this test program. He was one

9:1 Body In NASA Ames 12' Wind Tunnel

of the German 'Paper Clip' scientists, who immigrated to the U.S. after WW II. The group included Dr. Rudolph Hermann, my old graduate school adviser, and Werner von Braun of rocketry fame. Eric was a real pleasure to work with, and we spent many hours together both on this test and later in many flight tests at Edwards Air Force Base.

Midway through the program, the need arose to visualize the transition point from laminar to turbulent flow. I read much about various methods of determining transition and suggested we could use the 'China Clay' method, although I had no experience with it.

China Clay involves coating the model with a white, dusty particulate substance of a particular index of refraction. When wetted with a liquid of similar refractive index, the clay coating becomes transparent. As the liquid evaporates, the coating again turns white. Because a turbulent boundary layer evaporates the liquid at a much higher rate than a laminar layer, after a short 'development time' the areas of turbulent flow become visible. The nose of the body in the photo

Boundary Layer Transition Made Visible

above is laminar, with the bare aluminum showing through the China Clay. Aft of approximately the front quarter of the body, the flow is turbulent as is evident by the now-white coating.

China Clay is a tricky process. The clay particles are suspended in a lacquer base and sprayed on the model. The lacquer, after drying, binds the clay to the surface. Careful application is required to not change the contour or roughen the surface. Then, the surface of the coating is delicately sanded away, cutting through the suspending lacquer but only on its exterior surface. This opens the clay particles, allowing them to absorb the matching refractive liquid and make the clay surface temporarily transparent. While I was without experience, my old model making skills came in handy, and Jackson, my old mentor from Hokah, taught me how do a credible job with a spray gun. The impromptu NASA Ames session with China Clay was a complete success. I became the group's visualization 'expert;' I was astonished by how little it took to become an expert, but no one challenged my technique.

Other Wind Tunnel Work

I also had the good fortune to work in the Northrop wind tunnel from time to time. This was a fine facility for a smaller company to have as its own. I learned a great deal about experimental technique, data analysis and that raw data may not always be useful information.

Bruce Carmichael and I were exploring the effect of a wing/body junction on the transition of the boundary layer from laminar to a turbulent in the intersection. The joining of two aerodynamic shapes usually results in the formation of a vortex as indicated by the black wedge in the photograph, opposite. Here the visualization agent is naphthalene (mothballs) dispersed in a solvent and sprayed on the black surface. The black wedge indicates the rapid removal of the naphthalene by the turbulent flow in the vortex.

The tests extended over some weeks and we were almost finished

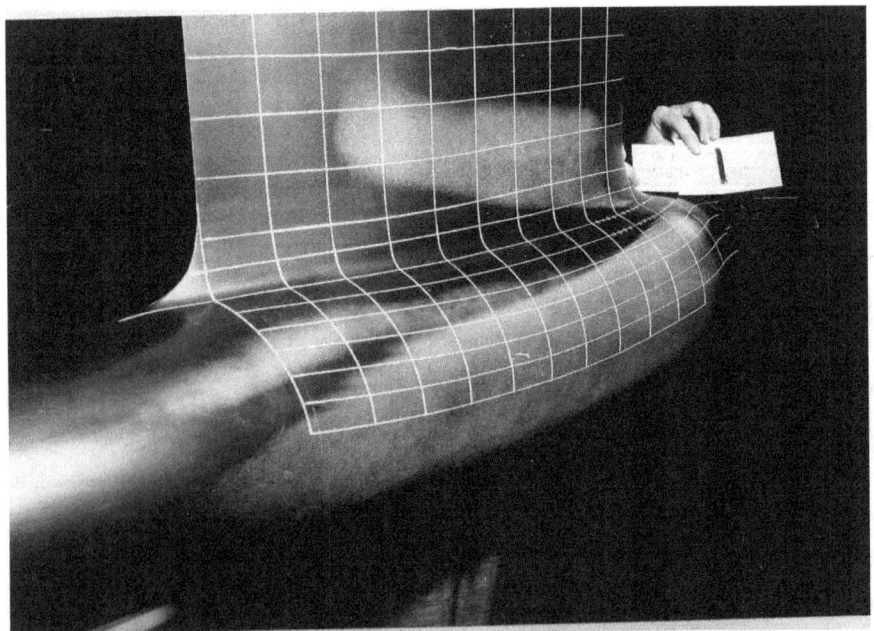

Wing/Body Intersection Model

with the planned test runs. It appeared we might have several hours of valuable and unused tunnel time remaining when our work was done. We were both interested in the design of high performance sailplanes as an avocation, and at the time there were many questions as to the drag of a canopy (personnel enclosure), when it was added to an otherwise low-drag, cylindrically-shaped body. We had an ideal situation: A highly developed body in place in the tunnel, substantial baseline data already in the bag and a couple of hours of free test time. Foregoing lunch, I carved a canopy shape from balsa wood, finished it smoothly with lacquer, and we were ready for some interesting personal experiments.

We completed the formal program as planned and fastened the canopy model in place on the basic body of revolution. We faired the canopy in place with modeling clay and began testing.

Plotting the raw data as we measured it, we expected it to follow some organized pattern. It did not. The more data we obtained the wilder it became. It showed some sort of trend, but if we were honest with ourselves the data plot more resembled the test pattern from a shotgun than a relationship between physical parameters. In short, it was a great disappointment. We made some changes in the variables but to no avail. The time was gone, and our grand experiment was a bust.

There's data and data … ; Ackeret always said,

"One must be careful."

As the experimental apparatus was being dismantled and the model removed from the tunnel, we sat slumped over the sheet of graph paper trying vainly to make something from nothing. It was hopeless. With a sigh and a great flourish, my friend Bruce drew a silly looking, 'S'-shaped curve through the data and threw down his pencil. The data were so bad that if we had one or two more scattered points, no rational person would have drawn a line at all.

Our day's hope died there on a piece of paper, with scattered data points and this strange line with the wiggle in it. We didn't even bother to take the plot with us and left it lying on the tunnel control console. We closed out the formal experiment, wrote a final report and abandoned our little side-journey into canopy drag.

* * *

In the mid 1950s a 'computer' was a person – usually a young woman and often with a degree in mathematics – armed with a Frieden calculator. If she were a class act, it was a '*Square-Root* Frieden.' Some months later, my canopy companion in crime was walking through Northrop's Computer Department – the young women with the Frieden calculators; every aircraft company had acres of them. Walking down an aisle en route to somewhere else, he saw a familiar figure from the corner of his eye. There, on a computer's desk, was the data plot from our failed canopy experiment; the funny curve with the wiggle in it made it unmistakable. Our discarded data was being used in some other calculation. However, the experimental points were removed, and the graph carried no information regarding its lineage. Furthermore, the young woman was locating points on the funny curve with a sharp, prick-punch. She was reading their coordinates for use in some other data manipulation process, using a magnifying glass to assure unerring accuracy!

In these days of the Internet, we often search for and find data available from unknown sources, with unknown lineage and reliability. One can find extensive data on the Internet, but we sometimes forget data alone isn't always useful information; perhaps *The Doctor* was right after all:

"Ackeret always said one must be careful to never read a report unless he knows the author personally." An extreme view perhaps, but it keeps one out of a certain kind of trouble.

The Tank

Before the days of computers and computational fluid dynamics, one of the ways of getting flow data around complex shapes was an 'Electrolytic Tank,' a facility simulating non-viscous, 'potential' flow around an immersed body. Again, it was not a common tool because it required a good equipment and extraordinary care to get good results. *The Doctor* had a classy setup housed in a small laboratory, carved from the back corner of our machine shop.

As with many esoteric experiments, the electrolytic tank is a simple device. Ours was constructed from a four by eight foot flat sheet of insulating material for a bottom, fitted with sides about eight inches high and filled with water. The tank walls at the ends (short sides) were conductive and connected across a power supply of several hundred volts. When powered, a current flowed through the water from one end to the other. The model, also constructed from an insulating material, disrupted this flow of current by squeezing the electrical path around the body of interest. The voltage change resulting from this distortion is measured with a probe, supported on a fancy carriage with precision x/y scales, allowing its position in the water to be accurately determined.

I was assigned to 'the tank,' along with Joe Sipe, to determine the flow around the intersection of a wing and a body. On this particular day it wasn't going well. The tank lab was close to the shop, and the machinists were frequently turning large machines on and off; we suspected the resulting large change in the electric line voltage might be causing the frustrating problems we were having with our fancy experimental apparatus. Finally, throwing up my hands in disgust, I said,

"Joe, let's calibrate this thing." Joe replied in horror,

"Oh no, we can't do that. *The Doctor* has told everybody to never calibrate the tank."

"Well, he never told me," I replied, "and I'm tired of this nonsense." I went out in the shop to find the shop superintendent, Jesse James, and said,

"See the big micarta cylinder up on the high shelf in stores? Please cut me a piece about an eight inches long." The 'potential flow' around a cylinder is simple enough to be completed by hand calculation. When compared with the experimental results, it would help us isolate our problems. Joe departed for his desk; he was not going to be a partner in this crime.

Office folklore conjectured that *The Doctor's* electrolytic tank work in Zurich, which set him up for the Air Force contract, might be compromised by new findings. While he wasn't outright, intellectually dishonest, he wasn't eager to revisit any experiments that might cast doubt on his prior work. Flow around a cylinder was just too basic and revealing; better the tank data be left just a bit misty to make room for some discussion and 'windmill' hand-waving

I drained the tank, put my calibration cylinder on the floor of the tank and sealed it in place. Refilling the tank, I began to make measurements; the results were outstanding. I was well along in the calibration process when *The Doctor* walked in, hands clasped behind his back un-sleeved, with suit-coat draped over his shoulders in European professorial style. He bent over to examine my experiment closely, grunted, said nothing, spun on his heel and left; what I was doing was obvious. A few moments later he returned, still hunched over, hands behind his back. He took another look at my apparatus and departed without a word. I continued working. Several minutes went by before *The Doctor* returned. He peered again at my experiment and said,

"Ya, vaat are you doing?"

"I'm calibrating the tank Doctor," I replied cheerily without looking up from my work. Long pause … then he said,

"Ya, how does it look?"

"Pretty good," I responded, "The worst data point I have is off from the theoretical value by only one part in 1300." The *Doctor's* face lit up as though it was Christmas morning. Wringing his hands eagerly and ignoring that agreement to within one part in 100 would have been more than good, he said enthusiastically,

"Ya, with a little more care perhaps we can even get it a bit better." In a couple of seconds I went from goat to hero … . I was now the tank 'expert.'

Fun on the Desert

A major milestone in the Laminar Boundary Layer program was the incorporation of the basic research into a flight test article. At this point, an airplane incorporating the technology wasn't possible, but it was necessary to explore the effects of altitude, contamination and engine noise on the delicately-stable laminar boundary layer. A flight test program was designed around a glove fitted to a Lockheed F-94, a two-seat version of the F-80, the U.S.'s first operational jet fighter.

The F-94's wing was fitted with a 'glove' over the inboard section of the wing, changing the airfoil contour in a limited part of the span, to a shape favorable to supporting laminar flow. The gloved section was deep enough to house an arrangement of thin slots in the surface of the glove with small plenum chambers below. This allowed a turbine-driven suction pump to draw off 'tired' boundary layer air, whose energy was reduced by friction. The removed air was

F-94 Fitted With Glove

replaced by higher energy air from outside the original boundary layer. Internally, the glove contained a vast array of pressure taps and tubes leading to a manometer board of liquid-filled glass tubes in the rear cockpit and read by an observer. The test observer was a problem.

While this was routine flying, with a seasoned airplane having no operational complications, the airplane had one nasty quirk. The longer transparent canopy, fitted in converting the F-80 to a two-seat configuration, had a tendency to rotate when jettisoned prior to an emergency ejection. Canopy rotation would sometimes decapitate the rear-seat occupant if he didn't have his head on his knees. The manometer board prevented a standard-issue man from assuming this position. Fortunately, our engineering observer, my good friend Bruce Carmichael, was about 5'4" and could just about get into head-on-knees position while wearing a helmet, but it was never quite certain just how well this would work in a real emergency.

On two occasions a bailout was avoided by some skillful piloting by our pilot, Jack Wells, who nursed the airplane to climb when the afterburner nozzle stuck in open position, preventing the engine from producing its normal thrust. Bailout not needed!

My small part in all of this involved flow visualization once again. While success was well documented by pressure measurements, the value of pictures is unchallenged. *The Doctor* wanted photographic evidence to show to Air Force program sponsors at Wright Field. I was enlisted to apply a China Clay surface to the glove and then spray the required propylene glycol development fluid on the glove at the end of the runway just prior to takeoff.

We reported for work every day at our facility near Hawthorne Airport and transported to Edwards Air Force Base – then called Muroc, after the dry lake where it was located – in the company's DC-3. Flight-test pilot, Jack Wells, was also somewhat of a 'stand-up comedian' before that appellation was part of the language. He would regale the commuters with stories of flying in Florida, chasing Northrop's 'Snark' missiles after launch.

The Snark was a troubled vehicle, a large, remotely controlled jet airplane, and for several years each launch ended in a crash into the ocean off Cape Canaveral, which Jack referred to as a "Snark-infested bay." His unparalleled descriptions of living with Florida's abundant insect population, and the popping sounds resulting from stepping on Palmetto Bugs were vivid.

If there was a limited contingent going to Muroc on a particular day, the company used a four-seat, North American Navion to carry the crew. In winter, the pilot would always carry a well-packaged copy of the "Los Angeles Times" we would drop to the caretaker of the Mt. Wilson Observatory. We would pass low over the observatory as we crossed the San Gabriel Mountains, just north of 'The City' and attempt to hit the parking lot with the day's newspaper. Located at about 6000 feet and visible from anywhere in the 'sunny paradise,' Mt. Wilson would sometimes be snowed-in for weeks at a stretch, isolating the caretaker. There was no formal arrangement; it was just one of those things essential for anyone flying the Navion to Muroc. The reward was a friendly wave and knowing you brightened someone's day.

In retrospect, this seems to have been an inordinate amount of flying-about for my 30 second contribution to a flight test. However, for some reason, no one at Edwards appeared able to spray just the right amount of fluid onto the China Clay surface. Too little meant it evaporated too quickly for the airplane to fly stabilized, on-point for a sufficient length of time. Too much, induced rivulets of fluid, an artificial roughness of the surface as the flight began, thus prematurely tripping the boundary layer to turbulence.

Somehow, I'm reminded of the days when utilities advertised 'Electricity is Penny Cheap.' The local electrical utility ran entertaining commercials to induce people to use more of their product. A staple television commercial in this series featured the various adventures of "Homer and Roy." In one of these, Homer sprayed about three shots from a paint gun at a framed canvas and miraculously produced the

Mona Lisa. Spray gun still in hand, he then turned to Roy with a wry smile and said,

"It's all in the wrist, Roy."

Office Environment

The *Doctor's* autocratic ways permeated the office environment. While one might have a long-term project such as the 'The Tank' or 'The Tube,' he would occasionally be assigned a 'background' research problem. Typically, *The Doctor* would pull a chair near your desk and without preliminaries would say,

"Ya, some day we must take a look at the effect of Reynolds Number on … . Would you look into this and make a report?" So, in addition project work, there would be time spent in the company library researching the literature on whatever was the item of *The Doctor's* interest. After a week or more, or perhaps a month or more, he would return and say,

"Ya, sometime back I asked you to look into … . Vaat haff you found out?" Having taken the assignment seriously and depending on the elapsed time, I would have a sizable file, with a summary paper and several possible approaches to expanding the current state of technical lore on the item of interest. *The Doctor* would accept the material with a smile and without looking at it, toss it aside saying,

"Ya, in Zurich once I made some measurements showing … and we will start wiss ziss and … ." After a couple of such outcomes, one took these 'backgrounders' less seriously, did a minimum effort and waited for the directed approach sure to come. While I always tried to be ready with something, Joe Sipe, who occupied an adjacent desk, wrote a play professionally produced by 'Players Ring' in downtown Los Angeles. Ken Rogers designed a helicopter he built in his garage; almost everyone had a 'thing' going on the side.

Information Control

Located some distance from the main company facility, we had a courier service that delivered supplies and technical documents from the company library. The service didn't work very well and it took forever to get something delivered. I inadvertently stumbled onto the 'slow problem' with the system. I went to *The Doctor's* office and although he was absent I noticed a technical report on his desk that I was expecting for some time. As I walked out with it, his secretary stopped me, pitching a small fit:

"No, no, no, no you can't have that; *The Doctor* hasn't approved it yet."

"It's a standard NASA report I ordered some time ago," I replied, "I don't think any approval is required."

"Oh yes it is," she replied, "*The Doctor* approves everything before it is distributed." When I asked him about this later, he told me this was his policy because,

"One should never read technical material unless he knows the author personally. I review everything for my people, so they don't waste their time." To make sure no time was wasted, *The Doctor* would stand in the doorway as people departed from work, checking to make sure they were carrying sufficient technical reading matter to occupy their time after dinner.

"Ya, Ackeret always said, one must be careful with what one does with one's spare time while one is young."

Poor Roger

Roger Moore, the ostensible director of the Boundary Layer Research facility, was the butt of many cruel jokes. While most of the professional staff understood his problem and the office politics, the machinists and tradesmen in the model shop took umbrage at Roger's many trips through their domain; they regarded his minute-by-minute visits to the model shop as some sort of spying operation. Often, when he'd stop in simple curiosity to look at a part being machined, the operator would suddenly increase the speed of the spindle or cutter, throwing cutting oil all over his face and suit and then, with profuse apology, proceed to wipe him down with a dirty shop towel.

On one occasion, a delicate part was undergoing a microscopic examination with a group of a half dozen or more awaiting turns at the microscope. Roger too lined up to have a look, but he didn't know what everyone else knew: the eyepiece of the microscope was coated with lampblack. So, while others approached for a careful for a look, Roger put his eye against the eyepiece and spent the remainder of the afternoon pacing his rounds with a black eye.

Two Doctors

Dr. Max Dengler was an enigmatic figure around the office: a real, official, Austrian aristocrat, complete with a nasty dueling scar running from one ear to the point of his chin. I never quite understood what he did, and it wasn't appropriate to ask Doctor Dengler much of anything; he made that clear by his demeanor. One day he mysteriously disappeared. He returned about a month later, to announce he received a second doctoral degree from his old Alma Mater in Austria, and hereafter he was to be known as Doctor, Doctor Dengler. Thereafter, he and *The Doctor* engaged in a European, culturally-based, hierarchical turf-battle over his title and the proper appellation to be used in addressing him. This European cultural war was great fun for Americans accustomed to first-name familiarity.

The End of the Trail

I began to tire of the paternalism and the dismal opportunity to advance beyond research flunky, despite the day-to-day satisfaction of working in a detailed research environment. When I began to think about a job change, *The Doctor's* paternalism took an ugly turn. One of my peers received a job offer from another company requiring a written recommendation from his current employer. At his request, *The Doctor* wrote a derogatory description of this man's competence and work habits. He was stunned, and I began to rethink just how I might seek another job. It emerged that *The Doctor* considered it a personal affront when anyone choose to leave his beneficent environs. Thus, seeking a new job took a different turn.

I don't recall how I became aware of it, but I learned of a University of Minnesota group working in the Aircraft Division at Northrop. Bob Katkov headed the aerodynamics group and working under him, Alson (Buzz) Fraser, ran a group devoted to inlet aerodynamics, my graduate school focus. Eventually, I sought out Fraser and explained my predicament. Buzz was a fighter pilot in WW II, quick of mind and decisive.

"Simple solution," said Buzz, "With your academic background in supersonic inlets, I can have Katkov request your transfer here. You can work under me for a year and then do whatever you like. I'll give you a good recommendation and have Katkov do the same."

When the request came through, *The Doctor* was furious. He fought my transfer politically and urged me to stay on with his group, but in the end I transferred to the Inlet Aerodynamics group.

The Airplane Business

The difference between working for *The Doctor* and the airplane development side of the business couldn't have been more striking. Instead of the luxury of exploring every little facet of flow configurations, the emphasis turned to getting the best solution to a problem within a defined schedule. I was initially assigned to the design of the supersonic inlet for a competitive program termed 'Long Range Interceptor' (LRI).

Although an official assessment said we the technically superior solution, we didn't win the program because 'it wasn't our turn.' I didn't understand the result at the time, but later, in my Washington-Pentagon years, I learned many of these development programs were a means to retain a competent 'Defense Industrial Base.' At the time of the LRI, Northrop won the T-38 trainer program a few years before. Ultimately, a training aircraft is a much more lucrative enterprise; the T-38 is still (in 2019) the Air Force's advanced training aircraft, having been a sustaining source of parts and maintenance contracts for over 60 years. On the other hand, the LRI program, won by North American Aviation, became the F-107, an airplane that went nowhere after the building of two prototype airplanes.

After losing the LRI program Northrop had a large engineering staff with little to do, however, it was necessary to keep a technical staff available, ready to bid on the next big airplane program to evolve. Such a staff was an essential part of a firm's bid, as were manufacturing operations, metal working machines and floor space.

To retain a staff, whose size is measured in acres rather than the number of individuals, is a different sort of challenge. People were often assigned to clean up loose ends left over from the chaotic days of a competitive design study, or even assigned 'busy work' such as computing the trigonometric tables to 'umpteen' decimal accuracy – remember, these were pre-computer days.

When hundreds of bright people are assembled in a vast open space, with little constructive activity to occupy their time, anomalous behavior is inevitable. I returned from lunch one day to find a black box on my desk with a neatly wrapped electrical cord attached. It looked like a manufactured item: engraved inscriptions, inspection decals etc. Most prominent was an engraved inscription below a large momentary switch. It read: 'Fuse Tester.' Wondering who delivered this neat device to me, obviously in error, I was overcome by curiosity. I unwrapped the electrical cord, plugged it into a wall socket and pressed the switch. The box emitted a sound like someone is being executed at San Quentin Prison, and all the lights went out in a ten thousand square foot area. Well of course, – a fuse tester!

I unscrewed the cover and found the switch attached to a large copper buss bar that put a dead short across the line. I reassembled it, re-wrapped the chord, walked a quarter of mile and placed it on the desk of the next absent victim. For several weeks, every few hours the lights went out in various parts of this multi-acre building as the little box did it's designed task effectively.

The F-5 Fighter

I was more fortunate than some of these people and assigned to the next big development program at Northrop: the supersonic F-5 fighter. This airplane was based on the T-38, minimally supersonic but lacking a well designed engine air inlet, the key to supersonic flight. In addition to detailed design work on the F-5's inlet geometry, one of my secondary duties was to work with the Preliminary Design Group that was determining the overall layout of the F-5. While not then-currently clear, this experience was pivotal to success in my consulting activities some 30 years later.

Preliminary Design at Northrop was not organized as a major independently staffed group, but rather as a small group of experienced designers, supported by specific skills and dedicated to a specific aircraft program. People with a variety of talents: structures, aerodynamics, inlets, electrical systems, hydraulics etc., worked in conjunction with groups dedicated to a particular aircraft. Their in-depth talents expedited solution to continuously evolving design problems. This led to an interesting set of pressures and the need to 'defend' your particular area of the design.

If there were no weight specifications, structural people would like to carve the entire airplane from solid material. Evidently impossible, the structural interests strive for minimum complexity, fewest piece-parts and openings. On the other hand, electrics, hydraulics, fuel supply systems and other auxiliaries never have sufficient passageways through the structure to route their essentials. They continually press to pass more and larger pipes and wire bundles through limited openings. Inlets, with their spacious tunnels, were always at risk of a sneaky bit of re-lofting, which could be difficult to detect without reference to layout drawings checked day-by-day. When the pressure became great enough in some particular part of the structure, the rumors would leak out:

"Structures is going to open another lightening hole at station 85." When this occurred, everyone would standby ready to pounce and get their pipe or wire into the preferred position. It was a dangerous and watchful time because much geometry was up for grabs in these times of flux.

Office Protocol

The office environment in the manufacturing business couldn't differ more from *The Doctor's* patriarchy. Instead of daily contact with *The Doctor*, I was given jobs for completion my way. Buzz was available for consultation at my behest, but formal contact with management came in monthly meetings in the office of Bob Katkov, where the entire aerodynamics staff assembled.

Katkov had a stunning young secretary who, by her interactions with his staff, made it evident her virginity could be a topic for historical study. Pleasingly structured, she often wore low-cut, peasant blouses, and mounted on hooker-heels she walked in such a way as to put the entire assemblage into motion. She caused such congestion it became necessary to move her desk from a main access aisle to an inboard location and less accessible for casual contact.

Since I didn't have any direct contact with Katkov, I never knew her name, but other female staff, whether out of disdain or envy, referred to her as "It." While she was well under thirty years old, rumor said she was in the process of divorcing her fifth husband.

At one of the monthly staff meetings, some 15 or 20 people assembled in a conference room along both sides of a long table. In mid-meeting, Katkov's secretary bounced in, walked the full length of the room with a message for him, delivered it and departed. As she walked past the long table she let out a shriek, recovered and walked on, unperturbed. Katkov asked,

"What's the matter with her?" After a long pause, one of the group replied,

"When she walked by here I grabbed her by the thigh; I just couldn't stand it anymore." Everyone chuckled and the meeting went on without further comment or repercussion. No legal violations, no lawyers, no sensitivity retraining classes, just another day at the office.

It was a different time!

Departure

After about year of inlet work I began to execute my plan for leaving the Los Angeles area. We made several trips to San Francisco and liked it, so I applied for a job with Hiller Helicopters and included Dr. Hermann, my graduate school adviser, as a reference. Unknown to me, Dr. Hermann was working as a consultant to Honeywell Inc. in Minneapolis. A job offer resulted from an interview he arranged with Honeywell Inc. Its major attraction was working on the inlet spike control for the Convair B-58 Hustler, the U.S.'s first supersonic bomber. I accepted.

My last weeks at Northrop were a nightmare. Much time was spent clearing my list of Confidential and Secret documents obtained from the company library over three years. General practice in the working groups required that classified material be kept in locked files, but the question was: Whose file? Once liberated from the library, an interesting document might be lifted from your section of a locked file and used by someone else without your noticing it was gone. Finding these, and clearing my records was a monumental task. I also assembled the collection of small tools, safety glasses etc. given to everyone upon joining the organization.

My last day came. In the morning, *The Doctor* made one of his rare trips to the 'Main Plant' in an attempt to convince me I should return to his group. He seemed saddened by my departure. After lunch it was off to my 'Exit Interview,' and then I intended to visit the old Boundary Layer Group to say my good-byes.

Reporting to the personnel department, I was questioned as to why I was leaving and what it might take to retain me on staff. After completing the interview I was told to step into the office next door. There I submitted the forms certifying the return of all classified material and again told to go to the office next door, where I returned my small tools, duly noted, and I was again asked to step next door. There I returned my company badge and identification and I was again told to go next door. I passed through the door and found myself standing on El Segundo Boulevard, blinded by the late afternoon sun. The door clicked shut, and when I tried to reenter, I found it locked behind me. There was no way to return to say farewell to my old friends, most of whom I never saw again. Now on the wrong side of the building, I was a mile from my car with a hollow feeling in the pit of my stomach. It was the end of an interesting, three-year, learning period.

* * *

Epilogue

Many years later, *The Doctor*, now a feeble old man in his 80s, was still working as a technical consultant at the NASA Langley Laboratory in Virginia. Laminar flow was almost a religion for him, and I don't believe he ever quit working on its deepest mysteries. In the mid 1990s, I found myself on a trip to the military side of Langley Field. After finishing my work I called *The Doctor* and inquired as to his health. He invited me to visit, and I searched-out his office in the labyrinth of NASA buildings. *The Doctor* welcomed me warmly; he inquired about how I'd spent the intervening 40 years, and with shaking hands he reached into his bookcase and opened a large notebook of formal reports on past work. The report he wanted to show me was one I wrote decades earlier. He complimented me on this bit of work and told me how it was still valuable in the work he was then doing. After an hour or more it was time to go; we shook hands and he walked me to my car with his arm on my shoulder. There was a spark of graciousness in the old gentleman after all; it just hadn't been visible in years past.

I still feel some regret that a golden opportunity to learn escaped because I rejected the constrained paternalism of the 'Old World,' but things are different when one is young.

"Ya, Ackeret always said one must be careful with what one does with one's spare-time when one is young." The time I spent with *The Doctor* proved valuable throughout the succeeding four decades.

7

Back To Minnesota

During our years in California, we were indoctrinated, almost unknowingly, by subtle psychological pitches placing the state on an environmental pedestal. Two-inch newspaper headlines might read: 'East Swelters' or 'Blizzard Grips Plains.' Unsaid: You're here in Paradise, basking in the sun.' Enjoy!

* * *

As we started up the California cost toward Oregon, there was a nagging feeling we were returning to some primitive existence. The California culture carried on a subtle, continuous sales campaign to assure everyone they were indeed living in paradise. It was difficult not to be affected.

We decided, although it was midwinter, we would see parts of the West we hadn't been able to cover during our years in California. The route was San Francisco, Oregon, Seattle, Spokane, Idaho, and Montana, with a stop in North Dakota to visit some of Betty's relatives.

Arriving in Minnesota just before Christmas 1956, we set up temporary housekeeping at the Lake Trail Motel, then found a house at 6001 Zenith Avenue North, in Brooklyn Center. Our little duplex in California was a bit cramped after Tim began to grow, and it was good to have a place for him, his big highchair and the cage for Herman, the parakeet. In 1957, the bird was his constant companion and wouldn't even let him cry in his crib without flying to where we were in the house and buzzing us to let us know all was not well.

We began to look for a house to purchase immediately; it became a weekend occupation we worked at diligently. We were influenced by California archi-

Tim, Brooklyn Center 1957

tecture and favored long, low styles tucked into the landscape: a rarity in Minnesota. A friend I met at work, Elmer Johnson, who just completed building a new house – with his own hands – encouraged us to build our own from scratch. Taking a leaf from Elmer's book, we began to make drawings, but the hammer and nails part was beyond consideration at this point in our lives. Getting started on a new job consumed most of our time and we decided to go with a general contractor.

At the end of about six months, while designing our structure, our landlord on Zenith Avenue decided to move back into his house. Forced to move, we found a house vacant for the summer and fall at 2218 Benjamin Street in Minneapolis, just a few blocks from work. After more searching, we discovered a lot in Arden Hills that didn't belong to a major builder of 'cookie cutter' houses: 1759 Venus Avenue for which we paid $1750. The following four pictures show the early progression toward turning our drawings into living space.

* * *

Betty and Tim inspecting our lot at 1759 Venus Ave. in 1957

The start of excavation was a big day.

The basement is complete and a rough floor covers the open hole.

The sticks begin to go up and we can get an idea of how the rooms will feel.

* * *

We hired a contractor, Western Homes Inc., to turn our drawings into reality. The firm was run by Vern and Laurie Johnson, who were a strange pair. Vern was a pilot and aircraft owner, and his wife was a tall, overbearing Amazon. Vern was very deaf and Laurie, somewhat the architect, was always yelling at him with a booming voice, referring to him as ***JOHNSON!***"

While there were three houses on Venus Avenue across the street, we built the first house in the entire block between Venus and Glenview Avenues. This created a problem when we needed electric utilities installed. Northwestern Bell and Northern States Power shared the responsibility for setting power poles. By mutual agreement, one would set the poles in this subdivision, while the other would provide the poles in an adjacent area. When we requested electrical service, NSP said,

"You'll have to contact Bell; they set the poles in that area." After many phone calls I managed to contact the proper authority in the Bell organization, who took the position:

"NSP set the poles in that area; you'll have to talk to them." Two months of phone calls and argument passed before the problem was resolved. Of the five poles required to give us electrical service, NSP set three poles and Bell set two. It was my first brush with corporate bureaucratic evasion done well.

Sewer and water service were easier: We drilled our own well, installed our own septic tank and its drain field. In March of 1958 we moved in and have been here almost 61 years as of this writing. However, much work remained to achieve a livable dwelling.

After surviving great downpours in California, we were determined that any house we built would look down on the surrounding lands. High lots mean complex landscaping, and the first order of business was to get the steep slopes under control. For enclosing the front entrance and both sides of the driveway we built walls composed of 17 tons of Kasota limestone.

The Wall

The picture above shows Betty working on the wall while Tim watches. She worked out positioning of the cut and broken stones and set the smaller ones. When I came home from work, I set the heavier pieces. They were randomly sized, and each piece moved several times before it found a home in the wall. We marked a few stones and kept a record of how many times they moved before they were permanently positioned. The average was three times, and we estimated we moved 51 tons of rock in this part of the project.

The Red Hat

Tim was always a part

of the building operations, and the dirt around the wall work was his 'sand pile.' The little red hat was almost a permanent fixture in those years. We still have it.

The wall has served us well and survived the forces of nature for more than 60 years as of this writing.

8

Honeywell Aeronautical Division, 1957

The incentive was an opportunity to work on the Convair B-58, the Air Force's first supersonic bomber. Dr. Rudolph Hermann, my graduate school adviser, set me up to use the inlet design skills he taught me in class.

* * *

I reported for work at Honeywell and was assigned to the B-58 supersonic inlet program, but this program was winding down, and my work on this fascinating new bomber was limited. A few months after my arrival, an economic downturn struck the defense business, and talk of layoffs began. An opportunity to bid on a rocket thruster for a spy satellite emerged. People with supersonic flow experience were scarce around an electronically oriented company, so I made a place for myself on this program. We were successful in the bid, and I designed the supersonic nozzles for the control system thrusters, shown opposite a bit larger than full size. It produced 10 pounds of thrust when connected to a 145 pound per square inch gas supply. Each drawing and calculation I completed disappeared into the mysterious chasm of 'black' programs, never to be seen again even for reference. I had a 'Secret' security clearance

wasn't, but it wasn't good enough for me to see my own work once it was stamped 'Top Secret.' I never knew what became of my little thrusters. 'Oh, what tangled webs we weave ... .'

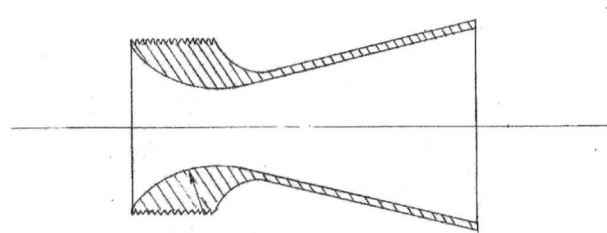

Satellite Supersonic Control Thruster
Internal Details and Dimensions Omitted

Pressure Transducers ... you can't test for everything

About this time there was a giant reorganization of Honeywell's engineering department, and I found myself assigned to a pressure instruments group working on a pressure ratio transducer. In these days of microprocessors and mathematically capable software, it is almost a trivial task to divide one number by another. In the 1950s this was formidable task done by fulcrums, pins and levers. Combining such a mechanism into a small, flyable device to survive with high reliability in the hostile environment of a jet engine was difficult. Sometimes, even the quest for high reliability can be troublesome, as we shall see.

Take note of the transducer in the picture, over and its con-

Pressure Ratio Transducer

struction. The round black objects are metal bellows that are connected to pressure sources via tubing connections on the bulkhead (the large circular plate on the left). Pressures fed to the bellows exert forces on the opposite ends of a beam, balanced on a moving pivot. The precise location of the pivot point determines the ratio of the two pressures. An electric motor drives the pivot point along the beam, constantly seeking a balance point between the two pressures. The result is a mechanical computation giving one pressure divided by the other. The balance point's position is transmitted to the pilot's instrument panel and displayed as a number on a dial.

A drawn aluminum case that covered the transducer mechanism was sealed to the bulkhead by an 'O-ring' residing in the circumferential groove. The bulkhead is of particular interest because of its role in a later part of the story. Pressure fittings threaded into the bulkhead provide for connections to the engine. For a small mechanical device operating in an environment of high temperature and punishing vibration, these transducers were unusually reliable. I believe some are still flying on B-52 aircraft today, 50 years later.

In late 1958 as jet airliners began flying, Honeywell wanted to work some of its military products into the civil aviation business. At the time there was a great controversy dividing the jet engine business: should engines be controlled by pressure ratio (the Pratt & Whitney philosophy) or by turbine temperature and fuel flow (General Electric). I was assigned as engineering support for a sales campaign to get pressure ratio adopted as a standard and began an extensive series of travels to aircraft manufacturers, engine companies and airlines.

We had somewhat of a 'leg-up' as the first Boeing 707s were flying with several airlines. They were powered by Pratt & Whitney engines, and pressure ratio instruments set their thrust levels. The company mounted an intense marketing campaign to convince the airlines and airplane manufacturers that 'pressure ratio' was the wave of the future. This campaign was my introduction to giving both prepared and extemporaneous, 'stand-up' presentations.

The airlines made reliability a prime issue, and Honeywell wheeled out its extensive record of military experience with this instrument. The anchor point of this transducer was its deployment in the North American F-100 (Super Sabre) aircraft. Military references were uniformly outstanding, but there was a nagging problem. Of the 500 instruments delivered to the Air Force, a few, perhaps a half-dozen, failed because of cracks in the large round bulkhead described earlier. Honeywell's Materials Laboratory undertook a long, difficult study of manufacturing methods and material certification that went back almost to the mines, where the materials originated. No answer to the cracked bulkheads was ever found.

Fast forward perhaps 25 years. I was between airline flights in Albuquerque, New Mexico, standing in the sun on a passenger walkway and enjoying the mountain views. This was before jet-ways and 'shoes-off' passenger inspections; passengers walked outdoors from the terminal to their airplanes. At the far end of the walkway was a New Mexico Air National Guard airplane, an F100, which had bumped its way down the equipment chain to service with the Guard. The legs of a mechanic extended from a belly-hatch, so I ambled to the end of the walkway and struck up a conversation.

Looking in the hatch, I saw my old pressure transducer mounted near the engine, still soldiering-on after many years. I remarked to the mechanic that I worked on these devices many years past and he commented on its reliability. He said, however, it had one major flaw: It was too hard to calibrate.

"We knew that," I replied, "but we included complete calibration stations and extensive instructions in an attempt to make the calibration task easier."

"Yeah, I know," said the mechanic, "but they fail so seldom we can never find the calibration rig let alone the instruction manuals."

"So how to you fix them?" I asked.

"Well, I've never had to repair one, but we're instructed, should one ever fail, we're to … – and removing a large Crescent wrench from his tool belt for emphasis – turn the pressure fitting in so tight the bulkhead splits. Then it becomes a replacement item I can draw from the supply depot and not have to bother with calibration."

High reliability can have dark underside.

Space

Space became a major playing field in the late 1950s, and I suppose it was inevitable I became involved somehow. The work I did came to naught because it was based on fallacious assumptions of the potential problems with manned space flight.

A major problem, if not *the* major problem of space flight, was regarded as isolation. Not much thought was being given to orbiting more than one person initially. The alternative, two or more people working in a confined cabin, posed severe personal interaction problems: the operative theory at the time.

A second problem was based on a lack of knowledge of the extent of cloud cover over the earth. In the event of total electrical failure above clouds, the astronauts would have no means of knowing when to start the reentry burn that determines the landing point.

There was a big technical push in many areas. The Russians orbited Sputnik and a dog. The race to put a man in space was on; seven Air Force and Navy test pilots were selected as the first astronauts. Lovelace Clinic in Albuquerque conducted extensive physical and mental testing with them to qualify for space flight. In the background, the Air Force's School of Aviation Medicine at Brooks AFB in San Antonio, ran an extensive biomedical program attacking what were considered to be major problems with humans in space flight.

Brooks also had what has proven to be an overly optimistic view of the future of space. They had extensive programs related to closed environments: oxygen/CO_2 exchange with growing plants, aquaculture involving both fish and plants and other exotic biological processes.

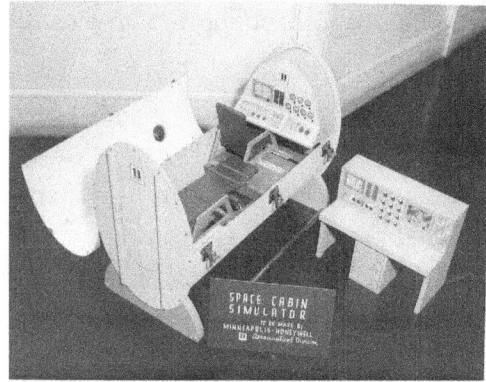
Space Simulator Model

Research in the area of personal isolation took the form of testing the mental stability and the physical stamina required to work complex tasks while enduring limited rest and peculiar work/sleep cycles. Herb Lindquist, in the Honeywell Human Factors group, had some contact with these problems and with the technical/medical operatives at Brooks. I had some limited experience in biomedical systems working with manned balloon flights. Out of personal interest, I had looked at the life support problems attached to extended, high altitude balloon flights. Herb and I put together an unsolicited proposal to the Air Force to build a test chamber supporting two men for 30 days. An electrical power cord was the only connection with the outside world. Much to our surprise, we won a contract to build a Space

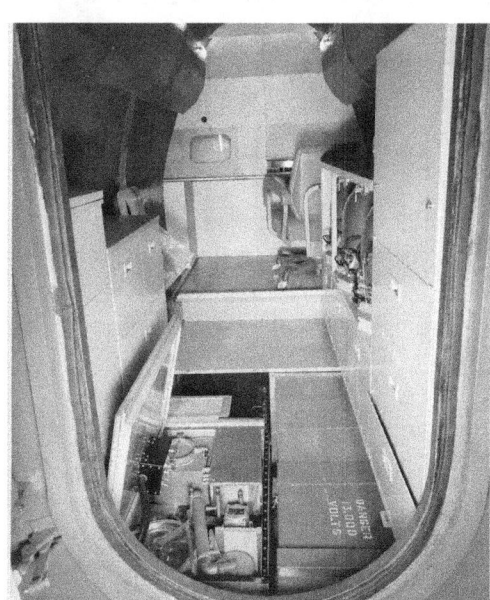
Space Cabin Interior

Cabin Simulator.

Because food supply and sanitary breaks for the crew undergoing tests would interrupt the isolation, the test capsule contained all oxygen, CO_2 removal, food storage and garbage handling for up to a 30 day test period. This included the reprocessing of urine to potable water. The model shown, – prior page – built to support the proposal, closely depicts the finished system. The oval shape allowed standing upright and space below the floor for life support systems and stowage and was structurally suitable for lowered pressures.

Tragedy

During the development of the various systems, we became very concerned over the possibility of fire in such a confined space. We expended much time with our materials laboratory, testing the flammability of materials used construction. Concerned with chairs and bedding materials, we began including those fabrics in our tests and found that calorimeter tests of cotton fabrics produced nearly explosive combustion, when ignited in a pure oxygen environment. This observation became important, when NASA chose a 100% oxygen environment for its Mercury and Gemini capsules.

In the infancy of space flight, weight was extremely important and pressurizing the capsule with oxygen alone made significant weight reductions. Since oxygen is only about 20% of the earth's atmosphere, the capsule's internal pressure could be reduced to only about five lbs./sq. inch of pure oxygen, resulting in a much lighter structure. We reported our findings relative to cotton and other fabrics to our Air Force technical staff, but we never knew whether the data reached NASA. Perhaps the design of the Mercury capsule and its follow-on Gemini cabin, were too far along to incorporate the structural changes necessary to accommodate the higher internal pressure required to include the moderating effects of nitrogen on combustion. For whatever reason, the dangers were ignored, and Astronauts Grissom, White and Chaffey burned to death, when fire started in the Gemini capsule during ground tests, many years after our warnings.

Earth Path Indicator

My second venture into the space business, while technically challenging, turned into something even more trivial. At the time of the Mercury capsule and the seven original astronauts, today's extensive communication system with control points around the world didn't exist. Secondly, the knowledge of the earth's atmosphere and the extent of cloud cover over the earth were matters of conjecture. The parachute landing system of the Mercury Capsule required a water landing. A total electrical failure, with the earth obscured by cloud, would leave astronauts without knowledge of when to start the reentry burn determining the landing point. We proposed and won a contract with McDonnell Aircraft to design what was essentially a spring driven clock whose 'face' was a small globe. This 'clock' would approximately track the Mercury capsule's position over the earth, so the astronaut would always have a rough idea of his location, regardless of cloud cover or the status of more sophisticated, electrically-driven systems.

This was a challenging mechanical design task. The basic mechanism was conceived by a talented designer, Leif Arnesson. The globe was mounted on a series of gimbals allowing the operator to make multiple settings to the globe's position. Adjustments included setting the position of the globe to coincide with the capsule's known position over the earth, adjusting the inclination of the globe's axis to the inclination of the capsule's orbit relative to the earth's axis and winding the driving spring. The best way to describe the instrument is to include the specification to which the instrument was built. The following descriptions are taken from the various editions of the Mercury Familiarization Manual SEDR104, December 1959.

*   *   *

Mercury Familiarization Manual SEDR104
December 1959

Specification

The earth path indicator consists of a spherical map (globe) of the earth gimballed and rotating in a manner to indicate ground position under the capsule. The indicator is spring motor powered and is capable of running 20 hours without rewinding. The globe, which is approximately 3.85 inches in diameter, will display the following geographical features:

(1) All continents

(2) All bodies of water having major dimensions of 300 statute miles (3) The sixteen largest rivers of the world(4) All islands having major dimensions of 500 statute miles(5) All known islands or island clusters separated from continents by 300 statute miles and having major dimensions less than 500 statute miles shall be identified by an 0.020 diameter circle.(6) The fifty largest cities of the world are identified by 0.020 dots.(7) 15° latitude and longitude lines are presented and numbered. Controls are provided on the face of the indicator to wind the spring motor and to adjust the orbit time, adjust orbit inclination and to slew the globe about the earth and the orbital axis. The touchdown area is displayed as a rectangle and the luminous dot inside of the rectangle being the point of impact. The landing area is 3040 nautical miles ahead of instantaneous orbital position above the earth as indicated by the fourring bullseye. The instrument is externally lighted by cabin floodlights.

*   *   *

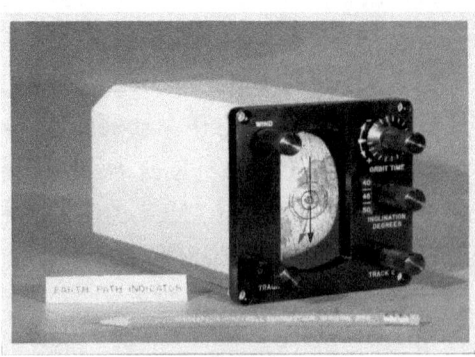

Earth Path Indicator Model

The picture, left, shows the mock-up of the instrument we designed and built in Honeywell's model shop in less than a week. It started me on a continuing process of being a corporate 'hair shirt,' when bureaucratic endeavors seemed to make little sense. I began to think perhaps I wasn't a good match with bureaucratic structures.

I promised the Mercury Program manager at McDonnell we would deliver a mock-up of the instrument within a week of award of a contract. They were working against tight deadlines and needed as many components, or models thereof, as early as possible in the program.

Honeywell was awarded the contract, and after completing the mock-up's exterior design I found a near-perfectly sized globe, masquerading as a 'piggy bank' at Woolworth's dime store. The EPI model was finished within a week, on a Thursday. With my week's promise running out on Friday, I took the model to Honeywell's Shipping & Receiving department, gave them the address and asked them to ship it by overnight express.

"Can't do it," said the supervisor, "it doesn't have an inspection stamp."

"But it's just a wooden block," I pleaded.

"Sorry, rules is rules," he replied. So I went off to Inspection.

"Can't inspect it without an Engineering Specification to check it against," said the man in charge.

"There's no specification other than size of the block and the dimensions of the mounting holes. I'll draw a sketch for you," says I.

"Won't work," he replied and then recited a litany of the required signatures required, which would require perhaps a week to collect.

"Thanks, I'll deliver it myself," I replied

"You can't do that," he answered, becoming indignant.

"Ever hear about briefcases and airplane tickets? Just watch," I retorted and wandered off muttering to myself.

The following morning I put the model in a briefcase, bought a ticket with a personal check (credit cards were uncommon in 1959) and was off on an early-morning flight to St. Louis. I went to the McDonnell Campus – fancy buildings with fountains everywhere –

and handed the mock-up to the Mercury Project Engineer. He was surprised and grateful. I was back at my desk shortly after lunch.

My boss sought me out almost immediately.

"Where have you been?" he asked.

"St. Louis," I replied. He responded angrily,

"I've spent the entire morning trying to keep you from being fired. Your trip has been driven to Vice Presidential level and everyone's mad at someone."

Without knowledge of a raging, internal political battle, I had inadvertently walked into a corporate brier patch. Unknown to me, the Shipping and Inspection Departments were carrying on an extended feud, and my short-circuiting 'The System' exposed a hole in their game. Now all the combined animosity fell on me, but I kept my promise to the customer, which to me was all that counted. From the political standpoint, there is now a quarter-inch thick section in the Honeywell Operations Manual describing how Inspection and Shipping are to deal with non-functioning, wooden mock-ups.

For the final product, the globe to meet the specification became a major effort. After much difficulty, I found a small company in a suburb of Philadelphia able to make a globe to replace the one from Woolworth's dime store. I still have one of the original globes, a spare from the project.

The Specification Globe

The Earth Path Indicators flew on all the test flights and on a few of the manned, non-orbiting flights. One was used for John Glenn's first U.S.

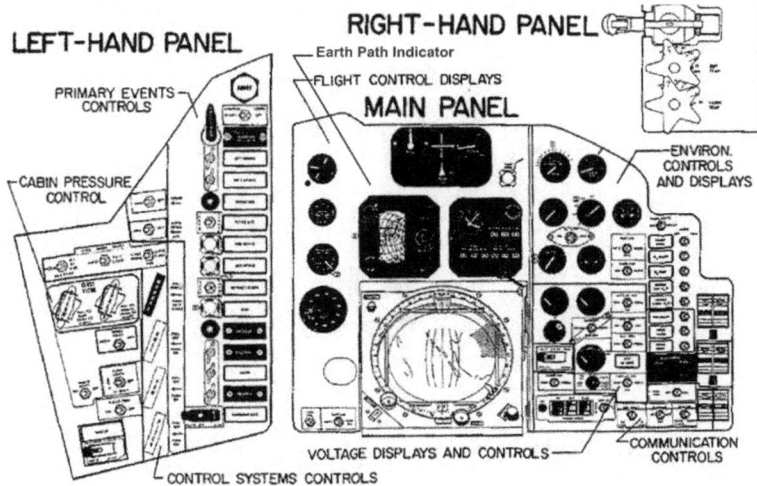

Mercury Capsule Instrument Panel

manned orbit of the earth. It is on display in the instrument panel of John Glenn's capsule in the Smithsonian Museum of Flight. I believe one additional EPI flew on the second orbital flight, but experience showed there was insufficient cloud cover over the earth to obscure the capsule's position for any meaningful length of time. The use of the EPI was discontinued thereafter.

A New Direction

At about this time, Honeywell acquired patent rights to a then-new class of computing and control devices called 'Fluid Amplifiers.' Again, my fluid-flow background determined the course of my professional life. I was transferred to the Military Products Research Group to explore the potential of this technology and attempt to turn its capabilities into products.

9

Honeywell Military Products Research

Fluid Amplifiers, so named because this class of device used low energy flows of air or liquids to control higher power fluid streams, were a technical area of high interest during the 1960s – 1970s.

* * *

Sometime in the early 1960s, Honeywell acquired patent rights to what were known as 'Fluid Amplifiers.' The three inventors worked at the Army's Harry Diamond Laboratories in Washington, DC. Just how Ray (Romald E.) Bowles, Billy Horton and Raymond Warren were able to extract the ownership of this technology, while still employed by the government, was never quite clear. Horton, somewhat unusually, became Director of the Laboratory shortly after the deal with Honeywell was consummated. All of this was not of great interest to me at the time; my interest was with the technology and the intriguing fluid mechanics problems.

After participating in the patent negotiations, I was transferred into the Military Products Research Department and charged with conducting explorations related to turning this technology into products.

Early Research

The early work done by the Harry Diamond group did not go far beyond basic observations of the phenomenological aspects of the flow of fluid (air or liquid) through a variety of configurations of passages cut into metal blocks. The first order of business was to explore these phenomena using large models permitting detailed pressure measurements and flow visualization techniques.

Fluid Amplifiers

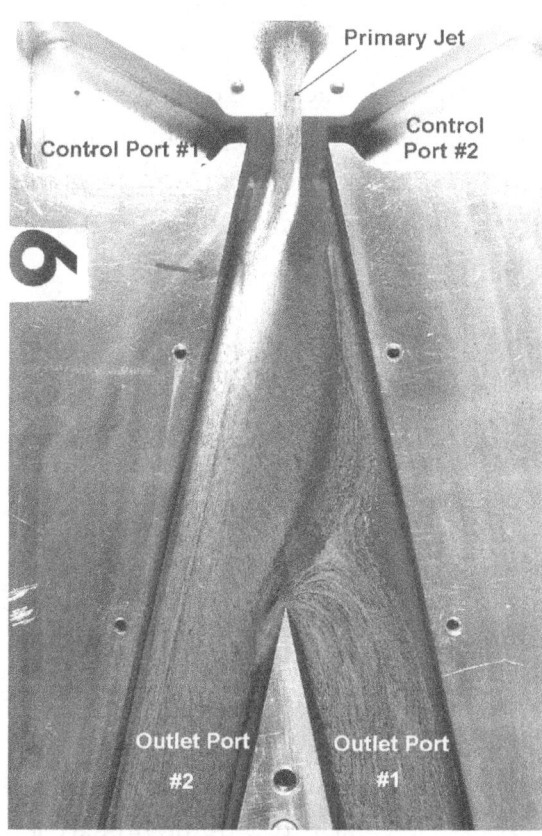

Bi-stable Fluid Amplifier

The basic fluid amplifier configuration consists of a primary jet, two control jets and two output ports. When operating in a bi-stable mode, the primary jet, when it begins flowing with no flow from the control ports, attaches itself randomly to either the left or right-hand wall. It can then be controlled to flow from either output port by pulsing it momentarily with a flow from the appropriate control port. A pulse of fluid from control Port #1 causes the jet to attach to the right-hand wall and flow from Output Port #1 and vice versa. Once primary flow is attached to either wall, the control flow can be removed. Only a pulse is required to establish the bi-stable output, and in a fluid sense it duplicates the action of similarly-named electronic devices: flip/flops

By altering the geometry of the long sidewalls, a slightly different configuration exhibits an analog or proportional output flow from the two legs of the device. The side walls are moved closer to the primary jet and the flow from the control ports is continuous rather than pulsed. When the flows from the control ports are equal, the primary jet flows down the center of the mixing cavity and divides on the wedge-shaped central divider. Increasing either control flow deflects the jet causing a differential flow from the output ports. The primary flow is swept smoothly back and forth across the mixing region by varying the control pressures. Because the control flows are small compared to the primary jet, the term a 'fluid amplifier' applies. From these basic configurations a variety of Boolean logic functions can be constructed from the bi-stable configuration and smoothly varying control functions from proportional fluid amplifier.

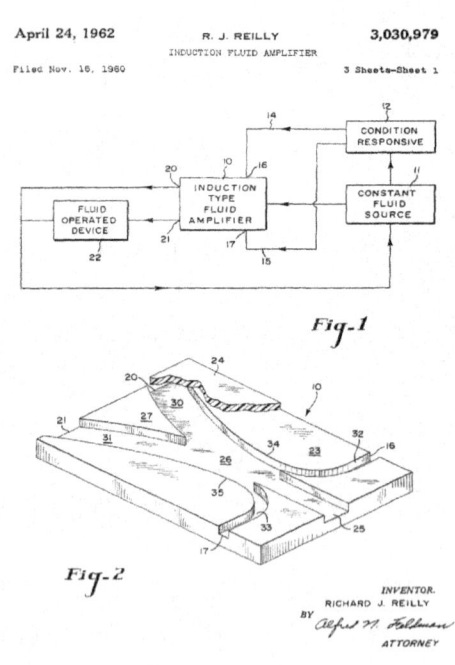

Induction Fluid Amplifier

While exploring the fluid mechanics of these devices, I realized the gentlemen from Harry Diamond Laboratories had missed an entire class of similar devices based on boundary layer forces. Without getting too deeply into the fluid mechanisms involved, the figure at left shows the control ports curved and aligned with the primary jet. Thus, the control flow induces the main jet to follow it rather than being 'pushed' across the cavity by a control pulse. The Patent Office lawyers, with little expertise in fluid flow, initially rejected the various claims as being not significantly different from the bi-stable device described earlier, but in the end they had to admit there must be some internal difference: the control flows produced the opposite effects. There followed a half-dozen different device patents based on viscous flow properties, for which I received a one-dollar stipend each from the company. In the final analysis, not much became of these boundary layer devices, but they may have influenced the negotiations between Honeywell and the Harry Diamond people: there was more than one way to 'skin the same a cat.' Once we began publishing papers and presenting them at technical conferences, the general field of fluid devices with no moving parts became a technology offshoot with great activity by many companies. Patents were filed profusely, and the Patent Office was inundated with these 'fluid things,' which all looked similar but performed differently.

It drove the Patent Office crazy. For a time they rejected all patent applications in this area, arguing these devices were 'just pipes with peculiar internal walls,' and didn't meet the patent criterion of novelty. It was as if they were to declare all electrical devices are simply variations of a wire, but ultimately, all these patents were allowed. Wags at the time said:

"Harry Diamond Labs patented Momentum and Reilly patented Viscosity." With the clearing of these patent thickets, the field was fertile ground for technical endeavor for over a decade. In the mid 1960s the suffix 'ics' was an essential to anything technological, much like the 'dot com' appellation of the 1990s. The technical field became known as 'Fluidics.'

Sensing Devices

Honeywell's interest in these devices was for use in control systems, which required sensors for physical parameters. Using air as the operating fluid, such system could function at very high temperatures and in nuclear radiation environments, limited only by the materials used to construct them. The military was interested in both environments, and with air or other gases as the active medium, fluid systems are applicable to many difficult control problems. Systems of these jet devices could perform logic and provide the amplification needed for input devices. Sensing devices often produce low-level signals requiring amplification. The reliability of such a system is enhanced if the input device also has no moving parts.

Vortex Gyro Angular Rate Sensor

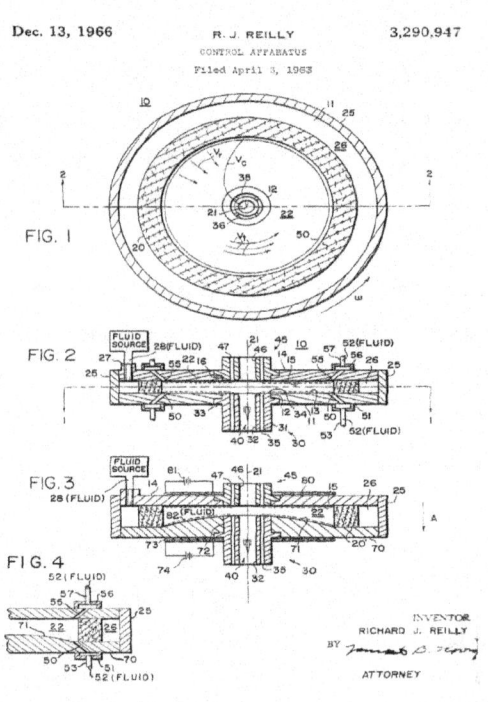

Vortex Angular Rate Sensor

While watching the flow in the bathroom sink, I observed that while the surface of the water had a slow, circular movement, the center of the flow was rotating at a high-speed. This appeared to have the potential for measuring rate of rotation of a vehicle, a rate gyro of sorts, having no moving parts, other than the fluid passing through it. We built a structure consisting of two flat plates, separated by a porous ring, through which a flow of air or liquid is induced from the outside diameter toward the center. The porous ring serves two purposes: first, it damps-out tiny fluctuations, making the fluid flow very smoothly, and secondly, it couples rotational motion into the flowing fluid. This does not mean the device rotates like a wheel but rather, when mounted solidly in a vehicle for example, it senses the vehicle rotates from north to west and generates a signal proportional to the speed of rotation during the turn. While these signals were weak and required amplification, the vortex rate sensor was a key component to a flight stabilization system. After some years work, we flew a small missile using the vortex rate sensor coupled to a collection of fluid amplifiers to control its flight.

Honeywell Develops New Spacecraft Fluid Control

Engineers at Minneapolis Honeywell Regulator Co. have developed a radical new control system for spacecraft, it was disclosed today.

The air force labeled the development a "technological breakthrough" and gave four engineers its Air Force Systems Command award for outstanding achievement.

The technique was described by Honeywell as an all-fluid control system that operates without moving parts or electronic components. Its simplicity makes it cheaper, more reliable and less subject to damage than other systems.

Honeywell said it is prevented by security requirements from disclosing just what control systems will use the new technique. It did say, however, that it has developed a "fluid rate sensor" that does the job of a gyroscope.

The technique uses the basic principles of fluid mechanics — principles that also are exploited in hydraulic brakes and automatic transmissions—but somehow does so without benefit of pistons and valves.

Honeywell has been working on fluid systems since early 1960 and considers itself the leader in the field.

In ceremonies today at Honeywell's aeronautical division, Lt. Col. Robert B. Hinck, commander of the air force systems command's Milwaukee contract management division, made the recognition awards.

The engineers who received them are Richard J. Reilley, 1759 Venus ave., Arden Hills, a principal scientist; Louis J. Guertin, 2231 Lakeaires blvd., White Bear Lake, systems analyst; Werner H. Egli, 431 NE. Pierce st., Minneapolis, senior aerodynamicist; Richard A. Evans, 2100 NE. Forest dr., Columbia Heights, senior design engineer; William J. Lewis, 17225 Manor rd., Wayzata, fluid systems project supervisor, and David L. Payne, 2409 W. Ninety-sixth st., Bloomington, design engineer.

The air force award is based on three things: a breakthrough in the state-of-the-art, extraordinary cost reduction and extraordinary increase in product reliability.

Vortex In the Southern Hemisphere

An age-old party question is: 'Does the water in the sink swirl in the opposite direction in the Southern Hemisphere?' The answer is: sometimes. In either the Northern or Southern Hemispheres, the water flowing down the drain will swirl in either direction almost randomly. The vortex flow is such a high-gain amplifier that the vortex will swirl in whatever direction the greater expanse of the fluid is disturbed. In a carefully arranged experiment, vortices will turn in opposite directions in the two hemispheres, but the effect is unlikely to be reliably observed in one's kitchen sink.

In an experiment set up by Dr. Ascher Shapiro of MIT, a tank some six or eight feet in diameter and filled with water, was allowed to settle undisturbed for almost a week to allow any tiny swirls from the filling process to dissipate. Located in an air-conditioned room, thermally induced fluid motion in the tank unlikely. An external plug was then removed from a small, center, exit-hole, and after a short time a counterclockwise swirl developed due to the rate of rotation of the earth and would do so in the opposite direction in the Southern Hemisphere. However, in a casual observation of a household drain, the swirl will develop in the direction of any random disturbance, which overwhelms the influence of the earth's rotation.

In the vortex gyro described above, we could measure the earth's rate of rotation with good response because unwanted disturbances were eliminated by the porous medium at the peripheral, external flow entrance. As small as this rate seems, it is relatively large compared to the requirements of a navigation system, where the **rate** of angular motion must be continuously integrated to yield angular ***position*** resulting from rates of change and the duration of such angular motion.

Variable Deflection Thruster (VDT)

With the capability to measure angular motion and the ability to amplify a signal, the control of an aircraft seemed at hand, but the final, force element was missing. In about 1961 B.G. Newman, an English scientist, published a paper that describes a jet attaching to a rounded surface and almost reversing its direction. This phenomenon can be superficially demonstrated by inserting one's finger into a gently flowing stream from a faucet. With the finger pointed downward and just grazing the stream, bending the finger slightly produces

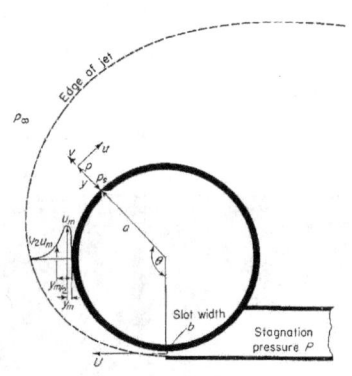

Flow of a two-dimensional jet round a circular cylinder.

large displacements of the stream as the flow attaches to the finger and is deflected as the finger is moved. The actual physics of this experiment differs from the condition with the jet submerged in surrounding fluid of its own kind, but it illustrates the jet attachment phenomenon.

In a variation of this configuration, we combined two jets on opposite sides of a cylinder. In this arrangement, we duplicated the jet on the bottom (above) with a second one at the top of the cylinder. The two attached jets meet in opposition and the resulting

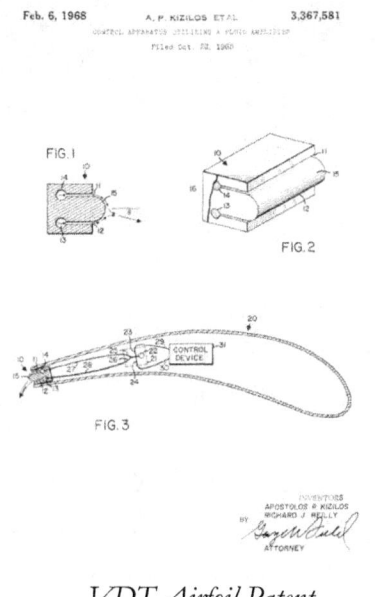

VDT Airfoil Patent

combined stream leaves the cylinder in their original direction (to the left in the figure) and will sweep through a total deflection of 180 degrees or more. Combining this arrangement in a truncated airfoil, with the cylinder/jet serving as the trailing edge, produced a jet flap for control without the need for a moving surface. The drawing from the patent doesn't show the application well, but it illustrates the general concept. Small models of this arrangement we bench-tested, worked well on the first attempt. We then looked for a vehicle that would expedite a proof of concept in flight.

I knew the aircraft field well, and we sought a military sponsor who would have access to a Model 18 Beechcraft, an ancient design dating from 1935. A few were still active as executive transports in the Navy. After locating an interested technical sponsor, the search was on for **the** airplane. The sponsoring agency found one such

VDT Test Installation On Model 18 Beechcraft

aircraft in Florida, the then-current pride and joy of a Navy Captain, who regarded it as **his** personal airplane. No one else was allowed to fly it. It was kept in pristine condition at the Pensacola Naval Air Station in Florida. With great reluctance, it was pried loose from the Captain's grip and flown to Airesearch Corporation in Burbank, California, for fitting with a vertical control surface incorporating our aerodynamic flap.

The Model 18 was well suited to this experiment. With its two vertical tail fins, it was flown independent of our experimental additions, using normal controls. Then, the standard controls were locked in fixed position and control taken over by our aerodynamic control system. Any realistic application of this control technique would be aimed at jet aircraft having sufficient bleed air available to drive the jet flap system.

Stable Flight Using VDT To Trim Dead Engine

The proof of concept test was specified as shutting down one engine, locking the two conventional rudders in neutral and maintaining controlled, stabilized flight, using only the blowing flap to balance the asymmetric thrust. The picture above shows these conditions being satisfied while the left-hand propeller is stopped. For the Beechcraft experiment we provided an air supply onboard as an independent system. A vibration-free air compressor (Roots Blower) was mounted in the Captain's well-preserved cabin and driven by a Volkswagen engine. The cabin became cluttered with machinery, and we crossed our fingers hoping nobody would ever need to leave the airplane quickly.

The program went on to a design study for incorporation into a jet aircraft, but I understand the program died sometime after I left the company.

The Salesman

I became involved with technology because I enjoyed solving problems related to airplanes, physics and fluid flow, and in a sense, I never had to 'work' in the same way many people dread Monday morning. Being an only child, I still prefer solitude to 'people activities' and will go out of my way to avoid a neighborhood bash, which might substitute for water-cooler camaraderie over a long weekend. Thus, it was an unwelcome surprise when I found the delights of an engineering career were often limited unless one brought his own money to the party. This meant *selling*. It meant being adept at small talk, traveling to distant places and talking, both one-on-one and sometimes to large audiences. These skills were key to success in the engineering world, not only with Honeywell but also in the consulting role I later pursued for over 35 years.

Honeywell had a large sales staff positioned worldwide, but they were not much help in selling research projects. Research, by definition, deals with exploring a concept, a capability or sometimes an abstract idea. A salesman selling research has nothing to put in his bag that he/she can pull out in front of a customer and boast about its size, large or small, its capabilities, it's color, or whatever makes it superior to the offerings of a competitor. In selling research the investigator has only a personal record as a base: I've done this, explored that, or succeeded in something resembling whatever it is the potential customer might want done. A salesperson, operating remotely, is unable to address this task.

This was a new world for me to tackle, skills to be developed and polished without much in the way of role models, or written guidance to be studied in the quiet of home or office. I had to get out in the world, make contacts, get beaten-up and try a different tack until something worked.

The Honeywell salesman knew strange locales, some potential contacts, had a car and an office but beyond these was of little concrete help. The delights of travel wear off quickly – nothing gets done in the way of home maintenance while you're gone – weekends become 'catch-up-on-the-home-work' time. I could not have led the working life I did if Betty not been so self-sufficient.

A major problem in this life, divided between detailed technological work and selling into the future, was the conflict between travel and maintaining technical skills. Unless I remained active in the laboratory effort, I would no longer be able to speak firsthand to the basics involved and would soon be no better-off than the dedicated salesman. While it was a stressful time of life, I came away from Honeywell with some useful people skills, knowledge of the Department of Defense organization, its contracting methods and the hidden, complex, political underbelly. These abilities were useful in many of my succeeding endeavors. I learned to detect the odor of a bluffer, when to be audacious, even outrageous and developed the courage to press accepted boundaries while feigning ignorance of them.

Some Practical Devices

About this time Honeywell Management decided they wanted to apply fluidics to some of their industrial product markets. This changed the focus of our work from the details of fluid mechanics to applying the technology to working systems. The research work on large fluidic devices led to families of smaller components more suited to practical applications. As shown left, these were palm-size devices produced by plastic molding with integral tubular spigots. This allowed interconnecting the elements with tubing to form logical systems doing useful tasks.

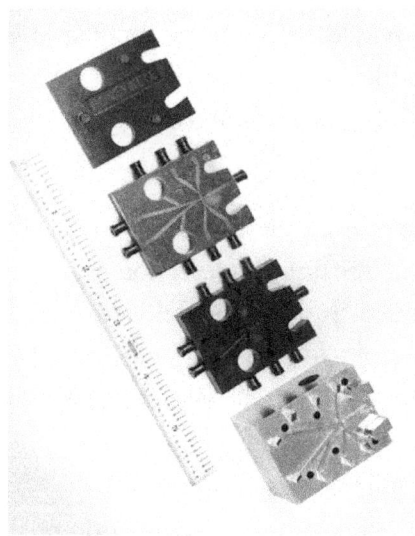

Early Fluidic Logic

As development progressed, we did away with many of the tubing connections by further reducing the size of the fluid amplifiers and interconnecting them with laminated layers having integral flow passages, over. As the various capabilities of these fluid components developed, we built a staff of about 10 engineers working on the various components and systems. While some work was supported by company funding, much

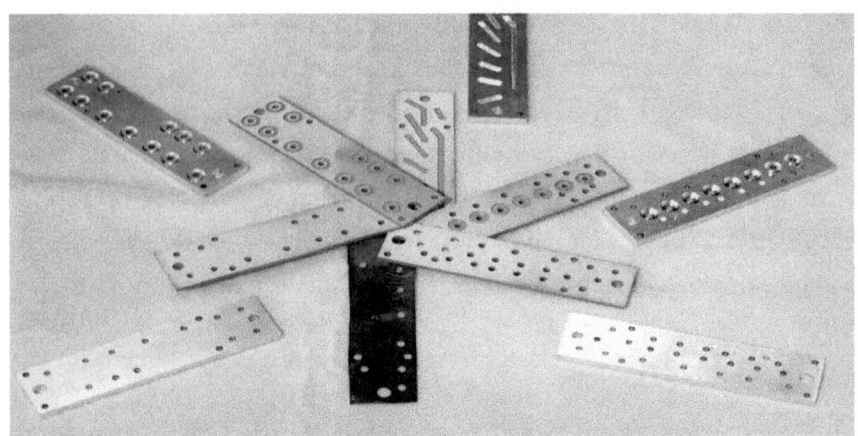

Layered Modular Construction

of the support for this work was brought in through government contracts.

The Air Force Office of Scientific Research, Office of Naval Research and several Army agencies provided substantial support. This required much travel time for me in addition to trying to keep current on the technology through work in the laboratory.

A Simple System

We acquired some revenue through a simple system for a major U.S. Army Arsenal requiring extreme reliability. Detection plugged primer holes in shell casings is a critical function in reloading used ammunition. These automated systems run at high speeds and attempting to jam an explosive primer into a plugged primer hole has dangerous potential. Thus, detecting a spent primer remaining in a re-loadable shell casing involves serious reliability issues.

Electrical systems are undesirable because of spark potential. Mechanical means for detection of plugged primer holes tend to get out of alignment or wear out quickly. A fluid amplifier running on air was a near-perfect solution:. A probe with a low flow of air connects to the control port of a fluid amplifier positioned in contact with the shell casing. A plugged primer hole causes the control pressure to rise, switches the amplifier, shuts down the loading machine and

Munition Plugged Primer Sensing

sounds an alarm. With no moving parts, no wear, no explosion potential and high reliability, the fluid devices covered many design concerns. We delivered a substantial number of these systems from our little research operation.

*   *   *

Commercial Systems

After several years of research, the company sought to use the findings from the military work to generate commercial products. We added a commercial products development group to our little research group. All the trappings of brochures, advertising and trade shows made for a somewhat tortured existence while operating under the defense related business umbrella.

A major thorn was the purchasing of materials and components under the auspices of the Military Products Procurement operation. For reasons too complicated to explain here, this group added a large and uncertain overhead cost to every item purchased. When we 'committed' to a purchase, the buyers added a nominal 15% to the cost of the item. We would then write that amount off in our budget as a hard and fast cost to our project.

At the end of the fiscal year, when everyone's books were re-

Page From Brochure

solved, the Purchasing Department, which displayed little fiscal discipline, just summed its entire annual costs of operation. They then divided that number by the actual cost of the material purchased over the year and applied the ratio back to the budget of the people they were buying for. Thus, our nominal, 15% 'estimated' burden expense became 20%, 25%, or in one year 41%, and voila, we were over our budget by the stroke of a pen and received a managerial thrashing for poor planning.

After a couple of years of this, one of the newly added engineers to the commercial products enterprise, Fred Merrill, came up with a creative solution. Some of our material purchases were out of the realm of the Purchasing Department: too small, too technical etc. These were made directly by staff, as petty cash items, reimbursed later. Fred, whose dedication to the success of the commercial venture was evident, came to me and said,

"Look, I've been using my own money for petty cash purchases and then getting reimbursed rather than drawing money beforehand. I've sampled the system and determined I can submit petty cash purchases up to $200 before anyone complains. I'm willing to put my own money into this for the front-end cost and we'll only have to purchase big items through Purchasing." How could I turn down a deal like that. Fred and I agreed if anything went wrong with this scheme we'd just give it a shrug, 'palms-up,' feign ignorance ('Who, me? I didn't know that.') and promise never to do it again.

Fred's system worked beautifully, and we operated on this basis for several years, getting bolder with each passing year. Trusting suppliers would give us time to pay even large bills by billing us in $200 increments. Fred took care of the float personally, and at one time he had over $3000 of his own funds invested. Everything worked smoothly until a major purchase for an injection molding tool came due and required Fred to pass $18,000 worth of petty cash vouchers in one week. Caught in a vise of our own making, we brought the enterprise back under the corporate tent, where the vagaries of company internal operations crippled the business aspects of the endeavor.

Annunciators, Sequencers and Such

Despite the corporate millstones, these men assembled some significant systems. Because the fluid devices required continuous flow of fluid (air, gas), the natural gas industry seemed a 'natural' for an initial stab at industrial applications. I wrote a few articles that were published in petroleum industry magazines. These generated a number of serious points of interest centered on the reliability of the 'no-

Pipeline Magazine Cover

moving-parts' devices.

We chose to work on a system detecting problems with reciprocating, natural gas engines for Trunkline Gas Company in Houston, Texas. Such systems are generally termed 'annunciators in industry parlance. The working fluid for these annunciators was the gas being pumped own the pipeline, and after passing through our instrumentation, the gas went onward to heat homes. The power to drive the system was free.

Once we delivered a few of these systems, and they operated reliably, Trunkline asked if we could build a startup sequencer and monitoring system for one of its new gas turbine pumping stations. Gas turbines are much more 'tender' than the huge reciprocating engines used for decades in compressing gas for transmission by pipeline.

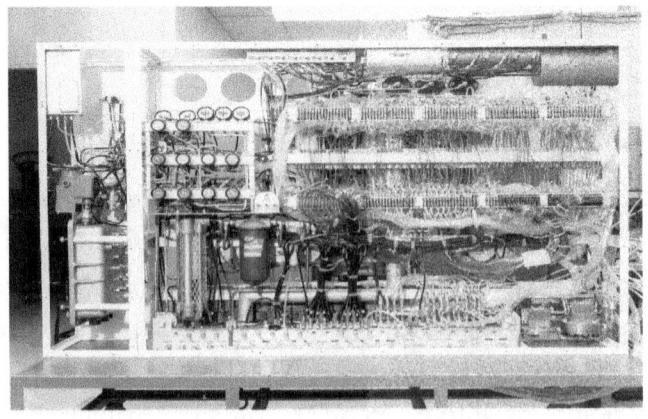

Shutdown Annunciator

Critical conditions must be satisfied at many steps in starting a turbine; the startup portion was a new challenge for us. The monitoring functions were much more extensive than those of the earlier reciprocating engine systems.

Gas Turbine Startup Sequencer and Shutdown Annunciator

While these systems functioned well and reliably, shortly after I left Honeywell, electronic integrated circuits came on the scene and rapidly became common and inexpensive. Their small size enabled them to be packaged in explosion-proof housings, mitigating the explosion potential of electrics, and one of the major advantages of the fluid systems disappeared. The fluidic field almost vanished for several decades, but recently I've been seeing articles about nanotechnology, published under the heading 'Microfluidics.' I haven't yet taken the time to assess the developments in this area.

10

The Lecture Circuit

As the fluid mechanics work at Honeywell progressed, I began writing technical papers published by professional society journals and articles on system applications for trade journals. These caught the eye of a number of universities in this country and Europe producing an interest in related research programs.

* * *

The educational world sought a part of the contractual funding being spent on the general fluidics area by the Department of Defense and NASA. In addition, the Advisory Group for Aerospace Research and Development (AGARD), the technical arm of NATO (North Atlantic Treaty Organization), expressed considerable interest and I participated in several technical information exchange programs under their auspices.

I received a surprising telephone call from Dr. J. Lowen Shearer, who headed the Mechanical Engineering Department at Pennsylvania State University. They had a major curriculum section dedicated to fluid power control, and he asked me to assemble a couple of day's lectures on fluid control devices. My boss at Honeywell thought this was good publicity for Honeywell if Penn State paid the expenses.

Thus began a whole new facet of my professional life.

After the Penn State lectures, Dr. S.Y. Lee, from the Massachusetts Institute of Technology, requested me to do a similar series of talks with a different twist: a more extensive series of lectures as part of a Summer School course on fluid power control. There followed a request from Stanford University and number of other state institutions, Kansas State, Oklahoma State and the University of Minnesota as well as the University of Toronto, the Technische Hochschule in Aachen, W. Germany and some smaller educational institutions in Canada and Turkey.

These activities were invaluable in developing contacts proved useful in my later life in the consulting business. Being able to find help with a difficult problem at the end of a telephone connection in a large part of the technical world can be exceedingly useful.

The Advisory Group for Aerospace Research and Development (AGARD)

In 1966 I received a call from Dr. S.Y. Lee, of the Dynamic Analysis and Controls Laboratory, at the Massachusetts Institute of Technology. He and his brother, Dr. Y.T. Li, were assembling a group of technical people to put on a traveling lecture series under the auspices of AGARD. Planning was in process for technical lectures at for several European educational institutions. There were also plans for a couple of days in Paris, which remained AGARD's headquarters despite the French withdrawal from NATO. While NATO relocated to Brussels, AGARD, for personal reasons of the principals, remained in Paris. The European lecture series, sponsored by AGARD, was presented in 1966 at the University of Turin in Italy, the Von Karman Aerodynamics Institute in Brussels and the Imperial College in London. Perhaps the best way to describe the tour is to include a copy of the internal AGARD report.

* * *

Report on Lecture Series on
Fluid Control – Components and Systems

1) GENERAL

Upon recommendation of the AGARD Guidance and Control Panel, a lecture series on "Fluid Control – Components and Systems" was organized by the Consultant and Exchange Programme in Europe in 1966.

Three different locations were chosen in order to make the series available to a wide audience. Speakers were selected from different nations to allow exchanges of information on the relative work being carried out in NATO countries.

2) SUBJECT

The subject was the utilisation of the dynamic properties of fluid in the form of jet or vortex in the design of fluid sensing, amplifying and activating elements.

Development work carried out in the direction of fluid suspension systems, such as air bearing, fluid bearing for instruments, and more sophisticated air cushion and active suspension systems were also presented.

3) SPEAKERS

Under the technical direction of Professor Y.T. Li, Professor of Instrumentation in the Department of Aeronautics and Astronautics at the Massachusetts Institute of Technology, the Speakers were :

K. Foster
Lecturer, Dept of
Mechanical Engineering,
Birmingham University, UK.

F. Giraud,
Scientific Director,
Bertin & Cie,
France.

S.Y. Lee,
Professor of Mechanical
Engineering,
Massachusetts Institute of
Technology, USA.

R.J. Reilly,
Research Section Head,
Fluid Sciences,
Systems & Research Division,
Honeywell Inc., USA.

H.H. Richardson,
Associate Professor of
Mechanical Engineering,
Massachusetts Institute of
Technology, USA.

L.B. Taplin,
Manager, Energy Conversion
and Dynamic Controls Labs.,
Bendix Corp. Research Labs. USA.

It was a different time; Trans-Atlantic travel was regarded as somewhat of a 'plum,' and not a chore. From Honeywell's standpoint, my travels were getting more complicated; the duration of the trip was two weeks, and my request to participate was initially denied. I applied for an unpaid leave of absence that was reluctantly approved. When the Director of Research asked whether he could accompany me to 'carry my bags,' I realized this was no longer a happy circumstance for the management, but I was already committed to the trip. This was an opportunity that proved to be a key to several minor successes in later life.

In 1967 AGARD sponsored me for lectures at Middle East Technical University in Ankara, Turkey and an International Conference in Varenna, Italy. During a stop in Paris, we discussed plans for a more extensive series of lectures to be given at educational institutions in nine NATO countries from Ankara, Turkey to Trondheim, near the Arctic Circle in Norway.

A Brush With Medieval History

Villa Monastero

The setting of Varenna on Lake Como in Northern Italy is about as pretty as one can imagine. The conference was held in an old monastery, Villa Monastero, overlooking the lake.

According to official records, the Monastery was built sometime before the year 1208, according to references in traceable documents. It passed into private ownership from 1569 to 1862, when it was extensively renovated. Internationally known literates, historians, artists and scientists extolled Villa Monastero since 1953, when this fine, old building became a Congress Center for advanced level studies. The villa has served as an international cultural and scientific center since 1963.

The conference was held in the Fermi Room, the old

Fermi Room (Old Chapel)

chapel of the monastery named after Enrico Fermi. Despite all the architectural elegance of the villa, the heating system in the Fermi Room was also from the 12th century and left something to be desired during the cold, rainy days, which persisted much of the week we were there.

We planned a vacation around this trip, so Betty and Tim could go along. Sightseeing in Paris, Switzerland and Rome consumed a couple of weeks before I departed for the Middle East, which wasn't a safe tourist spot. We enjoyed mountain hiking in Switzerland and seeing the wonders of Rome. Tim, who was 11, became weary of not being able to speak English to anyone but his parents. His crutch

Main Entrance of Villa Monestero

throughout the trip was a palm-size portable radio that would pick up "Voice of America" programs after sunset. He fell asleep with it every night.

After meetings in Paris and many letters, we hammered out a program and a contract to cover travel and expenses for the following year. These were formal international contracts that required defining the details of work statements, currency manipulations and a multitude of other first-time (for me) considerations. Each was a learning experience, but as my Dad used to say,

"Experience is often what you get when you're seeking something else."

* * *

When the 1968 contract arrived, we were scheduled to give two days of talks on fluidics at technical universities in nine of the NATO countries and Betty and Tim went along for much of the trip. Middle East Technical University was on the schedule, and since Ankara is not a real garden spot I again elected to do Turkey first, then have Betty and Tim meet me in Oslo. After talks at the University of Trondheim and the Norwegian Defense establishment, we were off to Copenhagen, Von Karman Institute in Brussels, and the Technical University of Delft in the Netherlands. Then it was on to Paris, just in time for the student riots of 1968. Betty and Tim departed Paris for home while I went on to Frankfurt, Munich and Naples.

Good Samaritans

In Naples I became seriously ill with a respiratory malady of unknown origin. I pulled myself together to croak my way through four two-hour talks over two days, retiring to a hotel room to lick my wounds at every opportunity. After completing my talks on the last day, I went to bed in late afternoon after closing the interlocking outside blinds, which let in no light whatever. I don't know how long I lay there half-delirious with a high fever and almost unable to breathe. Sometime later, I heard someone pounding on the door. I think it may have been the next day, or perhaps the day after; I've never been able to reconstruct it. I opened the door to find Assistant Professor Russo, from the University of Naples, and his wife. They became concerned when they tried to call me and receiving no answers, decided to check.

The Russoes brought a doctor friend to the hotel with prescription medications to treat whatever was 'going around.' Then they brought me meals for several days, until I was able to go out for food on my own.

Seeking breakfast out of the hotel for the first time, I passed a news stand and saw a huge, four-inch headline on the morning paper: "A Los Angeles Come Dallas." My high school Latin (rough translation): "To Los Angeles Comes Dallas," told me Robert Kennedy was 'morte' (dead), but I didn't know enough Italian to translate the article without a dictionary.

It was a sunny day, and I hopped a train to Porto Fino, where I knew US Navy put-in from time to time. When I arrived, the streets were teeming with American sailors who were able to tell me about how Kennedy was assassinated the night before.

I regained my strength quickly and returned home the next day via England, but without the help of the Russoes there might have been a different homecoming.

*　　*　　*

The following year, 1969, I was asked by AGARD to assemble a lecture tour on gas turbine control using fluidic devices. I collected a group working in the field:

    Elmer Johnson from Honeywell, who controlled a General Electric J85 jet engine using fluidics.
    Bill Boothe, from General Electric's gas turbine division.
    Lael Taplin, from Bendix Aviation Corporation.
    Keith Foster, from Rolls Royce gas turbine group.
    Dr. Herbert Schaedel, a professor at the Technical University of Aachen.

Two lecture series of several days were planned: one at the Von Kaman Institute in Brussels and one at the University of Pisa in Italy. My dad died a day or two before the Brussels conference, so I missed opening the lecture series but arrived in Pisa two days later, following the funeral. This was the finale of my junketing, and I left Honeywell in December of 1969.

*   *   *

Rescue By A Total Stranger

Aside from the NATO/AGARD conferences and lectures, during the late 1960s I often gave technical papers at international conferences on fluid mechanics and control systems. A Swiss engineer, Hans Glaettli, often attended these meetings. Glaettli and I long carried on a friendly (on my part) professional jousting match at technical conferences, but I'm not sure how Glaettli viewed our relationship.

He was a researcher from a prestigious company (IBM) in Zurich; he made sure you understood his position and carried himself with a somewhat haughty air. If I presented a technical paper saying something was white, I could be sure Glaettli would work a rebuttal into his talk saying it was black; confrontation seemed an innate part of his personality. For my part, I often responded with the demeanor of bumbling country boy from Minnesota – "No Mr. Glaettli, I didn't look at aspect of the problem; back home we've been busy with the spring plowing and ... ."

Glaettli and I had different approaches to technology. I had a somewhat intuitive understanding of aerodynamics and fluid mechanics and made conceptual leaps in a number of branches of the field, which I would follow with a supporting mathematical analysis. Glaettli's work was always sound, solid and meticulously constructed but tended toward small extensions of paths beaten dusty by other researchers: brain surgery on gnats so to speak.

Most of these conferences were held at universities, if the audience was small, or in large hotels with 'grand ballrooms,' which could accommodate larger groups. A facility in Essen, Germany was unusual and striking. The facility was built by one of Germany's major labor unions and lacked nothing in the way of amenities.

The lecture hall was an inverted, semi-conical shape. Think of a cone sliced from the point at the bottom to the 'base' at the top with the pointed end truncated at a tiny speaker's platform while the sides extended steeply upward from the stage, perhaps 35 or 40 feet. It seated several hundred people and each plush seat was fitted with its own desk and microphone that allowed anyone to question the speaker at any time. Labor unions live well in Germany.

Speaking there was eerie; the hall was darkened with only a spotlight on the small stage at point of the cone. Questions came anonymously out of the blackness.

At one of the talks I gave in Essen, I spoke of a device we were researching, which deserved mention but was not ready for 'prime time.' A voice, I'm quite sure it was Glaettli, came out of the dark with an insightful question revealing he might be working on something similar. The question went directly to the heart of a detail determining whether the concept was sound. I wasn't ready to reveal the 'key to the kingdom' and answered the question somewhat elusively. The voice came back immediately, taking a shot at the critical detail from a different direction: again an elusive answer. Twice more came the same question, phrased a bit differently. I began to wonder how to handle this persistence, when out of the darkness came another heavily accented voice:

"Mr. Reilly," it said, "you have answered this question now three times. The gentleman asking the question obviously has no experience with research apparatus, and nothing you say will further enlighten him." Beyond thank you, I was speechless. It was a welcome rescue from an anonymous friend, whom I will never know.

* * *

A Test of Time

Several years later, at a meeting in Frankfurt, I surreptitiously entered a technical conference late, after an extended lunch hour. I quietly found an empty chair. A tiny shaft of sunlight from an imperfect window-blind illuminated the watch of the person sitting beside me. I studied the watch closely noting the time; I didn't think I was *that* late, but I missed Glaettli's talk I so badly wanted to hear.

Having given my paper in a morning session I was now relaxed and wanted to shop for a watch. My old watch, a high school graduation gift, was getting tired and I longed for a Swiss self-winder. After a quick lunch I walked to the Frankfurt business district, which took more time than I expected. I looked at my neighbor's watch again; it had five tiny circles surrounding the center shaft carrying the hands. I recognized the brand, an Eterna, similar to the one I just purchased minutes before. The five circles were a trade mark signifying micro ball bearings used at critical points in the movement, a Swiss marvel of miniaturization. I didn't aspire to an Omega or a Rolex, so I purchased something I could afford. The Eterna was a fine watch, with a solid gold case and a reputation for long-term accuracy, but it lacked the prestige of a Rolex.

As my eyes became accustomed to the darkness I glanced at the wearer of the watch: To my astonishment it was Glaettli. When the session ended and the lights came up, we stood. I turned to him and extended my hand; we shook hands and exchanged pleasantries. I then asked him about his watch and told him I purchased its mate. "How do you like it?" I asked, "Has it been reliable?" Drawing himself to full attention he responded in his usual 'Germanic English.'

"I tsink it iss tza best, ferry preetcise," he answered. We exchanged some timepiece small talk, and I managed to work in a question of some delicacy, given the moment. Having noticed his watch was nearly 30 minutes fast – I hadn't been quite as late as I thought – I asked,

"Is Zurich in a different time zone?" Immediately sensing the thrust of my question, Glaettli replied,

"Oh no, I neffer set tziss watch. I haff it now tzirteen years, and it has gained in tzat time tsirtytzix minutes and tzikteen seconds, maybe tzseventeen. It is not so good atza one I had before. I had it all tru my days in tsa Swiss Ahmy. Twenty-one years I carried it, and tzat one gained only twelf minute tse whole time." I nodded as though I understood, but I didn't, really. More small talk; I bade him good-bye until next year's conference and we shook hands again. He motioned to me to pause while he reached into his pocket for a business card, which he presented with a flourish.

"Thank you," I said, "and by the way, what happened to your first Eterna watch?" Turning on his heel he replied over his shoulder without looking,

"I lost it," and strutted away.

I thought about this exchange off and on for some time, and then it dawned on me: A watch to Glaettli was not a timepiece but a long-term demonstration of a Swiss-precision, mechanical device; a test of time so to speak. Sometimes I just seem to have a knack for asking the wrong questions. I still have my Eterna; sadly, Glaettli lost his.

* * *

The Berlin Wall

Sometime later, at a meeting in Frankfurt, I made an acquaintance over lunch with an Assistant Professor from the University of (then West) Berlin, Uwe Ganzer. It was the time of the Cold War, and the Berlin Wall was the topic of much conversation. Ganzer invited me to visit him in Berlin and offered to show me around the city. I found a day's slippage in my schedule that might accommodate a day in West Berlin, if I could arrange the travel.

Without an East German visa, I couldn't follow Ganzer's rail route, because the Russians controlled travel through East Germany into West Berlin. Newscasts were often sprinkled with reports of Westerners being roughed up on trains by Russian guards. Even air traffic passed through the Russian controlled sector but was restricted to altitudes of less than 3,000 feet. The trip was somewhat tense.

With some quick exploration, I determined Pan American Airways flew a few flights into West Berlin each day, using Boeing 727s. I caucused with Ganzer to determine his schedule and booked early morning passage from Frankfurt to West Berlin for the day after Ganzer's return to Berlin. The flight departed just before sunrise and lasted about a half hour.

Tempehof Air Terminal

The entry into West Berlin's Templehof airport was memorable. On final approach, we slid down a canyon formed by tall apartment buildings. The airport was built as a monument to Hitler's National Socialist Party (NAZI) and is striking, even in the modern era, although constructed in the late 1920s.

The scale of the terminal building is difficult to comprehend. In the picture, the small white dots on the concrete apron are Boeing 727-size airplanes, and the circular arc is an array of boarding gates. They enclose both airplanes and access to them, protected from wind and rain by sliding doors rolling along the inner arc. The enclosed area, the dark region just inside the brick segments comprising the exterior surface, is large enough to allow a DC-3-size aircraft to enter and be completely enclosed. The passenger terminal, no miniature in itself, is the brick building just outside the center of the arc at the far right of the picture.

Ganzer met me in the terminal building, and we went to his office, where he introduced me to Ulrich Stark. Ulrich's history was interesting. Raised in East Berlin, he participated in a major escape of refugees from the Eastern Zone, sponsored by NBC News a year or two earlier. I recalled the feature, called "The Tunnel" and watched it with great interest when it first appeared. It made my day with one of the participants even more than interesting.

High point of the day in Berlin was a visit to a museum dedicated to the people who died trying to escape from the Eastern Zone during the cold war. The museum, located about 200 yards from Brandenburg Gate at 'Checkpoint Charlie', backed up to the 'Berlin Wall,' and was the starting point of 'The Wall.' 'Checkpoint Charlie' had great symbolism as the focus of the conflict between East and West. Brandenburg Gate, erected by Friedrich Wilhelm II in the 1700s, has long been a symbol of German victory in various wars and was, in a sense, the German 'Arc de Triomphe.'

En route to the museum, we passed by the Brandenburg, the nearby ruins of the Reichstadt and the Chancellery. Close-by was the spot where Hitler's body was cremated with gasoline after his suicide in the basement of the Chancellery.

The museum was located in the shadow of the East Berlin guard tower. The guards photographed everyone who stood on the viewing platform for a look into the Eastern Zone. Starke waited for me a block away; because of his involvement in 'The Tunnel' escapes he was not interested in being photographed by the East German police, who watched the museum entrance closely.

The East Germans vacated all the dreary gray buildings along the eastern side of the wall to prevent their being used in escape attempts. When Starke and his friends began to dig the tunnel under the wall, they started some distance back into the Eastern Zone and used a building's upper floors to secret the dirt excavated from the tunnel. Beginning in the basement of one of these buildings, the labor of digging was enhanced by the need to carry buckets of dirt to the upper floors of the abandoned buildings. A cursory look at the ground floor by guards, wouldn't give away the activity going on underground. The seriousness of the game of escape was recalled to me by a 2007 article in the New York Times.

East German Shoot-to-Kill Order Is Found

By JUDY DEMPSEY
Published: August 13, 2007
BERLIN, Aug. 12 — Seventeen years after German reunification, archivists have found the first written proof East German border guards had been ordered to shoot to kill anyone trying to escape to West Germany, including women and children. Deutsche Presse Agenture, via European Pressphoto AgencyA 1962 photo showed East German guards with the body of a man who was shot when he tried to cross the Berlin Wall. The seven-page order, dated Oct. 1, 1973, was discovered last week in the regional archive office in the eastern German city of Magdeburg. Though unsigned, it shows the Ministry for State Security, known as the Stasi, told guards they must 'stop or liquidate' anyone trying to cross the border. "Do not hesitate to use your firearm, not even when the border is breached in the company of women and children, which is a tactic the traitors have often used," the document said. The revelations, which stunned politicians here across the political spectrum, were made public just days before the 46th anniversary on Monday of the building of the Berlin Wall, which divided the city and became the symbol of the cold war. The wall was toppled on Nov. 9, 1989 and paved the way for the reunification of the city and the two Germanys.

The museum at Checkpoint Charlie was a tragic-comedic history of escalating attempts by East Germans to escape to the West and the countermeasures employed by military police to prevent such escapes. Initial attempts were crude: Get a car and drive at high-speed toward Checkpoint Charlie, scatter the guards and crash through the gate. The countermeasure was steel tank traps – geometry similar to children's jacks – made of heavy steel beams and arranged in a serpentine path to prevent rushing the checkpoint.

There followed an array of automobile modifications: 'floors' in a fender well to allow an escapee to drape over the wheel, hollowed out rear seats and arrangements to hang one's self beneath the vehicle. This was countered by mirrors on a long stick for viewing without soiling the guard's uniform.

One family escaped in a homemade hot-air balloon, which led to the restrictions on the sale of lightweight fabrics in the Eastern zone. Another ingenious escapee built his own underwater breathing system and escaped by swimming down the river Spree into the Western Zone. Several tunnels were dug during the time of The Wall, some with greater success than others. One of these originated in a cemetery; people carrying flowers 'in grief' for a relative would reach a point in mid-cemetery and suddenly disappear into the tunnel.

After Checkpoint Charlie, it was a wild ride around Berlin's high points terminating at the Kaiser Wilhelm Memorial Church. The old church, severely damaged by bombing in WW II, was rebuilt as a modern structure, but preserved the bell tower as a monument to those who died in the conflict. I spent a few minutes in the new chapel, a haven of peace and quiet in the middle of the Kurfurstendamm, one of Berlin's busiest avenues. Then it was off to Tempelhof and an evening flight back to Frankfurt. It was a memorable day.

New Church

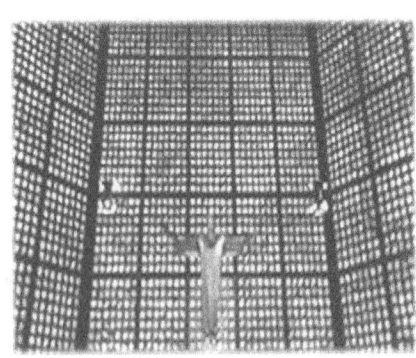

New Church Interior

*   *   *

So You Want To Lead a Band

Escoullier was an easy man to dislike. I called him from my hotel and was invited to visit Honeywell's Frankfurt offices for a late afternoon visit and a later dinner. Lolling about Escoullier's office for a few minutes and watching his interaction with employees, revealed an abrasive personality with an imperious, demeaning attitude toward his German colleagues. He seemed still to be fighting WW II and treated his subordinates as though they were occupants of a prison camp. Why a major corporation would choose a Frenchman to lead its German subsidiary in the receding shadows of WW II, was a mystery I never resolved to my satisfaction.

My visit to Escoullier's office was a courtesy call. While Honeywell management was never enamored with my AGARD activities, they began to expect my request for a leave of absence, for a couple of weeks each summer, to accommodate my foreign travels. The Director of Research decided to use my outside-funded, European trips to enhance his corporate relationships. He asked me to 'drop-in' at corporate offices in London, Zurich or Frankfurt, which is how found myself in Escoullier's Frankfurt office.

The business day wound to a close and we proceeded to a very fine German restaurant. I don't recall what I ordered, but everything else was memorable; the dinner didn't go well. Escoullier ordered trout. He spoke excellent English, so conversation came easily while we waited for our food.

When the food was served, Escoullier's trout was presented whole on the plate, head to tail. With the first tentative examination of his fish Escoullier exploded,

"@#$%& chef," he exclaimed in a loud voice, attracting the attention of all diners in the room. Not content with the initial uproar he created, he slammed his silverware to the table and continued: "The @#$%& chef stole the cheeks; they always do that." Our waiter rushed to the table and inquired about the problem; he was followed quickly by the maitre de and the manager of the establishment, investigating the noise.

"@#$%& chef stole the cheeks," he repeated in German while displaying the small, empty slits under the trout's eye with his knife. Escoullier then continued with a long tirade in German, which I was unable to understand.

Coming from a town of 400, where a spring-caught Catfish from the Root River was considered the height of seafood delight, I didn't even understand the problem. In fact, until then I didn't even know trout had cheeks let alone that cheeks were a sought-after delicacy. So, I just sat, somewhat puzzled, listening to Escoullier's continuing cascade of vituperation piled higher and higher on the absent chef.

As he spun on, the volume of his voice began to diminish, much as a balloon losing its inflation. His delivery resembled a child's windup toy, and I could almost see the key unwinding in the middle of his back. When he ran out of gas, it stopped turning. The three Germans watched impassively, arms folded, until he was finished. Then the maitre de responded to him in French – letting him know he understood his rudeness was not homegrown. He then picked up Escoullier's knife and fork and with a grand flourish, deftly opened the trout's mouth revealing the two cheek pieces, carefully excised and placed inside, for the diner's convenience, by the considerate chef. Without another word, the threesome turned and departed. We were left to eat our meal quietly with little conversation; after all, what else could be said? It was the perfect squelch.

As we finished our meal and left the restaurant I was tired, somewhat jet-lagged and looking forward to a good bed to recover for the next day's events. But it was not to be; Escoullier announced he was going to show me a genuine, down-in-a-dank-basement, German beer hall, an old fashioned rathskeller he explained. My hopes for retiring early faded as we descended into a noisy, smoky hall. A hundred or more revelers, some dressed in lederhosen, swaying, arms locked together, to the music of a Tyrolean band. Not being an imbiber, this wasn't what I had in mind for the evening. Escoullier ordered a pitcher of beer, I ordered apfelsaft (apple juice) and resigned to listen to the music while watching the level in Escoullier's pitcher recede.

Nearly an hour later and one pitcher down, I made polite motions to leave; Escoullier motioned me to remain seated.

"Not yet," he said, as if he were waiting for something and ordered another pitcher of beer. I wondered what 'not yet' meant, and I was to find out shortly. The evening was becoming a thorough drag; I began to wonder how I could terminate it gracefully and considered feigning illness but discarded it as an option. I ordered another apfelsaft and set about watching the level of beer in the pitcher recede for a second time. I'm sure Escoullier too, would rather have been somewhere else, rather than 'entertaining' me.

* * *

In the 1960s there was a television program called "So You Want To Lead a Band." Its entertainment format snared people out of the audience to lead one of the so-called 'big bands' of the era. I've forgotten which band it was, perhaps Sammy Kaye, but I'm no longer sure. The 'victim' was given a baton and the band forgot all it ever knew about music and smooth performance. It responded to every twitch of the amateur's baton, much to his/her embarrassment. It was great fun for the audience and humiliation for the victim. Yes, you're ahead of me; you already know what 'not yet' meant: I was yet to lead the band before being allowed to sleep.

* * *

The band took a break, and when they assembled again the leader came down from the stage and pretended to wander randomly through the crowd, finally stopping at our table. He removed his Tyrolean hat, complete with the feathers and the requisite 'paint brush' under its band. He dropped it onto my head; it was a bilious green.

In what was an obvious setup with Escoullier, he handed me his baton and motioned me toward the stage. I walked slowly, my mind racing as to how to recover and turn the tables on this connived set piece. I decided on a brash approach to put Escoullier and the band leader in their respective places. Recall, I'm not in a good mood by this time and I don't care what happens; it's time for me to have some fun.

I'm now in front of the band, hands on hips wondering just how to proceed, when the band begins to play some unfamiliar melody. I motion them to stop and they do. I'm not a totally lost soul, having played for several years in a small-town band back home in Hokah. Addressing the guy who seemed to be the number two dog in the pack, after the leader, I inquire:

"Do you know any American songs?" He looks both right and left at his colleagues and mutters something under his breath. Then he turns to me and says,

"Home On The Range." So we crank up and do "Home on the Range." It came out OK, but I'm not sure I had anything to do with that. We finish, and Number 2 looks at me quizzically with a shrug and a palms-up gesture.

"What other American melodies do you know?" I ask. The mini-conference with his colleagues is repeated, and he looks back with a shrug and a sickly smile of emptiness.

"How about "Deep In the Heart of Texas?" I inquire. A flash of a smile: Yes, they know "Deep In the Heart of Texas." We do "Deep In the Heart of Texas," and I have the crowd clapping their hands enthusiastically, – *The stars at night, are big and bright: Clap, Clap, Clap, Clap, deep in the heart of Texas* – at proper points by the finish. Another wild idea sweeps over me, but the bandleader begins to move out of the stage curtains. He points at his baton; he wants it back. I point it at him and tell him,

"The guy who has this (the baton) runs the show. You got me into this and I'm not done … yet." He recedes to his spot in the wings.

I turn back to Number 2, who is now sort of my buddy and seems to be enjoying this. "Deep In the Heart of Texas" was a hit, and I contemplated doing it again just for the crowd participation, but I decide to go for broke. I play my Ace.

"Do you know 'The Star Spangled Banner?'" It was a good bet; I knew the U.S. Air Force Base at Ramstein was nearby, and there was a chance the band was involved in events there, now and then. Yes, they know it. Good; it was a lucky guess.

I turned to the crowd and said,

"We're going to play the American national anthem. At home, when the Star Spangled Banner is played, everyone stands. I want everyone to stand." I start the music, then turn to the crowd and motion with the baton, everybody up. Nobody moved. Then one guy stood, then another and another and pretty soon the whole place is standing. I abandon the directing and remove my Tyrolean hat. Facing the crowd, I hold it over my heart while Number 2 completes the Star Spangled Banner. Then I salute smartly, bow to the crowd and clap my appreciation; the crowd also claps and there is quite an uproar as I hand the baton and the hat back to the bandleader. In retrospect, it would have been more gracious to add the German National Anthem as a finish, but my general mood at the time prohibited rational thought.

Driving to my hotel, conversation was sparse between Escoullier and me. In the extended silence, I couldn't help but wonder about German crowds. Perhaps it's not a fair assessment, given the circumstances, but if the right little guy with a small mustache and a bad haircut, were to turn up in a basement beer hall in, say … Munich, could he do it all over again? Hmmm … the Fourth Reich?

Lasting Friendships

The NATO-AGARD experience proved to be of lasting value. As an engineering consultant, after I left Honeywell, the contacts were invaluable. The AGARD part of NATO continued to operate out of Paris after the parent organization departed for new quarters in Brussels. It was a politically complicated relationship, because France was no longer a part of NATO. The coordinator of the technical lectures was a gentleman, Bernard Heliot, who flew U.S.-built P-47 Thunderbolt fighters during WW II. We had an immediate common interest in flying and carried on a lively email correspondence for more than 40 years.

After retiring from AGARD Bernard passed his time giving flight instructions for a French flying club, flying out of Toussus le Noble, an historic old airfield near Versailles.

Each time I visited Paris during our long acquaintance, Bernard

Heliot and Author

would manage to turn out a club airplane for me to fly – while he talked to French air traffic control – and roam about the French countryside. This was a real treat because flying in Europe is frightfully expensive – between $100 and $200 per hour in the 1960s/80s. The gasoline cost alone was between $8 and $10 per gallon in 1999.

The most memorable of these trips was a flight down the Seine River from Paris to the sea and then along the Normandy Beach landing site of WW II. I was able to fly at near water level and look up the cliffs of Omaha Beach in wonderment and sadness. It was sobering to think more than 3,000 of our people died, and several times more were wounded in a single morning, while climbing those cliffs facing withering German fire. The picture above shows Bernard and me after our last flight together in 1999; he was in his mid 80s. at the time. He joined the 'innumerable caravan' in 2016 at age 93.

Beyond Heliot, AGARD meetings introduced me Dr. Francois Giraud, who became my employer when I left Honeywell in 1969. Dr. Herb Schaedel remains a good friend and frequent correspondent. John Dawson, a nine-year client from Ottawa, and I exchange emails several times a month and we visit each others homes. Dr. Jean Thoma of Zug, Switzerland and I have a common interest in Thermodynamics and exchange frequent emails. He's been kind enough to send me copies of the textbooks he's written over the years; he's just finished his eighth. These friends and former clients, with whom I maintain contact, give me some assurance my work was appreciated, and they mean far more to me than the consulting fees I received.

AGARD was good to me.

11

Fired! (Well, sort of)

The British might call it being "turfed-out." – You get a small office for reading magazines, but your playground and its responsibilities are gone.

* * *

After nearly 13 years with Honeywell, holding a variety of engineering jobs, I advanced to managing one of four sections under the Director of Research for the Military Products Division. It was a group I built over about 10 years.

Research in the Military Product Group was no ivory tower operation, no lavishly funded corporate showcase of basic research for the good of mankind. The company funded little research per se. Funding came from two sources: so-called 'Independent Research and Development' (IR&D) funds and contract work for government agencies. Theoretically, we worked to develop products for seven divisions of the company engaged in manufacturing products with a military emphasis. In practice, it worked quite differently.

The small amount of money (IR&D) we received from the company, as 'seed corn' for new ideas and products, came from a percentage override on contracts for products the company sold to government agencies. Production contracts were priced in the usual way.

Cost of producing the product had to be verified as 'allowable,' then selling costs and administrative expenses were added. Finally, the government allowed the company to add an item of cost called 'Independent Research and Development,' an add-on of something less than 5%. This was the source of our seed money and termed IR&D in common parlance.

In reality, the professional engineering staff of each section under the Director of Research worked in an environment of divided loyalties: the interests of the manufacturing divisions against the raw survival considerations for the research group. The section manager allocated the IR&D money received at the beginning of the year to his first-line supervisors, then hit the road selling applied research to such organizations as the Air Force Office of Scientific Research, Office of Naval Research and NASA.

In addition to the heavy technical workload this was a somewhat unrewarding exercise. The more success I achieved in the contractual arena the less IR&D funding allocated to my section. It was a high pressure job. I struggled to keep up with technology in the laboratory. At the same time, managing the laboratory work-in-process and traveling to the sponsoring agencies were a significant part of the job. Without Betty's independence and ingenuity, I could never have kept up with the action.

There were further tensions: The semiannual treks around the country to the Military Products Group's seven divisions, only two of which were in the Twin City area. This entire exercise was a bit disingenuous, because we had to show how the IR&D money a particular division contributed to the research group furthered the division's welfare. This was often difficult because in reality, most of the IR&D funds seeded the best potential research and development contracts that might assure our group's survival. The fortunes of a particular division were secondary. This meant section leaders prepared an IR&D presentation with slides and handouts specific to each of the divisions. These presentations took some small corner of our overall activity and blew it up to look as though our entire effort was in the interest of the division at hand.

IR&D money was not manna the federal government dropped from the sky every morning. The small percentage the company was allowed to add to production contracts, in support of new development, was monitored by a board composed of people from the various government research agencies and academia. The board visited our laboratory every two years to evaluate the quality of the work being done. This, in turn, determined the IR&D override percentage the company could apply to production contracts over the succeeding years. The better the assessment of our work, the larger the percentage override allowed – small in any event.

In preparation for these visits, someone in the laboratory prepared an accompanying document the board members were supposed to read prior to their visits. Preparation of this document, which was approximately the size of the St. Paul telephone directory, was a major effort rotated among the four Research Section Chiefs. The author described not only the work of his own group but also of the entire department. My last year at Honeywell I was tagged with preparing the dreaded IR&D document.

After many weeks of writing, the final step in preparing the book was to insert the amount of IR&D funding used to support each of the programs described therein. The division's Financial Manager, Bob, supplied the financial data. As I began inserting the numbers to match with the corresponding words, the amounts appeared inflated. When I looked at my section, I discovered my group's numbers totaled to a value about 50% greater than the funding we actually received. I called Bob and explained my accuracy concerns. He said,

"They're OK; just use those numbers." I objected,

"Bob I can't do that, my section's numbers a just wrong and the others are likely incorrect also." He replied,

"I'll talk to the boss." He returned a couple of hours later saying,

"The Director said to go ahead and use those numbers."

"I can't do that Bob; the values aren't correct." I replied. After a couple more rounds of essentially the same discussion I finally said,

"Here's the report; it's complete and you can put in whatever numbers you like. I don't want my name on it anywhere, or be connected with it in any way." He left with the book I wrote.

Shortly afterward, I received a summons to the Director's office. A rather fiery conversation ensued. At this point, I didn't understand all the concern: The major part of the job – preparing the IR&D document – was done and done well, so why the big problem with the cost numbers. Only years later did I learn why.

A day later I was invited to a tense conversation with the cognizant Vice President, who accused me of 'not being a team player' and other, more dastardly appellations. I stuck to my position because to submit those inflated numbers for submission to a government agency was in essence a fraud, for which people – witness Westinghouse executives at the time – go to jail. I thought the whole thing would blow over, but a couple of months later I was offered a position as a Staff Scientist, reporting to the Vice President of Honeywell's Brown Instruments Division in Philadelphia. In addition to many other considerations, I never liked Philadelphia and never cared for striped prison attire.

My departure surfaced in a social setting several years after I left the company. One of the group commented that I should have known that at this time the Military Products Division launched an entirely new research operation in the Boston area. He remarked that this start-up was likely funded by reallocating part of the IR&D funds from the money assigned to the Minneapolis division. The existence of this new research activity was not disclosed to the government review board in the IR&D document I wrote, because I had no knowledge of it. This may not have been fraud, but it was perilously close, so I was glad I stood my ground at the time. As an aside, it might also explain why, whenever our section was successful in winning more contract support funds, the IR&D support for our section was reduced.

A reason for my being offered a face-saving 'promotion' rather than being discharged now presented itself: Corporate management thought I knew where the bodies were buried and wouldn't take the risk of dealing with a whistle-blower. Little did they know, I no idea of the real story; I only knew the numbers given to me were wrong. We often overestimate the power of an adversary.

In the past, I saw how management treated other senior staff in disputed situations: They were given a titled position with no staff and no real job. My 12-year record of achievements, many patents and letters of commendation from the company's top executives lost all meaning, and in the end they were not a redeeming factor. The organization circled the wagons, and the 'problem' was left outside the circle. I was determined not to spend 25 years reading magazines, in a small office, just to get a free lunch and a plaque of some sort. It was time for me to go . . . again.

12

Cytec Development Inc.

Win the battle, lose the war.
* * *

About the time I was getting the turf pulled from under me at Honeywell, one of the people I met during my AGARD lectures contacted me about joining him to help build a U.S. division of his French company. His focus was the development of a personal transportation system. Personal Rapid Transit (PRT) was the technology du jour; Richard Nixon was President and made a personal commitment to spending significant government funds on small vehicle transportation systems. It appeared to be a technological field with a great deal of momentum. Buses and trains were 'out;' PRT was 'in.'

Cytec Development was founded by Dr. Francois Geraud. Francois was French, grew up in Morocco and armed with a PhD from the Massachusetts Institute of Technology, he made somewhat of a name for himself in the transportation business. Working with a French company, Bertin CIE, he developed a 250mph train concept. The original test vehicle was both supported and guided by a film of air bled from its jet engine and injected into its supporting base and along an inverted 'T' section guide surface. The photo below shows the third version, large enough for 80 passengers, powered by a gas turbine driving a ducted propeller, rather than a jet engine, as in the original test vehicle.

Aerotrain Prototype

Based on this work, Francois set up a consulting business on Long Island to service a consulting contract Cytec was awarded by Ling Temco Vaught Inc (LTV), a subsidiary of Jones & Laughlin Steel Corporation. LTV was awarded a contract to construct the intra-airport transportation system for the new Dallas-Fort Worth Regional Airport (1969), and I was asked to work closely with LTV while also doing some aerodynamic consulting work on the 250mph. vehicle in France. In December 1969 I left Honeywell and set up shop in a small facility in Roseville, Minnesota at 1723 Terrace Drive.

In reality, Cytec-US evolved into concentration on the LTV relationship and the development of a control system for a small vehicle transportation system Giraud was building in France. My aerodynamic experience with the 'Aerotrain,' was limited to a couple of 250 mph rides on a three-mile test track near Orleans, France.

Terrace Drive was a short street in a St. Paul suburb lined with simple warehouse structures, block long buildings divided into rental modules housing hopeful, small businesses. There were many such structures in the Twin City area in the 1960s and 70s. Control Data Corporation made hundreds of millionaires in the area, growing from a simple starting point into a giant international business. Real estate investment firms traded on this success and hope, as hundreds of startup businesses were formed during that period.

The business suites were sections from buildings several hundred feet long street-side and 125 feet deep, divided into structurally convenient modules 40 feet wide. 'How many modules do you want?' The module layout included 20-foot deep, finished strip along the street-front, containing a single office and a conference room with an entrance/secretary's foyer between. Businesses started and failed by the month and if one were lucky he could acquire a space with some leftover, installed amenities abandoned by a prior occupant. The rear space was raw, open structure; do your own improvements. In our case, we were able to acquire a module only 60 feet deep, with the rear part of our warehouse space occupied by an adjacent company.

One of my Honeywell subordinates, Glenn Merrill, asked to join me, and I hired him soon after startup. Later we acquired a secretary/receptionist from the company next door, when it filed for bankruptcy.

We purchased used shop machinery: a Bridgeport milling machine and a South Bend lathe along with welding equipment and other small tools. We were able to buy some high quality electronic instrumentation equipment from another bankrupt firm. Our early efforts were directed toward electro-mechanical control devices to support the French personal rapid transit system. While Merrill and I worked together on the design of the control system, I spent a substantial amount of my time in travel and general support of the LTV contract, leaving the building of instrumentation to Glenn.

LTV – Garbage In, Garbage Out

The LTV contract was a real frustration from the outset, and early-on we became involved in the control system for the Dallas/Ft. Worth Airport transit system. Some architectural detail is necessary to understand the nature of the problems we encountered.

* * *

Initially, the DFW airport terminal layout was an architect's dream slowly reduced to reality, step by step. The early design was based on three separate, circular, terminal buildings. The side facing the runways contained extending gateway fingers projecting from the periphery of the circles to the parked aircraft . Street-side structure housed the functions interfacing with the city: bus and automobile access, baggage, car rentals etc.

The circular buildings were to be connected with a personal transportation system permitting passengers to board the transit vehicles anywhere on the circle and ride around the circle from the boarding gates on the runway side to the service area on the inner side and vice versa.

To get from one terminal building to another the three circular terminals were tangent to one another and the individual transit systems meshed at the tangent points as do teeth on a gear. As with gear wheels, the local transit systems in the individual terminal buildings turned in opposite directions. This allowed the vehicles in adjacent terminals to drop into available slots, as gear teeth do, making it possible for a passenger to move from one circular terminal building to another. LTV invited Cytec to submit a proposal for the design of a system to control this beast. It all sounded good from the vantage point of a dreamy architect with airbrush drawings, but the nuts 'n bolts of making this system work were a different matter.

*   *   *

Cytec France employed a brilliant mathematician, Dr. Marcel Kadosh. Kadosch analyzed the three-circle control problem and solved it with a closed-form, mathematical solution he presented in two, tightly constructed, pages of equations. After our presentation to the engineering team at LTV, they smiled disdainfully and pointed to a foot-high stack of paper on the conference room table. It was the printout of a computer simulation of the entire system done by the Batelle Research Institute in Cleveland, Ohio.

This was the early days of computers that were often displayed in a 'glass house' along some prominent, street-facing portion of a company's headquarters. All of this 20th century wonder required public display. Analytical responsibilities were divided; an engineer would document his problem then submit it to the computer department for analysis. The computer interface employee was a high priest of sorts, who took the engineering operative's problem and its mathematical description thereof, for translation into computer language.

Today, one takes his own problem description to his desktop computer and gets an answer in seconds or minutes; in the late 1960s one 'turn' of an attack on a problem often took a week or more. There was plenty of room for error in the process. Nevertheless, Dr. Kadosch's brilliant solution to the DFW Airport transit system was buried under several pounds of paper submitted by Batelle, so we licked our wounds and went away.

About a year later I received a call from Jim Gathings at LTV. Jim was one of the 'straight-up-and-down' characters in the LTV assemblage of characters. Embarrassed by the treatment Cytec received a year earlier, now he was seeking our help.

A serious problem occurred in the computer analysis of the DFW transit system. A deeper dive into the computer analysis built around the Batelle model, showed some stations in the simulated system received no vehicle service for three or four hours. Then all the vehicles in the entire system would pass through one station like a gigantic gems on a necklace, separated by a 'safety separation' of a few feet. The call came in: Could we come to Dallas and discuss a 'debunching strategy' for operating the system effectively?

We came away with the Batelle computer program and the strange results it was producing. Starting from the beginning, a very peculiar picture emerged; consideration of time and space were confused in ways both simple and destructive. In establishing the size of the vehicles – they each carried between 15 and 20 passengers, size yet to be chosen – the Batelle computer model ignored the time required for loading and unloading the vehicles. To make the problem even more simple, the computer model used vehicles of ZERO length. These zero-length vehicles could hold any number of passengers the computer high-priest chose to assign. The passengers boarded and disembarked in ZERO time. This created a hopeless mess, but one obvious problem was solved by zero-length vehicles: when it came to finding a slot in the meshing gears, a zero length vehicle was conveniently allowed to fit-in anywhere. Dr. Kadosch started from the beginning and designed a functionally new transportation system.

If you travel through the DFW terminal today you see the result of the redesign, done by our little startup company. Gone are circular transportation systems and the 'meshing gears.' People walk around a semicircle from gate to gate. To get from one terminal to another they either walk or go to the inner ring, where trains pass by on a regular and orderly schedule. The vehicles also serve hotels and parking facilities along the airport service roads.

One more difference from the original design: Kadosch told LTV and the DFW Airport Authority the redesigned system would never be able to handle the then-anticipated traffic in the year 2000. It would be interesting to verify this with current traffic data, but I suppose no one ever will. This whole program was my first experience with computer modeling and the true meaning of 'garbage in, garbage out.'

The Cast of Characters

Working with LTV was perhaps the strangest experience of my working life. The management of the LTV program fell under the umbrella of a new transportation division with its eye on the same pot of government money that led to the formation of Cytec. It was composed of an eclectic collection of individuals from the Chance-Vought airplane division (the V in LTV), who had been 'kicked upstairs.' I never quite understood the organization chart.

The DFW project was under the direct control of one of the kindest men I've ever worked with, Bill. As cordial as he was, he had a serious problem: He was the only true alcoholic I've ever known. The so-called three-Martini lunch was just a start for Bill, and anything that didn't get done before lunch didn't get done that day. Bill began his lunch order with three Martinis, which he lined up in front of his plate in precise geometric order. He began to shake visibly when only one untouched Martini remained in front of his plate,

"Waiter, waiter," went the urgent call.

Bill answered to a Vice President, Jim, a man who was weak, both physically and psychologically. He some evident health problems and was being outmaneuvered by a staff engineer, Walt. Our tactic, being unable to deal with Bill much of the time, was to attempt to work with Jim by arranging for a working dinner meeting after Bill collapsed at lunch. Somehow, Walt would always discover where we were having dinner and would appear out of nowhere to join our party. Walt could drink prodigious amounts of alcohol and remain alert, while poor old Jim would slowly slide under the table. Walt would then proceed to make agreements on behalf of the line organization that would not be kept.

On most occasions, my trips to Dallas would start on Sunday for a Monday morning meeting with Bill. However, if Bill came out of the Monday morning staff meeting bearing a conflict with our meeting, it was all over. Bill would say, "We'll talk about it at lunch," and predictably, nothing would get done that day. Often I'd leave for home on Wednesday or Thursday having accomplished nothing.

Walt was a real enigma. I never quite figured out what he did for LTV, but his passion was *GOLF!* Arranging for the company's executive golf tournament, held annually in Hawaii, took up much of his time. At odd times, I would get a call from Walt to come to Dallas, for a discussion of some specific technical problem. I would tell him,

"Walt, you have people on your own staff better qualified to give you advice on this problem." He'd reply,

"That's all right; come on down, and we'll talk."

The meetings in his office were another weird happening; they revolved (literally) around golf. His office was decorated with a green carpet serving as a putting green. A hole in the middle of the floor was marked with a protruding flag. While we talked, Walt would pick up his putter, position the ball around his office and practice putting by aiming his shots at the flagged hole. For this Cytec received a thousand dollars per day. In 1971, a thousand dollars was real money.

After a couple of hours of putting and conversation, I would catch the late afternoon airplane home. These were quick trips but long days: Early morning to Dallas, late arrival home.

Transpo-72

In 1971, the Urban Mass Transit Administration (UMTA), predecessor of the Federal Transit Administration (FTA), funded four companies at $1.5 million each, to set up a demonstration, 'Transpo-72,' of their automated guide way transit (AGT) systems at After two years of working with LTV and the control system for the PRT system being built in France, we had something that began to look useful, and we were invited to bid on one of the four contracts. $1.5 million would be a real kick-start for our little transportation endeavor, and we put forth a real effort on our proposal.

To shorten the story, we bid and won one of the four slots for a demonstration system. The other winners were Otis Elevator Corp., a subsidiary of United Technology, Rohr Corporation of San Diego, a major builder of aircraft sub-assemblies for Boeing and Douglas Aircraft, and the University of West Virginia teamed with Boeing Aircraft. Otis and Rohr had serious financial muscle behind them, and the University/Boeing team had a real head start. The team was well funded by UMTA over several prior years for the development of an innovative transit system. They were in a favored place in the competition, because UMTA wanted to show off its baby.

Several other major companies, such as Ford Motor Company and Bendix Aviation Corp. entered the competition but didn't win a spot. Financially, we were outclassed, and we would soon to learn how political rough and tumble really worked, because we tried to compete with the 'big dogs' in the pack.

Political Hard Ball

Ford's entry in the competition was particularly mundane; it was not innovative, forward-looking, or outstanding in any way. One of the sketches I recall was an Econoline commercial van, perhaps with electric power and some sort of automated control system; in any event it was not a winner.

After the winners were announced, I was invited to Washington to negotiate the details of the supporting contract. The first day's meetings went well, and it appeared we were on our way to an official contract to build one of the demo systems. About 10 a.m. on the second day of negotiations, we broke for coffee and attending to biological imperatives. In the men's room I was positioned, perhaps by design, at a urinal alongside UMTA's chief negotiator.

"This is all going pretty well," he said encouragingly, "but you should be aware you're going to have sign this," as he handed me a piece of paper across the intervening barrier between the two facilities. 'THIS,' was a single sheet of paper, obviously typed hastily in the dark of the night, on somebody's ancient portable typewriter. Not only was the typewriter in poor state of repair – the letters randomly appeared above and below the typed line – and hadn't even been cleaned in some time. The 'o-s' and 'e-s' were filled-in and appeared as large, round, black dots peppering the page.

As I read 'THIS,' my heart sank. As a contractor, Cytec would be required to submit all purchase orders, greater than $50 or $100 – I've forgotten the exact number, but it was ridiculously small – to UMTA in Washington for prior approval before any purchase could be made. Anyone who has ever worked with the U.S. Government, particularly in the Washington arena, knows this is an unworkable arrangement. Signatures require weeks to months, and for Cytec this meant we would need to have cash available to cover every expense and purchase, while the paperwork was cooking in Washington. Further, we were to deliver a working system set up and running, at Dulles Airport outside Washington, in a bit more than a year, so any purchasing delays were intolerable.

To put a cap on the problem, signing 'THIS' committed Cytec to a penalty of $150,000 per day, for every day our system didn't run during the 10 day Exposition. In short, we were required to deliver a million and a half dollars to UMTA if the government-imposed signature delays prevented completion of the project on time. In reality it was the perfect excuse for dislodging a troublesome winner . . . 'not financially responsible for a contract of this size.'

In retrospect, I suppose there was legal recourse, since the original solicitation contained none of the impediments implied by 'THIS' and legally couldn't be added after the fact. However, we didn't have the funds for a legal team to sue the government, if it would allow itself to be sued, so it was a moot point anyway. After much discussion with Giraud, we withdrew our proposal and Ford replaced Cytec in the Exposition. In effect, Cytec U.S. died in a men's room in the Department of Transportation and I was left with the knowledge of how the fire hydrant feels after a big dog passes by.

Epilogue

This was my introduction to real power politics. I wrote many technical proposals at Honeywell, with a near-perfect win record, so the win with UMTA was not a surprise to me but the aftermath was. I thought I knew how to do business with the Federal Government, but I was a rank amateur compared to those pulling the big levers.

In the late 1960s and early 70s there was much interest in Personal Rapid Transit to replace buses and rail systems. The only way to finance such systems almost demanded the Department of Transportation tap the Federal Highway Trust Fund, amassed from the Federal Tax on gasoline. Each attack on the trust fund brought out the lobbyists from the automobile industry, and money from the fund was never diverted from roads and bridges to PRT.

In the middle of his first term as President, Nixon vowed to break the country's dependence on the automobile by proposing a multi-billion dollar backing of innovative systems to replace automobiles in urban areas. This new attempt to fund these systems with the Highway Trust Fund again generated a huge tension between government and the automobile industry.

When Ford Motor Company didn't win one of the four Transpo 72 system contracts, Henry Ford II was furious and proclaimed Transpo-72 would not go forward without Ford's participation. Ford went directly to President Nixon to complain, and in my opinion, a deal of some sort was cut.

John Volpe, ex-governor of Massachusetts, was Secretary of Transportation under Nixon, and we had some connections with him via Giraud's wife's family, who were well-connected socially and politically, in the Boston area. We learned that Volpe was ordered by Nixon, to make room for a Ford participation in Transpo-72. Cytec was the obvious choice for elimination, and it was expedited with an old typewriter and a short conversation at the urinal, a fit setting.

While some of the above is hearsay, credence of sorts appeared within about three months of Cytec's elimination. Henry Ford II, during a speech dedicating a new Ford manufacturing plant, said he would support opening the Highway Trust Fund to permit the Transportation Department's backing of new transportation technology: Quod Erat Demonstrandum, a quid pro quo, or in the vernacular, 'tit for tat'.

Life Goes On

We reduced expenses at Cytec U.S., moved to smaller quarters on Fillmore Street in Minneapolis and continued to work on the control system required for the PRT system, called VEC – short for Vector, a mathematical quantity having both magnitude and direction – Giraud was developing in France. He landed a contract for a demonstration

La Defense Grand Arche

system that in 1972, carried over a half million passengers at La Defense, a major business complex on the site of the defense of Paris during the Franco-Prussian war. It is an area of many high-rise office buildings and regarded as Europe's largest business center. The test system was about 700 feet long and carried passengers between two major sub-centers of the district. The system delivered 'exceptional performance' according to the government's appraisal.

Vec Drive/Control Chain

VEC was unique in that it combined the propulsion means with on-line control. Propulsion was by linear electric motors, whose permanent-magnet armatures were about a foot and a half in length and linked together in an endless chain loop, left.

The armatures were supported on four small 'ski' bearings running in oil lubricated troughs on either side of the magnet. The vehicles were primarily supported by rubber-tired wheels, with a small portion of their weight resting on the chain to provide motive force. Once resting on the chain, the vehicles could no longer vary their spacing, and the control system was reduced to finding a non interfering space on the chain and various safety interlocks. The propulsion chain is visible in the brochure photos. The success of the La Defense system led to a permanent installation at the FNAC, the largest French retailer of cultural and consumer electronic products: books, CDs and DVDs, computer software and hardware, television sets, cameras, video games etc. The VEC connected this shopping center with the Montparnasse subway station and carried two million passengers in 1977, long after I secured the facility on Terrace Drive and left Cytec for other means of earning a living.

Data Logging

In St. Paul we had another arrow in our quiver. Giraud developed a project control technique he called PROTACFI – Program for ... something or other, in French. The fundamental concept was a means for controlling the costs and estimating the progress of a project. Managerially, it is ineffective to have a middle manager attempt to estimate the status of an activity, when the person doing the work knows its status best. PROTACFI involved the worker in estimating the time involved to build a small part of the overall task. When reporting his/her time record for a week, the system re-

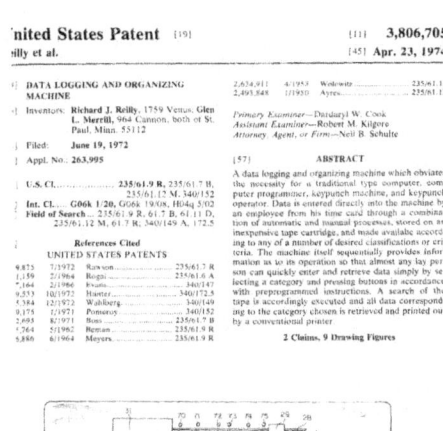

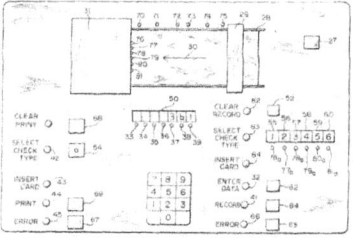

Data Logging Patent

quired reporting not only the time spent on the job but also the best estimate of the time required to complete the task, as the worker understood it. A manager reviewing time records for the week could see when the original plan and the progress estimates began to diverge. Divergence could indicate the job was going badly or the worker didn't understand the task. In any event, such reporting quickly focused attention where it was warranted. A professional paper on this technique, presented at a European business conference in Vienna, received high accolades.

A major problem with the technique was it was labor intensive and needed computer support. This was before the time of the ubiquitous personal computer. It was also before the time of the credit card with the magnetic stripe that could store voluminous data and be read in a single pass through a reading device.

At the time, the credit card industry was choking on bits of paper, imprinted from shopper's credit cards at the point of sale and read by optical readers. The impressions made from a credit card were of unpredictable quality, and there was great difficulty in discerning Os from zeros, '3s' from '8s' etc. Any impression with a questionable reading was diverted from the automated system to be read by a human operator; there were many such diversions.

Giraud dearly wanted to make PROTACFI some sort of industry standard for job cost control, so he funded Cytec U.S. to come up with a reliable means of data entry and the reading thereof. We contrived a technique for converting numbers and letters into eight-bit ASCII code, a common computer coding format. By embossing a plastic card with rows of dimples in eight-bit ASCII format, a paper card with interleaved carbon paper could be imprinted with rows of dots rather than English letters. It was much easier and more reliable to read the presence or absence of a dot on paper, rather than discerning the subtleties of 'Os' and zeros, threes and eights.

Glenn Merrill and I worked many months to refine the basic concept and produce a prototype data terminal. Two patents resulted

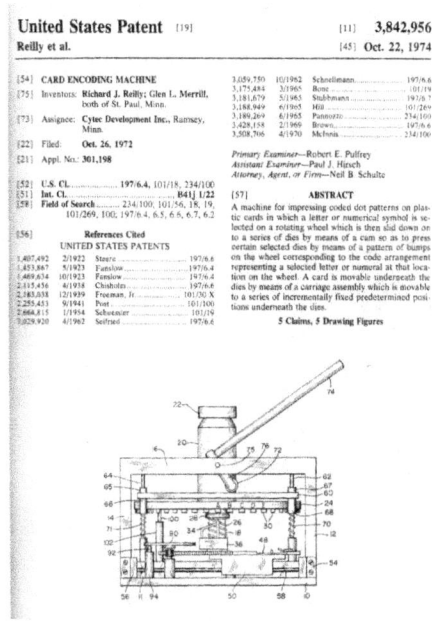

Data Card Embossing Device

from this effort: One was for the overall concept for reading cards and manipulating the data and the other for a machine to emboss the plastic cards with the chosen data, a slow typewriter to produced raised dimples corresponding to letter characters.

In summary, we produced only one machine we shipped to France for use by Cytec-France, because there wasn't sufficient funding available to support continued refinement of the system.

The Inevitable

Merrill and I struggled to keep the U.S. branch of Cytec going for several years after the loss of the Transpo-72 contract. We scrounged consulting and product development jobs such as electronic brushless electric motor controls for 3M Company and a 'Loop Back' controller to test telephone lines for ADC Corporation, but to no avail. We closed the doors in 1974. Merrill returned to Honeywell and I took a job with one of our clients that produced test instrumentation for the telephone industry. Technically, it wasn't an attractive choice, but after the recent turmoil it promised an orderly existence.

The job was not well defined by the company's President; it was, at its base, simply an invitation to 'join the family.' I should have been more careful and more insistent on a better job description. Live 'n learn, as you will see in what follows.

13

ADC Magnetic Controls Company

I've had three encounters with psychologists during my working years. All turned out badly. The psychologist described here likely engineered my demise.

* * *

My short career with ADC marks the darkest period of my life. Its President was an 'Old Honeyweller' and seemed to place an unwarranted value on ex-Honeywell employees. In trying to keep Cytec U.S. afloat, Glen and I did a number of consulting jobs for ADC with good results. Now and then, the President would ask,

"Why don't you join the family here?" These questions I answered with an offhand comment showing lack of interest. The company manufactured a number of low technology and unrelated devices for telephone companies: transformers, plugs, jacks and other wire-wound components. In addition, they were designing a line of test equipment for the telephone world. Despite little interest in this industry and only a smattering of electronic capability, haphazardly self-taught, Merrill and I produced several new technology devices for ADC, over a period of about two years.

Finally, with Cytec's activities winding down, I succumbed. The

President gave me a final push,

"What kind of salary would it take to get you to join the company." I tossed him a salary figure I was certain he couldn't meet, and he replied,

"When can you start?" Thus began a long, dark night.

Manufacturing Nightmare

At the outset, I was put in charge of a troublesome manufacturing operation. Its product centered around an electronic, printed circuit board, whose function I've long forgotten. This board was assembled manually by a crew of female assemblers headed by an older gentleman, Mr. A, who seemed to miss obvious clues in analyzing his production processes.

The division had a horrible 'work-in-process' inventory: hundreds of uncompleted boards going nowhere. My first task was to fix this bottleneck. Mr. A resented my insertion into his domain and was hostile at first.

These boards were manually loaded with parts inserted from 'kits' of parts collected from many vendors, then soldered into place by Mr. A's assembly crew. Parts arrived randomly from vendors and stored in 'kits' – metal bread pans – on coded shelves, and not released to the assemblers until 100% of the required parts were in-hand. However, it seemed there was no coördination between the purchasing of parts and the expedited collection of the most needed parts.

When the first part for a kit arrived, Mr. A would buy another bread pan, insert a parts list, check off the first part received, shelve it and wait for more parts to arrive. As a result, there were hundreds of partly filled kits awaiting anything from one to tens of parts.

The required action seemed obvious: Go through the bread pans and rank order them by the number of missing parts. Then, looking at the parts listings in each pan, construct a 'short list' of the missing parts and seek action from the purchasing group to put pressure on vendors for specific parts. To shorten the story, within two months the operation was turning out between three and four times the number of assemblies than in the recent past, and with no increase in staff. The group worked harmoniously, and Mr. A warmed-up, perhaps because I made him the hero in all of this.

Things hummed along happily for about six months; the President seemed was happy, Mr. A was happy, I was not. It just wasn't much of job for someone interested in research and development work on more complex problems. Maybe that's personal arrogance, but it is the way I am wired.

Suddenly, the President reorganized the entire company along functional lines. My little assembly operation joined a Manufacturing Division under a Vice President and moved to an out-state manufacturing operation in St. Peter, Minnesota. I became Vice President of Engineering for the entire company.

The Telephone Business at ADC

Telephone companies are a bit strange. Functionally they are all similar but insist on the uniqueness of their major systems. ADC's test equipment division depended on some major phone companies – New York Telephone, New England Telephone and the 'Baby Bells,' – for a large part of its business. To satisfy these customers' insistence on uniqueness, ADC laboriously redesigned its equipment for individual customers to suit almost identical requirements, but it rear-ranged certain details to yield a unique operator interface. This struck me as expensive, time-consuming and needless.

To cut cost and improve efficiency I looked at the test equipment problem functionally. After we isolated the individual functions common to the entire customer base, the engineering group designed individual functional packages to be mounted into a standard equipment rack, in any arrangement the customer desired. The package was individualized by topping the product with the customer's corporate logo and sometimes a unique operator's interface panel. Thus, the customer could boast of his 'built-to-order' test system, while ADC could set up to produce common modules. It worked well for both interests.

As this work progressed, the President seemed happy but not so his 'Assistant To,' another 'Old Honeyweller,' RW, who took a distinct disliking for me; I ignored him. He was a consummate boot-licker, and he seemed to occupy a world whose ethical standards were self devised. The President would leave town for a single day, and RW would come around to demand a written report for the President, briefing him on events during his absence. It seemed senseless and needless, and my response would often be,

"RW, go away, I have better things to do. If the President has concerns about what happened today he can pick up the phone." I was never good at politics, especially brown-nose politics. Some other second-tier executives referred to RW as 'Sneaky Snake.' Perhaps I should have paid more attention.

The Psychologist

Shortly after the reorganization and my promotion, the President announced he was inviting a management consulting organization to 'look at the company.' This would include detailed testing of all executive personnel. The consulting company was the Hay Company, a respected national business consulting firm headquartered in Philadelphia. The Hay inquisition lasted most of a week and included communal meetings, with the entire executive staff in attendance, as well as individual, private meetings.

Somewhere along the line, IQ tests on adults were branded as invalid unless given on an individual basis. IQ testing of children or youth relies on everyone having a somewhat standardized background from the public school system. In later life, adult experiences vary so widely that standardized tests are invalid. My turn in the 'IQ barrel' consumed an entire afternoon late in 'Hay Week.' My interrogator was a Ph.D psychologist whose name I've forgotten.

Testing began with the Minnesota Multiphasic, including the 'forced choice' section: 'Would you rather be lazy, stupid or mean?' Pick one; it's the rule. We then moved into the IQ section that began with reproducing a series of figures formed by equilateral triangles, red on one side and white on the other. It probably has a standardized name in the psychology business. The triangles are all equal in size and produce a variety of geometric figures, when properly arranged. The two colors allow added complications.

For the test, the tormentor shows the victim a figure constructed with a particular arrangement of red and white triangles. The 'unfortunate' is given a short time to memorize the configuration. He/she is then required to reproduce the figure with the loose triangles and scored on the time elapsed to do so.

I have a pretty good memory for geometric things and correctly produced the first required figure. The interrogator noted the time and intoned,

"Very good." It was then on to #2, which I also reproduced quickly; no comment from the master. After #3 he said,

"You've done this before or you've practiced somewhere." I never saw his test before, had no prior knowledge of the test and so stated. We went on to fill his test matrix in silence but under a dark shadow; I felt the investigator was convinced I was cheating the test somehow.

The next test phase was a question and answer session, which may have been my downfall. The questions were disparate in order and content, designed, I think, to keep the victim off-balance. This too went well for a while, but I was getting weary of the torture, and I began to answer the questions in a manner incorporating the sense of the question, rather than a simple answer. A particular sequence comes to mind:

"Who wrote Faust?"

"Goethe."

"Correct. What does it mean when I say, 'One Swallow doesn't make a summer?'"

"It means don't count your chickens before they hatch," I replied. Not a precise parallel but close enough. And so it ground-on through the afternoon.

An improbable turn of events occurred later in the afternoon. Somehow, I don't recall the exact progression of the dialogue, but I asked the questioner a clarifying question and his response suddenly reversed our roles. One question led to another and another, and eventually I was interviewing the psychologist. Ultimately, he confessed that he began his formative years with dreams of being a doctor, an MD. He flunked out of medical school and he settled on this psychology gig as a distasteful second choice. My previous experience with an 'industrial psychologist,' some years earlier, led me to wonder whether this was a setup snare of some sort, but eventually he broke down into near tears, so I concluded his distress was genuine. When the interview was over, I was left wondering how he was going to score my test, since a significant portion of it was consumed with my interviewing him. I was to find out several months later.

The Hay Company left town, and life settled into the routine. Nothing was ever said about the results of the consultant's sweep through ADC. I remained curious about how my own results were scored. In the aftermath of the entire episode, I felt some compunction about how I handled the interview. Gaming the interrogator during the question and answer test, was probably not a good idea, but he generated the role reversal himself in the later stages of the interview. In curiosity, after a couple months elapsed, I asked the President about the Hay Company results. He seemed annoyed and sort of brushed the question away saying,

"Well, when the subject is brighter than the interviewer, these things don't come out well." The response was brusque and terminated without further elaboration.

Christmas 1975 was not a merry one. A few days before Christmas, I was engaged in a year-end financial review of my programs with the company's Chief Financial Officer. He expressed great satisfaction with our revamping of the product line. Profit margins were up because of the ease of customizing the telephone products using our functionally modular design.

Less than three hours later, just in time for lunch, the President called me into his office and told me to clear out my desk, because my services were no longer required. There were no prior warnings or any other indications of trouble, so I asked what was bringing about my dismissal. The response was even more puzzling than the dismissal itself:

"Your subordinates are more loyal to you than they are to the company," he replied, an obvious attempt to evade the truth. There was no point in pursuing the matter further, but despite much soul-searching I never have been able to untangle the mystery. Was Sneaky Snake involved in my demise? Were my psychological test results a factor? I'll never know.

Every life must have a few mysteries. After numerous accolades and a rapid promotion, poof: I was driving home with a box of professional books and a potted Norfolk Pine, which once graced my office.

We lived through an unhappy Christmas, and shortly after we set off on a long anticipated trip to Africa. The firing evolved into a blessing in disguise. Hard work and interesting technical programs filled the next 35 years, but I never held another five-days-per-week job.

14

Dark Days and Saviors

It was a difficult time, but many helpful people appeared when needed and eased the pain.

* * *

Christmas of 1975 was not very merry. Betty and I have always lived frugally and tend to be savers; we had no immediate financial problems. Our house was paid for; there was money for gifts and food for the table. Nevertheless, being fired from a job, especially without an honestly expressed reason, was a severe emotional shock for both of us. I didn't spend much time licking my wounds and immediately attacked the business of finding a job. A few weeks later we embarked on a trip to Kenya to see the big animals. It was helpful in burying the vestiges of ADC.

In the process of trying to keep Cytec alive, we built a substantial engineering consulting practice on Cytec's behalf that withered away during my period of employment with ADC; I began looking for a standard-issue job.

I had maintained some business contacts. When I left ADC on the Friday before Christmas, I began to restore these connections; on the following Tuesday I had a luncheon meeting with Charles Richard Soderberg, President of Brown-Minneapolis Tank, regarding a position as Vice President of Marketing. Brown, a 'black-iron' fabricator of a variety of steel products. It was not a thrilling objective for one interested in research and development, but it was a job. After some negotiation over a period of weeks, Dick and I settled on a working arrangement that gave me my old Honeywell salary for half-time consulting work. This left me with half my time and then some, to seek full-time employment or other consulting work. Dick became a good friend as well as an employer.

I began keeping daily notes of all my activities and telephone calls as of August 1975, and these records recall a period of frenetic activity. I pursued interviews with 3M Company, Medtronics, Economic Laboratories, Fluidyne, Rosemount Engineering and a broad spectrum of other smaller companies. Within about two months I had established consulting activities that matched what Brown Tank was paying me as a retainer, so immediate income was nicely solved. Nevertheless, I followed employment ads in the Wall Street Journal and the local papers and responded to any glimmer of possible intersection of need, experience and interest.

This was a pretty depressing period. On many days, I was driving nearly a hundred miles covering jobs, interviews and luncheons to set up other interviews. Nights and blank days were spent typing letters in response to employment ads.

While I was a reasonably good typist, I wasn't perfect, and the days and nights spent typing letters were trying. Personal computers were yet to come on the scene, so an error in typing meant retyping, fixing the error and making yet another error somewhere else in the text. For me, the great contribution of the personal computer, and its associated printer, is the liberation derived from knowing you never have to retype a page. That sword hung over each keystroke as I neared the end of an otherwise perfect letter; it was so debilitating I would do almost anything not to begin the last paragraph: Another cup of coffee, throw a few Frisbees for the dog, a trip to the bathroom induced by the coffee, and so it went. These were hard days.

Bill Ogden

Another problem with this period was the lack of an office where I could meet people in something other than a revamped bedroom at home. Bill Ogden, a former a Vice President of the First National Bank of Minneapolis, rescued me. I don't recall how Bill came into my life, but he was starting his own business consulting firm, International Finance and Management Group. A lawyer, working both internationally and domestically, he was beginning from a far higher level of business contacts than mine. While he was in no position to hire me at the time, he recognized my problem and graciously provided me with telephone answering services, legal advice, business cards with a 'suede-shoe,' downtown address and an impressively furnished conference room to use as needed. There are times in life when one needs a little help or a quiet conversation on a dark day. Bill was one of those providential people who crossed my path in a time of need.

Harley Davidson

Out of hundreds of letter written during this period, I received only one, live offer. Harley Davidson Motorcycles offered me a job as Chief Engineer, which in retrospect might have been a pretty interesting job. Betty and I flew the Cessna to Milwaukee for an interview and to look about. While the interview went well, the Vice President of Engineering appeared as an intolerable, petty tyrant based on a day's observation of his dealings with his subordinates. While it was an interesting job, I didn't need one badly enough to work in such an environment. I respectfully declined the offer.

Over the next month, there followed several calls from the company President, inquiring as to why I declined the offer. The second call upped the monetary offer, which was pretty generous from the outset. I declined again. After another telephone conversation or two, the President called to say,

"We've made you two pretty good offers, and you've declined. We can only conclude you have some objection to our executive structure. If that's the case, we're prepared to make adjustments to our executive staff if you will come with us." Finally, I declined; if the VP of Engineering could be 'adjusted' out of the place, I anticipated a possible similar fate. I'd been to that school; lived and learned.

World Food Systems

Some of my consulting work embraced some pretty strange stuff. During one of my trips to Washington, DC, I made the acquaintance of Mel Bandle, the President of World Food Systems (WFS), a company engaged in large-scale, industrial food preparation and serving throughout the Middle East.

It was the time of the great 'Oil Shock' of the-mid 1970s, and oil companies were endeavoring to meet the demands of that market. At the same time, the Middle Eastern countries were on a building spree spending their oil money. The indigenous population of the Middle Eastern countries, spoiled by oil, typically didn't engage in manual labor, so most oil field work was done by expatriates from less wealthy countries.

These laborers lived in miserable conditions: barracks if lucky, burned out buses left over from terrorist attacks if they were not. The only touch of the good life was the food; good food prevented riots, and this was the WFS business. Economic activity was intense all across the Middle East, with oil outbound and structural steel, building materials and commercial goods being imported. At this time, the harbor at Dubai was so clogged that some vessels were lying at anchor for one to three months, waiting to be unloaded. World Food's cargoes were perishable, and they were desperate to find a way to get goods from ship to shore.

After reading about tethered balloons being used for logging in the northwestern U.S., WFS saw the ballooning experience in my résumé. They asked me to devise a balloon-borne unloading system. I worked for several months devising a cable tethered guide system to move loads from ship to dock, but all-in-all it was a cumbersome system that required a team of experienced balloon handlers to function reliably. In the end, I believe WFS settled on what is known as 'break-bulk' delivery: Shiploads of food went to Athens, where the major containers were broken-down to smaller packages and delivered overland by refrigerated trucks, a difficult, torturous trip, which finished the job.

Rosemount Engineering

As with many of the small jobs that sustained income during these transitional months, I relied on companies that played into my basic background of aerodynamics and fluid flow. A call to my old boss and mentor, Richard DeLeo, turned up an immediate consulting opportunity with Rosemount Engineering, a very successful aeronautical instrumentation company, which grew out of the University of Minnesota's Rosemount research group. DeLeo gave me my first professional job while he was at the University, and now plugged me into an air and liquid flow meter development based on a flow phenomenon known as the von Kármán vortex street. The Kármán street is the result of a flowing fluid – air or liquid – passing from the laminar flow region – a very slow flow rate – to a turbulent condition at higher flow rates. Since much of my work at Northrop Aircraft was based on preventing the transition from laminar to turbulent flow as long as possible, I was quickly productive.

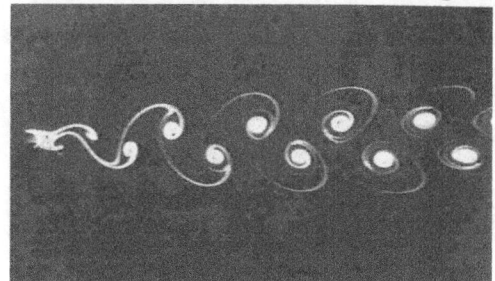

von Kármán Vortex Street

Objects of proper shape immersed in a flowing fluid produce the von Kármán phenomenon illustrated in the photograph. The flow direction is from left to right; the periodic vortices, shed from the immersed object, are made visible by injecting smoke into the flow just upstream of the object.

The spacing of the vortex pattern shown in the picture varies with the flow velocity. This is what makes the phenomenon interesting to an instrumentation company. By counting the number of vortex passages against a time base, the velocity of the flowing fluid can be determined. Thus, the vortex phenomenon converts analog information – flow rate – into a frequency, and when combined with a

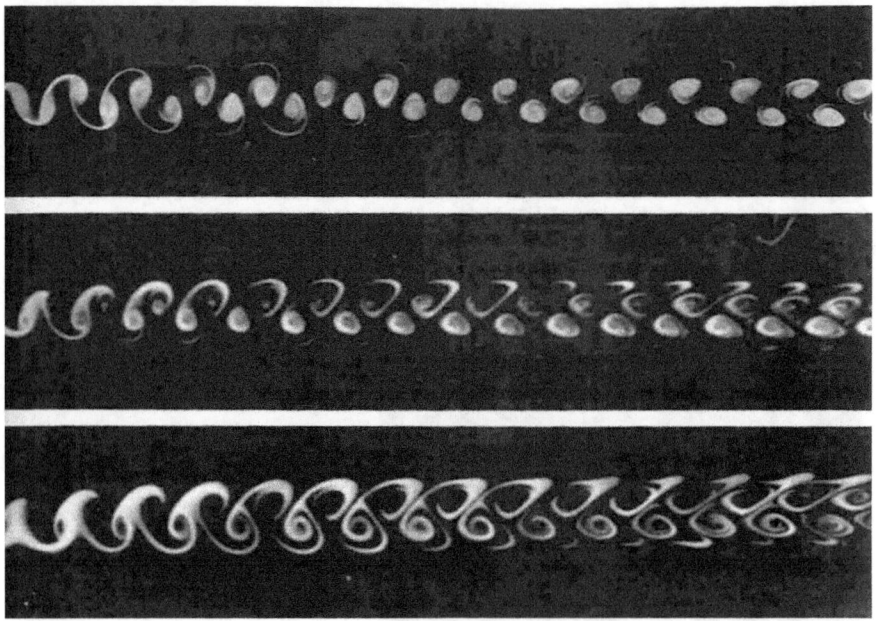

Multiple Karman Vortex Streets

counter, provides a digital measure of flow velocity. That's the easy part of the story.

Since the von Kármán street occurs over a limited range of flow velocities, one object of the Rosemount studies was to explore the shapes of immersed objects to extend the range of effective velocities. Another objective rearranged of one or more immersed objects to reinforce the effect of multiple streets for easy reading of the vortex passage. Hot-wire anemometry readily senses the passage of a vortex, but the delicate nature of this laboratory instrumentation almost precludes its consideration for use in an industrial environment. Multiple vortex generators, properly arranged, might generate pressure pulses sufficiently large to permit sensing by a static pressure transducer connected to a tap in the wall of a pipe. We succeeded in producing such an arrangement and I left the program in the hands of a Rosemount employee, whose task it was to design the electronic circuitry required to produce a salable product.

BrownMinneapolis Tank

Along with this bread-and-butter engineering work, the work with Brown Tank centered around President Dick Soderberg's desire to raise the company's level of technology by acquiring a technology company whose products fit Brown's fabricating capabilities. We focused on energy and energy conversion technology that achieved a prominence wrought by the "energy shock" of 197475. Along the way there were some diversions.

Watching day-to-day operations, it was evident Brown had serious difficulties with controlling and accounting for work-in-process in their extensive shop operation. They were not ready for a full-blown computer department but needed a better means of accumulating hours worked against various projects being handled simultaneously. Thus, in addition to my search for higher technology, I used Giraud's job costing techniques from my Cytec work and set up a computerized job tracking and costing program, using a remotely located computer service company. Logically named 'Service Bureau Corporation,' it was a subsidiary of IBM. This program ran well and was updated daily by Soderberg's secretary, Martha. She was an older woman and somewhat frightened by the entire computer business. She was shocked by the Service Bureau software program, which responded to any minor procedural errors by posting:

"What?" on the screen. Martha always felt there was someone on the other end of the line watching her every move.

The Barges

Barge After Launching

During my consulting period at Brown, their pressing problem was a major US Navy program for building 20 or 25 fuel barges for the U.S. Navy. It was a program well on its way to bankrupting the company. One barge was completed and a second was under construction.

The company's location, some 10 miles or more from water, made it necessary to build the barges in roadable modules that were assembled on the shore of the Mississippi River, south of St. Paul. The barges were about 100 feet long with a beam of about 20 feet and supported on large, rubber-tired dollies for transit. Launching meant simply pushing them side-ward into the river. As best I can recall, the modules were about 16 feet

Barge Launch

wide, in the fore and aft direction of the finished vessel. Transportation to the Mississippi shore at night, with police escort, minimized traffic interference.

Assembly on the riverbank became a huge problem because the modules were seriously distorted upon arrival at the assembly site. The material was precision cut and the modules carefully assembled at the plant, but matching the modules to one another, along the 20-foot beam, produced gaps of two to three inches corner to corner. The operative answer, at the outset, forced these edges together by welding heavy cleats to the exterior of the modules and applying hydraulic clamping forces to bring the module into contact with its mate. Along with introducing tremendous stresses locked into the finished vessel, the labor cost was untenable. Additional difficulties at the plant increased the frustrations at the river and brought projected final costs far exceeding the fixed-price Navy contract. The company was seriously considering filing bankruptcy and canceling the contract. Soderberg asked me to take a look at the problem.

After watching at the assembly process at the river for a few minutes and discussing procedures with the foreman on the job, the problem and a solution were clear: Completion of each module in the manufacturing plant included installation of the deck plates. The heat from the long welds distorted the hull structures and installing the decks locked in the distortion. With the deck plates attached, the hull modules became a rigid box structure, and it was nearly impossible to return them to their designed, rectangular state.

Lessons from my old mentor in Hokah, Ken Jackson, taught me a great deal about thermal and dimensional control during welding; the solution presented itself immediately: Don't put the decks on in the manufacturing plant! I used a shoe box to illustrate the solution.

The proportional dimensions of the barge modules were very similar to a classical shoe-box. I placed boxes side to side along their long dimension to simulate the length of the barge. With a single box in hand it was easy to show how easy it was to twist a topless box.

Placing the cover on the box and securing it with Scotch Tape demonstrated how rigid the box became. Taping on a few covers, with a deliberate bit of twist, produced the exact situation existing at the river assembly site. The solution: Ship open-top modules to the river, quickly join the bottom hull segments in situ and add the deck segments after alignment.

The solution worked as expected, and I was drawn into organizing the production process for all products. Using Gantt Chart methods, we smoothed production by having parts arrive at their assembly point on an as-needed basis. Thus, great quantities of small parts were not stacked around the plant and potentially lost before being incorporated into an assembly. Between reorganizing the plant assembly process and improving the module assembly at the river, we cut the labor hours from about 22,000 to 13,000. The company survived and made a substantial profit on the remaining barges.

These results led me to a seat on the company's Board of Directors, where I served for about three years until the company was absorbed in an acquisition.

Coal Gasification

Along with the barge work, I continued to pursue the upgrading of technology for Brown Tank but still limited to 'black-iron' fabrication. The time was during the 1974-75 "oil shock," and alternate energy was the watchword. Much emphasis was on coal in various forms or processes. Gasification of coal to convert its energy content into something useful for residential heating was a government focus. A major federal government research program, subsidized to the level of several billions of dollars, sought to produce clean, 'high BTU,' gas for mixing with natural gas and handled conventionally.

There is another way to produce a useful gas product from coal: so-called 'low BTU' gasification. Increasing the energy to a level approximating natural gas – high BTU – requires a corresponding high technology process for packing more hydrogen molecules into the coal gas at high pressure. In turn, this leads to expensive infra-structure: retorts with steel walls 3" thick, heavy piping and complex controls. In contrast, Low BTU gas is produced at atmospheric pressure in a simple structure. The major disadvantage of low BTU gas from coal is that it is dirty and not suitable for transmission in pipelines; energy conversion near the point of use is essential. There is a niche market for such energy sources: foundries, municipal heating plants and other users of concentrated heat energy. Furthermore, low BTU infra-structure is nicely suited to fabrication in a black-iron shop, such as Brown Tank, because the entire process operates at relatively low pressure without complex structure. After much digging through the literature and analysis, it seemed the low BTU process was a good match for Brown's black-iron shop and represented a reasonable incremental jump in technical sophistication that could be achieved with the current staff. More exploration isolated the Wellman-Galusha process, a patented piece of industrial chemistry for producing low BTU gas, currently unused and owned by a Cleveland based company.

The Wellman-Galusha process is simple: It is fundamentally a furnace overloaded with coal. Coal is introduced into a cylindrical chamber and ignited. Once the fires are burning well, more coal is placed on a grate above the fire and fed air saturated with water vapor. The high temperature of the air/steam mixture 'cooks' the coal above the grate and combines it with

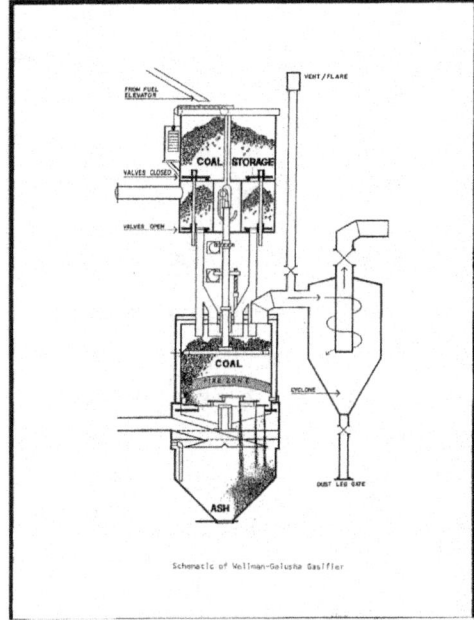

Coal Gasification

the water vapor, cracking the water into hydrogen and oxygen. The resulting mixture of carbon monoxide and hydrogen, cleaned in a cyclone separator, passes-on to a nearby, energy-using process. Combustion of the carbon monoxide/hydrogen fuel mixture from the process recovers energy from the coal at an efficiency level exceeding 90%. In the right setting, it is a clean and highly efficient means of producing energy from coal.

The W/G process was a near perfect fit with the capabilities and objectives of Brown Tank, so Dick Soderberg and I decided to visit the company owning the Wellman-Galusha patents.

Team Building in Cleveland

In the clamor surrounding alternative energy sources during the 'oil shock,' we were never able to negotiate a reasonable business deal with the Cleveland firm, whose name I've forgotten. In the process, however, we discovered some interesting management techniques. Although we assembled an effective team to rescue the barge program, in Cleveland we learned there were other methods of team building.

Dick Soderberg was a man of high integrity; his word and handshake were as good as any written contract. However, he had serious management problems at Brown.

Brown Tank, as the name implies, built tankage: city water towers and somewhat complex, build-to-print structures for the chemical and petroleum industries. Because of the nature of the business, it employed laborers represented by two unions: boilermakers and pipefitters. The mix of work could not always be neatly defined, and whether a particular job fell to one union or the other was often a subjective decision. Some of these bitterly-contested decisions were driven to Soderberg's level and his decision would leave him in the wrathful wake of one union or the other. The retaliation often took the form of 'sickouts' and general absenteeism. This infuriated a man of his integrity; he never adjusted to it.

Dark Days And Saviors

At an early morning meeting in Cleveland, we exchanged pleasantries in the President's office of the company holding the W/G patents. An overview of the company's business confirmed it too was a black-iron shop, having a high degree of overlap with Brown's business, a pretty good fit for an acquisition, with the coal gasification patents as a bonus. The introductory conversation completed, we were invited to tour the manufacturing area.

The shop floor was familiar, not unlike Brown's except for the workforce: The company, located in a tough section of West Cleveland, displayed some rough edges of the workforce — such as swastikas painted on the shop walls. Soderberg, ever mindful of his own labor problems, couldn't resist commenting,

"I'll bet you have a real absentee problem here." The President replied,

"Actually we don't." Soderberg brightened and responded,

"I want to hear how you deal with that."

We finished the tour and returned to the President's office for further discussion. With absenteeism never far from the top of his list of concerns, Soderberg opened the conversation;

"I want to hear how you handle absenteeism." The President replied,

"We don't have a problem with absentees. I guess it all stems from a union negotiation 10 or 15 years ago. We somehow convinced the union to sign-on to a contract that included an incentive-pay component. We break our shop workers into teams of eight to a dozen people headed by a work director. The work director is not chosen by management but elected by the group. Management breaks jobs into into work packages and the work director negotiates with management, defining the number of hours targeted for the package. If the team makes or exceeds the 'bogey' they get a bonus, now at an extra 25 cents per hour, for work done on the package, or they can take compensatory time off at the discretion of the group."

There was a long silence while we absorbed this island of free enterprise in a union sea. The President leaned back in his chair and absently examined a spot on the far wall somewhere near the ceiling. At last he broke the silence.

"I guess the last absentee incident we must have been 4 or 5 years ago. We pay every Friday at noon. One of the 'boys' had been out all week, 'sick,' but turned up late one Friday morning just in time for paychecks. I found out later this wasn't the first time it happened. Checks were passed out at noon, and some of the folks left for a ritual lunch. About 3 o'clock that afternoon they found the slacker in an alley, about a half mile from here, dead … ." His voice trailed off.

"No, we just don't have absentee problems." he concluded.

That's peer pressure! It's difficult to believe 25 cents an hour can lead to this sort of retribution, but it might be a hard world in Cleveland. Were we deceived by a spinner of yarns? Perhaps, but the story was presented as fact.

Wind Shear Instrumentation

A good friend, no longer with us, often commented on the irrational enthusiasm for patenting a 'good idea:'

"A patent and 50 cents – it was an earlier time – will get you a cup of coffee at 'Honest Bill's' on Johnson Street" – a neighborhood restaurant in Northeast Minneapolis, commonly known as 'Nordeast' by its mostly immigrant, local residents. The comment pretty well summarizes the monetary value of my patent collection.

On June 24, 1975, Eastern Airlines flight 66 crashed while landing at Kennedy Airport in New York, killing 115 of the 124 passengers aboard the Boeing 727. Investigation of the accident attributed the cause to a meteorological phenomenon known as wind-shear. The term *shear* describes the rapid change of wind speed with changing altitude. When shears appear at higher altitudes the result is a bumpy ride; near the ground they may bode disaster. As an airplane climbs or descends through such conditions, it must have sufficient thrust to accelerate the entire mass of the airplane to accommodate the rate of wind-change-induced reduction in airspeed. Similarly, in a shear of opposite direction, reducing power maintains the desired airspeed. Ordinarily, a shear in this direction is not as serious as the condition where wind speed is decreasing in the course of the flight path, provided the pilot is alert and makes the correct decisions.

With the impetus of Eastern 66, I began to look at the problem from the standpoint of basic physics and aerodynamics. Two reference frames must be dealt with simultaneously. As a simple mass, the airplane must obey Newton's laws in an inertial reference frame, but as a flying machine, the laws of aerodynamics determine the parameters of safe flight. In a wind shear, both realms must be satisfied.

In stable, non-maneuvering flight, e.g. during approach to landing, it is common practice to fly a constant, stable airspeed until near touchdown. All other things being stable, if airspeed begins to change without the pilot's changing the engine thrust or moving the flight controls, a shear could be detected by comparing the rate of change of airspeed with the rate of change of the inertial speed – ground speed. Some large airplanes have inertial measurement systems producing a measurement of acceleration in the inertial frame that could be compared with the rate of change of airspeed. I did a number of tests with my airplane, by rigging a rate of climb indicator into the airspeed measurement system, to measure its rate of response to abrupt thrust changes.

After many calculations the idea seemed to have merit, so I sought a discussion of the operational problems with Jerry Fredrickson, the Chief Pilot of Northwest airlines. He expressed great interest and provided me with more data on specific airplanes to aid in my calculations. Later, after filing a patent application, I discussed a proposed system with Honeywell who verified my calculations but decided such an instrument was not of interest to the company.

Lacking other options I submitted the idea to Phil Klass, a Senior Editor of "Aviation Week and Space Technology," a respected publication of record in the aviation industry. Phil obliged me with a well written, page plus article. He tells the story better than I.

* * *

Avionics
Airborne Wind-Shear Sensor Developed
By Phillip J. Klass

[Article text from Aviation Week & Space Technology by Philip J. Klass describing Richard J. Reilly's development of a simple, modest-cost airborne wind-shear sensor (AWAS) tested in his Cessna 170, with sections on Instrument Approach, Acceleration Sensor, Abrupt Throttle Changes, and Costly Equipment.]

Phil Klass Windshear Article

I met Phil Klass years earlier as he was doing an article on the Space Cabin Simulator program, described in Chapter 8. He enthusiastically entered into telephone discussions. After reviewing some of my analyses, he produced an article that sparked real interest in the industry. I received many inquiries as a result. They ranged from crackpots to major instrument manufacturers and one from a potential, direct competitor. The latter, as developed from later patent applications, appeared to be a digging for more information to include in their own patent application.

Ultimately, I received an offer from Fairchild Semiconductor to purchase licensing rights to the patent, which issued in 1980. It was not a lucrative offer but paid for my patent costs and for a couple of trips to paradise: New Jersey. It had significant royalties attached; however, Fairchild never pursued the device with any real diligence.

So, I headed for Honest Bill's on Johnson Street and had a cup of coffee on Fairchild.

* * *

A Range Of Clients

As I began to build a meaningful consulting practice I worked with many smaller clients. These included:

Casey Copters (Canada): Installation design for helicopter heater

The Donaldson: Company: Study of flow through filters.

Honeywell Inc.: Analysis of airflow through an office building

Sanders Associates: Design analysis of an electronics 'canoe' added to the bottom of a Grumman Gulfstream aircraft.

United Technologies Research Laboratories: Fluid temperature sensor for 3000 degree measurements.

YamatakeHoneywell Ltd.(Japan): Variety of business contacts in the U.S.

The breadth of these activities relied on the mathematical nature of the Aeronautical Engineering Curriculum at the University of Minnesota in the 1940s and 50s. Its analytical approach to problem solving differed from to the more application oriented curricula offered by other engineering disciplines of the era. Mixed with an interest in classical physics and the practical experience infused by my old mentor, Ken Jackson, while growing up in Hokah, I was able to study and solve a variety of problems.

15

Hush House

I entered into the Hush House Program almost by accident. It evolved into a $49 million techno-political odyssey lasted more than four years and changed the way the U.S. Air Force conducted ground testing of jet airplanes and engines.

* * *

While seeking to expand my consulting practice into areas of more personal interest, I discovered a small, aeronautically-oriented firm in St. Paul, Minnesota. It was internationally recognized as a quality builder of jet engine thrust stands and test cells. As an adjunct to these major structures, Aero Systems Engineering (ASE) was also developing computerized data acquisition systems. With my numerous contacts in NATO countries, jet engine control experience and knowledge of computers, I presented myself to Lars Broberg, the President of ASE, seeking consideration for a job with multiple roles: international marketing and writing computer programs related to the acquisition and processing of data from jet engines under evaluation in their test cells. I proposed a contractual relationship involving a fixed retainer for approximately half my time and a percentage commission for products I either developed or sold. My proposal was enthusiastically received, and we began negotiating a formal employment agreement. Simultaneously, I began extensive travel and technical presentations to the U.S. Air Force at Wright Field. Working without a completed contract, Lars and I traded contractual papers for legal review for nearly two months, when a major snag developed.

Lars Broberg, a good, practical engineer, struggled with the business aspects of running his enterprise. A Swedish firm, Granges-Nyby, acquired ASE as compensation for non-payment of bills, and Lars bridled under the big corporate yoke, which didn't fit his entrepreneurial style.

Granges was a large firm, a sort of Swedish General Electric but smaller and also with broad interests. ASE, more or less a nuisance to Granges, was placed under the care of one of its executives, who was appointed as Chairman of the ASE Board of Directors. I met the man, Alaric Wachmeister, in the process of negotiating my employment agreement; he was a real gentleman, and we got along well.

Early one afternoon, while working on a barge program at Brown Tank Corporation, I received a call from Lars Broberg.

"Alaric Wachmeister is gone and we have a new Board Chairman, Olof Muten," Lars began.

"That's an interesting turn of events, Lars, what does it mean?"

"I don't know," Lars replied, "but he'd like to meet you sometime."

"That's fine with me Lars, I'd like to meet him too."

"He's from Philadelphia, and he's here now; he would like to talk to you."

"It's pretty difficult, Lars, I'm dug-in deeply on a problem here; perhaps we could meet early this evening or have dinner together."

"He wants to see you **NOW**!" said Lars, with a note of real urgency in his voice. In retrospect, he sounded frightened, and I was soon to find out why. With some difficulty, I interrupted what I was doing at Brown and drove to ASE some 20 miles away.

Lars nervously met me at the receptionist's desk and ushered me into a temporary office set up for Olof Muten. He then departed immediately. There sat Olof, royally posed in a massive executive chair. Olof was also a Swede, who emigrated to the U.S. some 25 years earlier. He was a tall, steely-eyed man who arose, somewhat reluctantly, to shake my hand and sat down again. I was not invited to sit and didn't. Leaning back in the reclining chair, hands clasped behind his head, he glared at me with his penetrating, soulless, blue eyes; the entire ambiance gave me the feeling I was not among friends.

"I understand we have tendered you a contract," he opened.

"That's correct, sir," I replied, quite formally.

"Are you going to sign it?" he asked.

"Everything is quite in order," I replied, "but there are a couple of small details remaining; I'm sure we can work them out." Olof smiled and leaning forward for emphasis said,

"Then you're not going to sign it, *just as it is?*"

"No." I said. "The remaining details are not a serious problem and have only to do with disposition of contingent fees, should I slip on a banana peel." Without hesitation, Olof picked up a copy of the contract and with a gleeful flourish, tore it into many small pieces, which he deposited in the wastebasket. Then, displaying a slight smile, perhaps smirk better describes it, he turned and said,

"Good! I don't want any f***ing consultants around my place anyway." The shot came with unrestrained savageness. I had already sized him up as a bully and responded instantly. Taking my briefcase from its resting place on a chair, I smashed it down on the desk in front of Olof. He jumped; I think he was fearful I was going to throw it at him. Still standing and looming over him, I moved closer and met his now wide-eyed gaze, eye to eye.

"That's fine with me Mr. Muten," I said, "fortunately, there are enough decent people in the world, so I don't have to work for a SOB like you." I didn't use the acronym. I closed my briefcase slowly, meticulously setting the clasp and without further words, turned and departed for the front door, about 50 feet away.

I didn't mind how it came out. If I had stayed and groveled for a job on his terms, I would forever squirm under his heel. My situation was not urgent anyway; I had enough other clients to keep bread on the table. Lesson reinforced: Never rely on a lone source of income.

As I walked toward the door, I was both inwardly disturbed and yet somehow pleased with being relieved of the burden this relationship would have carried. I hurried my return to Brown Tank to resume work on the problem of the day the SOB had interrupted. Midway to the door, I felt an arm around my shoulder. It was Olof, walking with me. I pretended not to notice and continued toward the exit.

"Mr. Reilly, why don't you come back to my office, so we can talk? Maybe I want to keep you around here." I ignored him and kept walking. When we arrived at the door, Olof reached ahead and prevented me from easily opening the door. Pleadingly he said,

"Please come back to my office. Let's talk." Back in his office there was no talk other than about my contract that we changed immediately, on my terms, and signed. Thus began one of the finest, most trusted, working relationships I ever .

Olof and the Hush Houses

As our conversation turned to other topics, Olof made it clear he viewed ASE with some disdain, which was not unwarranted. Without the acquisition by Granges, bankruptcy loomed. Its stock was depressed, and as an entity in itself, was in a state of negative net worth. Olof reoriented the conversation:

"A couple of weeks ago, I had a phone call from my old friend, Ole Lund (the President of Granges-Nyby). He said,

'Olof, I've acquired this f***ed-up little company in St. Paul, Minnesota. Could you fly out there and see what it is and what you can do with it?' So, here I am. Do you have any ideas as to what we might do to put this place on the map?" Based on the conversational flow, the words carried some indication he wanted bragging rights with his old friend, Ole Lund and perhaps some other captains of industry back in Sweden. He wanted to do something BIG.

* * *

While working the prior month or two with ASE, I learned the Swedish parent company, Granges, had constructed several jet engine aircraft test cells for the Swedish Air Force and one for the British Royal Air Force. For many reasons, the time was right for the U.S. Air Force to adopt this technology. These test cells, termed 'Hush Houses,' were out of the ordinary then. Instead of clamping exhaust mufflers around the tail of an aircraft they were acoustical hangars, which enclosed the entire airplane. Further, the Swedish system used no water to prevent the meltdown of the muffler tube, a major environmental plus.

The Hush House used the aircraft under test as the primary nozzle in an ejector-type pumping system, and the engine induced flow of the large quantities of outside air required to cool the exhaust stream. From my early experience with exhaust gas cooling at the Rosemount Labs of the University of Minnesota, I understood the technology and began to spin a potential, major program for Olof.

What Is A Hush House?

By way of orientation, it might be well to illustrate what a Hush House is. The name was assigned by the original builder of these facilities, Granges-Nyby, headed by Olof's friend Ole Lund. Jet airplanes are noisy things. By the mid 1970s, ground testing of aircraft and engines became a nuisance, as opposed to a symbol of national power and pride, and mufflers of some sort became required by popular demand. The typical muffler consisted of a large, acoustically treated pipe that collected the jet exhaust products, quieted and cooled them. To keep the sound from escaping at the exit of the pipe, it was fitted with a large box enclosing only the tail of the

Individual Muffler

aircraft. The entrance to the attenuating pipe was usually of cruciform shape, fitted around the tail surfaces and rear fuselage of an aircraft, and all the contacting edges were padded to prevent damage to the fragile control surfaces. In addition, a feeble attempt was made to stop the high frequency noise from escaping forward, by hanging form-fitting boxes over the aircraft's inlets. To achieve a close fit, both the front and rear enclosures required a different design for each individual aircraft-type in the Air Force inventory. To protect the pipe from destruction by the exhaust flame, cooling water was injected into the jet efflux in huge quantities, many hundreds of gallons per minute.

The Hush House is different: It encloses the entire airplane and utilizes air cooling. Acoustic baffles along the sides of the hangar contain the engine noise, while cooling air passes freely into the interior.

The Hush House's appearance was timely. The Hush Houses Granges built for the Swedish Air Force did not receive much industry publicity at this time and were almost unknown in the U.S. The air-cooling technique solved many peripheral problems, and the timing was correct from several different

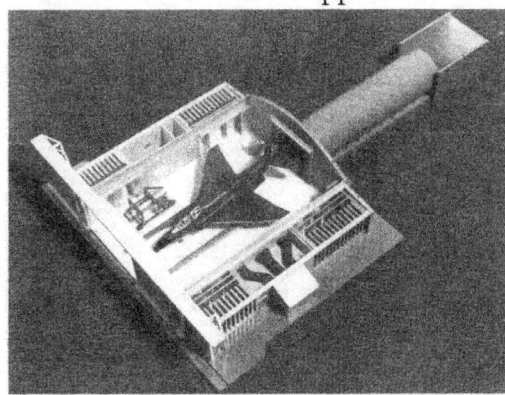
Hush House

perspectives.

Environmentally, air pollution was a serious public concern. Spraying water into the exhaust efflux of a jet engine quenched the combustion in the trailing jet and created a voluminous plume of dark, black smoke as unburned fuel burned poorly in the muffler tube. The effect was particularly bad in the after-burning mode, which expelled a substantial amount of unburned fuel from the engine.

Further, the fuel contained residual sulfur that mixed with the cooling water and produced sulfuric acid. The resulting fine, acidic mist fell on cars and vegetation and resulted in lawsuits for damages, despite attempts to place the facilities in remote locations. The lawsuits became a nuisance to the Air Force. The frosting on the cake emerged when the U.S. Air Forces deployed in England, were forced to stand-down for an entire, previous summer by a drought-induced lack of water. Water shortages created domestic problems and forced termination of almost all engine testing.

From an operations and maintenance standpoint, the timing was also fortuitous. The McDonnell-Douglas F-15, was in flight test and soon to be deployed. The General Dynamics F-16 was close behind in development, as was the Northrop F-17, which with some modifications, political infighting and more engine thrust, became the McDonnell-Douglas F-18. Exhaust silencers would have to be developed specifically for each of these airplanes, because the tight-fitting, cruciform structures to enclose the tail surfaces and aft fuselages of the different airplanes were necessarily of different shapes.

Operationally, the shape-fitted structure to enclose the tail of the airplane requires precise, time-consuming positioning of the airplane. Occasionally, damage resulted when the task was rushed or not carefully performed. The environmental considerations, upcoming development costs for new aircraft test cells and the operational benefits, all made the acoustical hangar an obvious choice for the future.

An added benefit for the dry, air-cooled system, was the elimination of the sulfuric acid that attacked the mild-steel structures of the water-cooled noise suppressors themselves. The water-cooled mufflers, with all their other limitations, required overhaul every two or three years. Because of the corrosion, they never lasted their contractually guaranteed, six-year life.

The stainless steel construction of the Hush House hot sections minimized maintenance. The final clincher: When an aircraft is moved to a different base, the custom-fitted exhaust mufflers had to be uprooted and relocated, along with all the associated logistics, whereas the Hush House fitted all aircraft in the inventory up to its maximum size capacity. It was a 'perfect storm' setup for the Hush House. However, as is often the case, logic stands aside while bureaucracy and politics rule. It would take a long journey over a tedious trail to bring success within reach.

Olof's steely-blue eyes danced as I spun this scenario for him; then he asked,

"What are our chances of selling Hush Houses to the U.S. Air Force?" Now it was time for the cold shower:

"Small," I replied, "perhaps as small as half of one percent. We will be trying to change the entire Air Force testing methodology and bucking entrenched Air Force functions. Many jobs will be eliminated or reassigned with adoption of the Hush House testing concept. We will face many tough battles."

Olof loved it. He walked to a window, paused in momentary contemplation, then turned and without equivocation said,

"Let's give it a try." With that we were off and running, and Olof never looked back. Later, he would brag how he decided to go forward, even though Dick Reilly told him the chances of success were less than two percent. He moved the numeral two from below to above the line (2 vs 1/2), probably to not appear foolhardy. However, neither of us understood we were embarking on a four-year adventure, and Olof would never see the end of the ensuing complex game to which he had committed his reputation ... and perhaps the company's very survival.

Throughout the next 39 months Olof never wavered. In the final days, he solved the ultimate financial problem, imposed by the Air Force purchasing organization, in an attempt to scuttle a hard-won contract.

Politically, the Hush House introduced serious tensions within the operational structure of the Air Force. It eliminated ongoing design and building of acoustic mufflers to fit individual aircraft. Moving these test facilities from base to base with changing deployments of aircraft, would no longer be required. Millions of dollars could be saved annually. The downside of all this: The Air Force had an entire logistic organization at Wright Field dedicated to the design, building, moving and repairing of the custom-fitted mufflers, worldwide. They weren't having anything to do with the universal hangar that would put them out of business.

Bringing about the this transformation was a long and difficult process, with many inexplicable deviations along the way. Wisely, the Air Force insisted on tests with USAF aircraft but pleaded it lacked the funds to build a test facility. We arranged to test USAF aircraft and engines in a facility the Swedes built in England some years earlier. The tests were successful in every respect, and by a strange quirk of fate, I wrote the Air Force's final report, which assured the test results were presented unambiguously.

As the report circulated through the system, the Hush House concept came under fire from the builders of the entrenched, individual, water cooled mufflers working in concert with USAF procurement functionaries. This effort set off an internecine battle between San Antonio Air Logistic Center and the Commanding General of U.S. Air Forces Europe. This dispute was settled by a year-long investigation and a hearing in the U.S. General Accounting Office, where we finally prevailed. The resulting contract, originally slated for $39 million, ultimately escalated to $49 million with the addition of features and variations not contained in the original proposal.

Sadly, Olof, who never wavered during the nearly four-year ordeal, was never able to savor the success that he felt was essential to the survival of ASE. Two weeks before the final award of the contract, he was thrown from horse while 'riding to the hounds' near his home in Pennsylvania. He suffered a serious head injury and never full grasped the winning of the last of the many battles we fought along the way.

I have written a book, "The Hush House Affair," published by Amazon, which recounts this four-year odyssey in chronological detail, but a short version of the story was published contemporaneously by "Corporate Report" magazine, an Upper Midwest "Business Week" of sorts. While the writer, Don Larson, captures some of my personal frustrations along the way, he doesn't properly credit the nearly providential appearance of many people who were key to the final contractual success. Nevertheless, his summary article serves well to summarize a difficult, four-year journey.

* * *

PERSONAL PERSPECTIVE *Don W. Larsen*

Looking for a Fat Government Contract?

Let's assume for a moment you're the head of a small manufacturing company doing about $7 million in annual sales. You're pitching for a very large contract from a single customer, a $45million contract – about six times your present annual volume. The customer is the U.S. Air Force, and it's impressed. Negotiations are conducted, you convince the people involved you can produce the product, and the contract is awarded to you.

Sounds simple, doesn't it?

Well, a Twin Cities firm recently went through this very exercise, with the same happy result, but it was far from simple. When Aero Systems Engineering, Inc., St. Paul, signed a $45million Air Force contract for 25 elaborate shelters in which to test jet aircraft and engines, the event marked the conclusion of an almost unbelievable tale of battling in bureaucratic jungles. It should be a good warning to any small company seeking government business.

A knowledgeable independent consultant, Richard J. Reilly of St. Paul, deserves much of the credit for Aero Systems' eventual success in getting the contract. Over the years Reilly has learned how to effectively cut government red tape, but the Aero Systems job proved even an expert can be, at times, overwhelmed in dealing with bureaucrats.

The Aero Systems Air Force saga started more than four years ago. In October 1976, when Olov Muten, chairman and chief executive of the small St. Paul firm, decided he wanted an Air Force contract and was ready to bet his company on the outcome, he hired Reilly to fight for it, even though Reilly warned him there was less than a one-percent chance a firm as small as Aero Systems could land such a whopping job.

The contract was awarded to Aero Systems 39 months later. Reilly devoted most of his time to the project, traveling more than 150,000 miles in five countries and making more than 2,000 long distance phone calls. Bureaucrats in Washington still scratch their heads over such a large award going to such a small company. The $45million award is the largest single support equipment contract in Air Force history, and Aero Systems is the smallest company to get any type of large government job. Yet, even after the contract was awarded, the complications weren't over. There was still another nine months involved in fighting protests from those representing firms had lost the job.

But the choice was far from capricious. Success in landing the contract can be attributed to three factors:

• Aero Systems is one of the few companies in the world with the expertise to build a complex shelter in which to safely and efficiently test a jet aircraft engine.

• Muten, Robert Lucas, Aero Systems President, and others at the company, had the faith and patience to keep plugging along during the months when it seemed the frustrations weren't worth the prospect of losing the company.

• Reilly's experience in dealing with the complexities inside the bewildering maze, where government contracts are awarded was the key to convincing military authorities Aero Systems could actually deliver if it got the project.

Reilly's credentials are impressive. An aeronautical engineer with extensive graduate work in gas dynamics, compressible fluid flow and supersonic inlets for aircraft gas turbines, Reilly not only understands the technical aspects involved but has a background in the business end of this field, as well. He has been an engineer and research scientist for several Twin Cities companies, including General Mills, Honeywell, and Rosemount Research Center. He holds 15 patents, has written more than 20 technical papers, and has been a guest lecturer at several universities in the U.S. and Europe.

One of Reilly's first hurdles in winning the Air Force contract was to convince the military authorities of the superiority of Aero Systems' air-cooled testing principles over the water-cooled system the Air Force has been using. Air Force brass told him the system used by the military was satisfactory, even though the technicians in the field admitted to Reilly they were having immense problems. Hundreds of meetings with Pentagon officials and Air Force officers at installations around the country and even in several foreign nations were necessary before the real selling job could begin.

Many of the meetings were major disappointments to Reilly and some were attended only by Reilly himself. Once, for example, Reilly had lined up an important session in Washington, D.C., with several Air Force equipment and logistics people. When he arrived in the nation's capital, after making the arrangements by long distance calls from St. Paul earlier, he went directly to the meeting. Only one official showed up, and he had no authority to take any action. The others had all canceled out because of the "extreme" weather. It was 13 degrees above zero in Washington. It was well below zero when Reilly left St. Paul.

Even getting the necessary information from the military to comply with its own instructions proved difficult. On one occasion, Reilly was told he couldn't get the life-cycle cost data he requested without using the Freedom of Information Act, a tedious process. He finally got the data after a lengthy delay.

Midway through the three-year struggle to get the contract, Reilly was told he needed an Air Force research and development program to get a National Stock Number before the operations people could consider purchase of the equipment. The research and development people said he didn't qualify for it because the Aero Systems equipment was an existing product and not eligible for an R&D program. Catch 22!

Slowly, methodically, Reilly removed one roadblock after another. The winning of the contract has cost Aero Systems hundreds of thousands of dollars, but it has been worth it. The *company is already involved in fulfilling the terms of the contract. Manufacturing facilities are being constructed in Crockett, Texas, and soon 150 workers will be constructing the 25 testing facilities.*

Companies in this area might be considering seeking government contracts to beef up their operations should give serious thought to the problems encountered by Aero Systems. It's a routine procedure for firms such as Honeywell, Control Data or Univac, but for a small or medium-sized firm, the prospects of doing work on a large scale for the government are mighty slim. CR

Don W. Larson is senior editor of CORPORATE REPORT *and publisher of the* Business Newsletter.

A small, paperback book entitled, "The Hush House Affair" (150 pages), tells the entire story in chronological detail. It has received excellent reviews on Amazon for its description of the government procurement system. Two reviews are shown below.

Great book

A well written, interesting,and informative book on what goes on in the government procurement process of new products in development. Although very interesting it would also make a good text book for any company lacking experience in development of new products for the government.

Good read

Superbly written fascinating account of four year procedure to improve USAF jet engine testing.

The book is available from Amazon.com and is best searched under the author's name: Richard J. Reilly.

16

Cuyuna Corporation

Tax considerations and retirement planning forced a change in business format.

* * *

With the signing of the $49 million contract and the demise of Olof Muten, I expected termination of my consulting contract with Aero Systems. However, the need for an Erection and Maintenance Manual (E&M) resulted in an extension of my Hush House activities. I was retained to photograph the fabrication of all components, their joining into sub-assemblies and final erection into a functioning test facility. All figures were then assembled into step-by-step, procedural narrative. Betty and I moved to San Antonio for about six months to close out the Hush House saga.

While in Texas it became evident my employment status was getting beyond a simple consulting relationship and we needed a personal retirement platform. A corporate organizational structure was required for individual protection and the construction of a 'defined benefit retirement program.' The Texas state corporate application forms required a name at the top of the forms. Both Betty and I had an interest in Native American culture and historical figures, so we decided to give the corporation an 'Indian' (Native American) name.

We tried several names indigenous to the American Southwest and all were previously used, so I decided to use a Minnesota-related name, and out of urgent need, the Cuyuna Iron Range came to mind; it was likely an unencumbered name in Texas: Cuyuna Corporation. I didn't know the history of the name, but it didn't matter at the time.

Some years later, back in Minnesota, I was doing some unrelated research in the Business Library Section of the St. Paul Public Library. On a whim, I sought historical references to the origin of the 'Cuyuna' name, but I found none. However, I thought it must be Indian.

I sought the help of the librarian, and she traversed the sources I had already explored and several more, all without success, but in the process she became intrigued. The Cuyuna Iron Range was well known as having supplied much of the iron for the high-rise buildings of the east coast in the 19th and 20th centuries, and she had difficulty accepting there was so little information on its origins.

Many years later, perhaps a decade, the telephone rang and a female voice inquired,

"Are you Mr. Reilly?"

"Yes," I replied.

"The Mr. Reilly interested in the Cuyuna Iron Range?" she asked.

"Yes."

"Oh good," she replied, "it's been such a long time. However, when we couldn't find anything on the origin of the name, Cuyuna, I became hooked. Ever since, I've looked for some background, not intensely you understand, but I've never forgotten your inquiry. Today I was looking for something else and ran across a plausible story that may solve our problem. It relayed the following bit.

'A man named Cuyler Adams discovered the Cuyuna Iron Range. Convinced there was a mineral lode awaiting discovery in the region, he endured great hardships during his exploration; in fact, he narrowly survived. When he returned to civilization and faced with the necessity of naming his claim, he decided to name it by combining his name with that of his dog, Una, whom he said was responsible for his survival and contributed as much to the discovery of iron as his own personal endeavors.'"

I was surprised by the story and the durable interest of the librarian, who not only focused so long on the problem but also remembered my name. Note that she referred to it as 'our problem.'

So much for Indian names; we did business under the name, 'Cuyuna Corporation,' for 36 years, visited 27 countries and were gainfully employed in 16 of them.

17

NASA Contract

Once enmeshed in a technical problem you may never get away.

* * *

Working for a significant time on any engineering program is a lifetime commitment within a company. As time passes, assignment to other endeavors, promotions and even transfers to other company divisions doesn't mean your responsibility for earlier work has ended. The material stored in one's brain is inevitably sought and tapped for a variety of reasons.

I left Honeywell and the fluidics game in 1969. In 1992, while working with a Canadian company on a flight test program at NASA's Dryden facility in the California desert, I received a call from Honeywell's librarian. She had received a call from someone at NASA Dryden, inquiring about a fluidic temperature sensor. The fluidic work at Honeywell had long ceased; however, the librarian remembered me and gave me the name of Rodney Bogue at NASA Dryden. Because I was working at Dryden at the moment, initial contact was quick and easy.

Bogue and I reviewed the results of a NASA Dryden-sponsored

contract with Honeywell from the 1960s that measured temperatures up to 2200 °C (4000 °F) using a fluid oscillator. NASA wanted a 10,000 °F sensor. We agreed that a limited-scope program to extend this technique to 10,000 °F, would necessarily concentrate on a review of high-temperature materials developed since completion of the original program.

Other areas for limited study included related pressure instrumentation requirements, dissociation, rarefied gas effects and analysis of sensor time response. The potential for measuring extreme temperatures, using fluid oscillator techniques, stems from the fact the measuring element is the fluid itself, however, the containing structure remained a major problem.

As a result of these discussions, I prepared a proposal covering the agreed-upon work statement and was awarded a contract for $25,000.

While it is unlikely the casual reader would be interested in a deeply-grinding assessment of the program's results, a few pages, extracted from the final report, are included to give some flavor of the work accomplished. The formatting is not elegant, because the material is presented as full-page copies of the original document pages, reduced in size to fit within the page-format of this book, leaving blank spaces below the extracted material.

NASA Contractor Report 186025

Program for an Improved Hypersonic Temperature-Sensing Probe

Richard J. Reilly
Cuyuna Corporation
3909 Peak Lookout Drive
Austin, Texas 78737

Prepared for
Dryden Flight Research Facility
Edwards, California
Under Contract NAS2-13457

1993

National Aeronautics and
Space Administration

Dryden Flight Research Facility
Edwards, California 93523-0273

INTRODUCTION

This program is, in a sense, a continuation of NASA effort begun more than 25 years ago. At that time, interests within NASA saw need for a temperature sensor to measure very high total temperatures in compressible gases. NASA Dryden sponsored a program with Honeywell Inc. which produced instrumentation, based on fluidic techniques, capable of measuring to a level of 2200 °C (4000 °F). For a more complete introduction to the current program a short history of the earlier NASA program is included as Appendix A.

The current program focused on the problems to be solved if this technology is to be taken to temperatures of approximately 5500 °C (10,000 °F). The most difficult area is that of material followed closely by the pressure transducer technology required to get pressure pulse signal out of the fluidic other concerns, regarding dissociation and continuum flows in rarefied environments, were explored by a limited analysis.

SUMMARY

The fluid temperature sensor is unique in that, for gaseous fluids, the fluid itself is the measuring element. As a result it is not necessary for any solid material to be brought to ultra high temperatures to accomplish a measurement. The oscillation frequency of a fluid oscillator is very nearly a linear function of the square root of the absolute temperature of the gas flowing through it. In the mid-1960s, NASA sponsored a development program which successfully measured air temperatures of 2200 °C (4000 °F) using this technology. The current program explored major questions relative to applying this technique to measure temperatures of 5538 °C (10,000 °F). Measurement of temperatures of this magnitude may be possible because the temperature gradient between the flowing fluid and survivable material temperatures is accomplished across the boundary layer of the gas.

The major objectives of this program as defined in the statement of work were:

* Define NASA areas of application for measuring ultra- high temperatures as a guide for developing a design specification

* Review progress in the development of materials for use at high temperatures

* Review developments in the field of high temperature, high frequency pressure transducers

* Explore effect of dissociation and rarefied gas effects on performance of the fluid temperature sensor

Conclusions

Since transducer technology has not advanced relative to high temperature capability, effective cooling will be required to get information out of the sensor via pressure sensing techniques.

Material developments have not advanced high temperature materials to a level which will permit the fabrication of an fluid temperature sensor whose oscillation cavity operates at 5,500 °C (10,000 °F) without cooling. It may be possible to build a simple, uncooled oscillator cavity for long term operation up to 1650 °C (3000 °F). For 5-10 hour life in a cycling environment some materials may allow use of an uncooled cavity to temperatures of approximately 1900-2200 °C (3500-4000 °F).

For measurements to 10,000 °F, designs based on refractory metals, having reasonable oxidation resistance, should be explored. High thermal conductivity combined with efficient cooling of the oscillator cavity may offer the best hope for an ultra-high temperature sensor based on fluid techniques.

Recommendations

Reproduce a sensor design developed under the earlier program but using high temperature materials developed by NASA Ames material developers. Objective: reestablish the technology base and evaluate fabrication techniques needed for advanced materials.

Design a sensor cavity from a refractory metal and incorporating extensive cooling passages. Evaluate, by analysis, the feasibility of rejecting enough heat to sustain cavity surfaces to temperatures below serious oxidation levels. Conduct experimental verification. Objective: determine the potential for heat transfer techniques to support a 10,000 °F sensor for long term use.

Explore potential materials and fabrication methods with the aerospace firm which has offered to participate in a cooperative effort. Objective: obtain better, first hand knowledge of material capability and to determine suitability of various high temperature materials for diffusion bonding.

Begin a search for an oscillation detection technique which overcomes the limitations of pressure port length and temperature capability imposed by pressure transducers.

APPLICATION AREAS

Discussions with personnel at NASA Dryden Flight Research Facility and NASA Ames Research Center isolated the following application areas:

- Supersonic Flight Test and Research
- Atmospheric Reentry Measurements
- Propulsion System Measurements
- Wind Tunnel Applications (Free Stream and Boundary Layer)
- Arc Tunnel Measurements Materials Research

Each of these areas has its own operational environment and related requirements. In general, the flight research application seeks the highest possible temperature capability while other measurement capabilities are more restricted and better defined physical constraints. Research applications can also tolerate more "care and feeding" such as auxiliary cooling and pretest calibration.

Flight applications carry the usual, well defined, needs for resistance to shock, vibration etc. with pressure and temperature ranges determined by the flight envelope of the vehicle. For manned vehicles, the temperature sensor can usually be constructed using the same materials or techniques as the vehicle itself. Since the sensor is small and has no moving parts, it can be relatively massive in external configuration giving it ruggedness, strength and thermal mass without adding significant weight to a flight system. Reentry systems could possibly be designed to survive on energy sinking techniques relying only on the thermal mass of the instrument. Measurements for longer flight applications might consider periodic measurements with an extending and retracting probe with cooling applied during the retracted phase.

Wind tunnel interests expressed a need for high temperature boundary layer profile measurements which brings consideration of miniaturization and vertical cascades of individual sensors. This leads to rarefied gas considerations, i.e., the mean free path of the gas molecules relative to the size of the instrument.

The operating environment is largely oxidizing, whether in the flight atmosphere, the wind tunnel or in the propulsion setting. This severely restricts the choice of materials and requires that otherwise promising material candidates, carbon/carbon composites for example, be protected with oxidation resistant coatings.

RAREFIED GAS EFFECTS

The expressed need for reentry instrumentation and for miniaturized sensors for boundary layer measurements led to the following limited exploration of real gas effects.

Reentry conditions and flight at very high altitudes is often conducted at high Mach number which results in extremely high gas temperatures. Typically, at Mach numbers of approximately 6 and above, so called "real gas effects" come into play. At the related elevated temperatures, molecular vibration, dissociation and ionization effects become important. A rigorous discussion of these issues is beyond the scope of this program; however, a limited analysis, dealing with mostly with low density effects, was conducted for the purpose of shaping the general problem areas. As a result, conclusions from this analysis should recall the limitations and be used with care.

Calculation of Knudsen Number

The aerodynamic and heat transfer effects encountered in a flow field change when the gas no longer acts as a continuous medium and the molecular character of the gas becomes important. In general, this occurs when the mean free path, γ, of the molecules is of the same order of magnitude as some characteristic dimension in the system. This condition is sometimes described in terms of the Knudsen number, K, defined as:

$$K = \frac{\lambda}{d}$$

Knudsen number can be expressed in terms of the more familiar aerodynamic parameters, Mach number and Reynolds number.

$$M = \frac{V}{a} \quad \text{and} \quad Re = \frac{Vd\rho}{\mu}$$

* Define potential sources for fabricating experimental temperature sensor.

NASA requirements for an ultra-high temperature sensor were explored during discussions with research personnel at Ames and at Dryden. The nature of research at both facilities demands that materials and technology chosen for an advanced capability temperature sensor must be capable of operation in an oxidizing environment. There was common interest in the rapid time response that is characteristic of the fluid temperature sensor. While measuring capability to 2500 °C (4500 °F) is adequate for materials research, re-entry instrumentation needs a 10,000 °R capability. Mach 10 in a standard atmosphere produces total temperatures in the 8,000–10,000 °R range. Considering other potential applications in the propulsion field, all NASA users work in an oxidizing atmosphere.

Materials for fabricating a 10,000 °R sensor are a difficult problem. Carbon/carbon is an attractive but disappointing option. While carbon increases in strength to temperatures of approximately 2200 °C (4000 °F), it begins to vaporize at about 425 °C (800 °F). Some refer to it as "frozen smoke." The structural properties of carbon/carbon have spurred a great deal of work on protective coatings but no really successful coating has been developed for the oxidizing, thermal cycling environment required for temperature sensor applications.

Ceramic matrix composites present even more complex problems. The conventional considerations of strength, fatigue, bending modulus and creep resistance remain important. In addition, thermochemical compatibility between the ceramic matrix material and the reinforcing fibers comes into play. Because of the rigors of an oxidizing environment, most non-oxide materials require oxide protection systems as with carbon, especially after microcracking begins in the matrix material. As a practical matter, because of oxidation problems, potentially useful ceramics for temperature sensor fabrication are mainly limited to oxide/oxide (oxide reinforcing fibers in an oxide matrix) composites.

Pressure transducers with high frequency capability have made limited progress since the earlier NASA programs. Threshold levels and resolution have been improved. However, high temperature capability, as required for temperature sensor applications, has receded somewhat. This has occurred because, by placing emphasis on ease of use, some manufacturers are incorporating amplifier circuitry into the transducer body. This limits the operating temperature to the capability imposed by the semiconductor materials rather than the limit of the basic piezoelectric element (quartz for example). Although basic transducers are still available, the high temperature "special use" versions used previously are no longer available.

Dissociation effects will become important somewhere in the temperature region of 2800 °C (5000 °F) and above. A limited analytical study of the dissociative effect was made by comparing the speed of sound in a gas, with γ = constant and with γ computed from tabular values in reference 1, up to 6400 °R. At this temperature, with this data source, no dissociative effects were evident. More work, with experimentally determined real gas parameters at higher temperatures, is required to adequately define the dissociative effects.

The Cuyuna Corporation has only limited capability to fabricate and test experimental temperature sensors. Discussions with several instrumentation manufacturers have determined that one major manufacturer of airborne total temperature sensors is interested in cooperating with Cuyuna in developing an advanced version of the basic sensor design. Another large aerospace company has offered a cooperative effort on material development.

and the total temperature by:

$$T_{to} = T_o\left[1 + \frac{\gamma-1}{2}M^2\right]$$

If it is assumed that the temperature sensor inlet will operate behind a normal shock, the following relationships apply:

$$\frac{P_{t2}}{P_{to}} = \left[\frac{(\gamma+1)M^2}{(\gamma-1)M^2+2}\right]^{\frac{\gamma}{\gamma-1}} \left[\frac{\gamma+1}{2\gamma M^2-(\gamma-1)}\right]^{\frac{1}{\gamma-1}}$$

$$\frac{T_{t2}}{T_{to}} = \left[\frac{2\gamma M^2 - (\gamma-1)}{\gamma+1}\right]\left[\frac{(\gamma-1)M^2+2}{(\gamma+1)M^2}\right]$$

$$\frac{P_2}{P_o} = \frac{(\gamma+1)M^2}{(\gamma-1)M^2+2}$$

$$M_2 = \left[\frac{(\gamma-1)M^2+2}{2\ M^2-(\gamma-1)}\right]^{\frac{1}{2}}$$

The viscosity of air was computed as a function of temperature from the following relationship:

$$\mu * 10^{10} = 0.317\ T°R^{1.5}\left[\frac{734.7}{(T°R+216)}\right]$$

Atmospheric values for pressure, temperature and density were computed from the equations of reference 3. Then, using the above expressions, Knudsen numbers were calculated for various Mach numbers and altitudes. These data and intermediate values of interest are presented in tabular form in Tables 1-A, 1-B, 1-C, and 1-D for a sensor inlet opening of 0.020".

The data from these tables are plotted in figure 1, showing Knudsen number as a function of altitude and Mach number. The figure shows that the larger values of Knudsen number occur at the lower values of Mach number and the data pack very closely for Mach numbers greater than $M=4$ or 5. This results from the assumption that the sensor will always operate behind a normal shock. Inspecting the intermediate data in the tables indicates only minor changes in M_2 beyond $M=5$. Further, V_2 and ρ_2 conspire to hold the Reynolds number, based on sensor port dimension (0.020"), remarkably constant.

Based on the foregoing criterion for free molecular flow we see that nowhere in the altitude range to 200,000 feet and Mach number to 20 does the Knudsen number approach 10. However, the Knudsen number criterion of "a few percent" is approached for nearly all Mach numbers at altitudes in excess of 120,000–140,000 feet.

APPENDIX A

A Short History of Fluid Temperature Sensors

Early Work

The fluid amplifier concept originated at the Army's Harry Diamond Laboratories in the early 1960s and by 1964 a variety of concepts and configurations had evolved. The Laboratory's work included some of the earliest known work on the use of fluid oscillator concepts for measuring temperature. References 1 and 2 cite temperature measuring work dating to 1964 and 1965.

Honeywell Developments

In 1960 Honeywell purchased licenses to fluid amplifier technology and started a fluid mechanic laboratory to research the basic operating principles of these devices and to develop products incorporating air and liquids as the working medium. One of the areas of focus was the temperature oscillator.

By 1964, under the contractual sponsorship of the Aero Propulsion Laboratory of Wright Patterson Air Force Base, Honeywell's temperature sensor work had progressed to the point where a temperature oscillator was incorporated into the primary control loop of a General Electric J85-5 jet engine.

In other areas, Honeywell developed a fluid angular rate sensor, which had no moving parts. In 1963, combined with other fluid amplification devices, the fluid rate sensor was the heart of a control system used to fly a demonstration missile flight with compressed air as the working medium and no electronics. This program was sponsored by the Army. The fluid rate sensor operating on oil was also used in a hydraulic, single axis rate damping system for helicopters. In general, the driving force behind this technology was simplicity, high temperature environment and immunity to the nuclear electromagnetic pulse.

NASA Sponsored Work

In 1965 NASA Ames Laboratory contracted with Honeywell for a series of research programs to explore the potential of fluid oscillators for temperature sensing in various hypersonic wind tunnel applications. The Air Force sponsored work for jet engine measurements had resulted in relatively large devices. Because one of NASA's prime interests was in boundary layer measurements, the work concentrated on miniaturization.

Earlier work was used as a starting point but the difficulties of small size soon became apparent:
    * Viscous losses in small passages attenuated the magnitude of the pressure pulses

* Signal wave forms were distorted and dominated by noise at higher total pressure levels
* Machining tolerances became critical and surface finishes better than 15 microinches were required on all internal flow passages
* Diffusion bonding became the only feasible means of assembly so this imposed another overriding requirement on material selection in addition to the already severe environmental requirements. At these temperatures, adhesives were out of the question and welding introduced undesirable thermal stresses in relatively brittle materials. Ultimately these problem areas were overcome with engineering compromises which resulted in a number of successful instruments.

Three temperature probes delivered under the contract; two "low temperature" (temperatures to 2300 deg. R), designated Probe A and B, and a high temperature version capable of operation at 3500 deg. R. The low temperature probes are shown in figure A-1 (Probe A) and figure A-2 (Probe B). The two low temperature probes had the same internal oscillator configuration figure A-3, except for the signal tube exit which had to conform to either a straight or a swept back pylon. The high temperature probe is shown in figure A-4 along with it's internal dimensions figure A-5.

Geometric Compromise

The probe internal geometry was developed using a a variable geometry model which could be clamped together for rapid configuration changes. Selection of the optimum exit orifice location was dictated by signal waveform shape and signal-to-noise ratio which are major indicators of oscillatior performance. Exit orifice size and location coupled with transducer sensitivity and location were the prime parameters investigated. They were investigated over a wide range of inlet pressures.

While some research measurements showed that oscillation could be maintained down to absolute pressures of 0.1 psia the practical lower limit for these wind tunnel applications was about 1.0 psia. Transducer sensitivity available in 1967 resulted in a capability to detect oscillations at 4.5 psia for Probe A and to 1.3 psia for Probe B. A typical characteristic plot, taken from a Probe B configuration, is shown in figure A-6.

Final configurations resulted from a balancing of thermal, mechanical and pressure measurement considerations. In general, more sensitive pressure transducers also exhibit temperature interactions so must be cooled and/or located farther from the oscillator. Internal passage length attenuates the pressure signal, limiting the distance the transducer between the transducer and oscillator. Smaller oscillators give lower pressure pulses, simply because there is less total energy in the flow. Transducer developments since the mid 1960s might change the design optimizations and result in temperature sensors with better performance and extended range of operation.

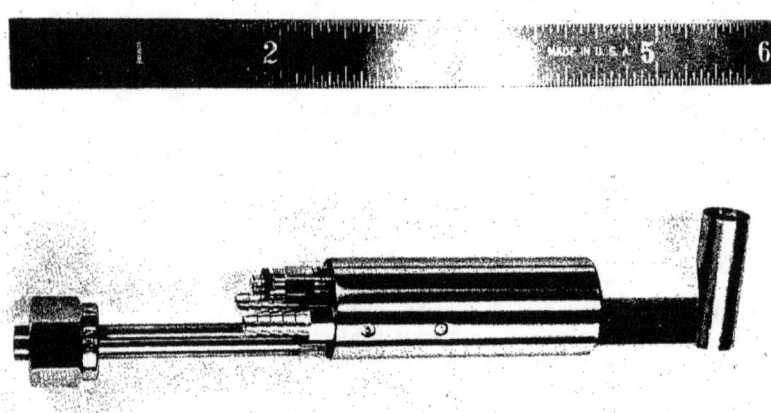
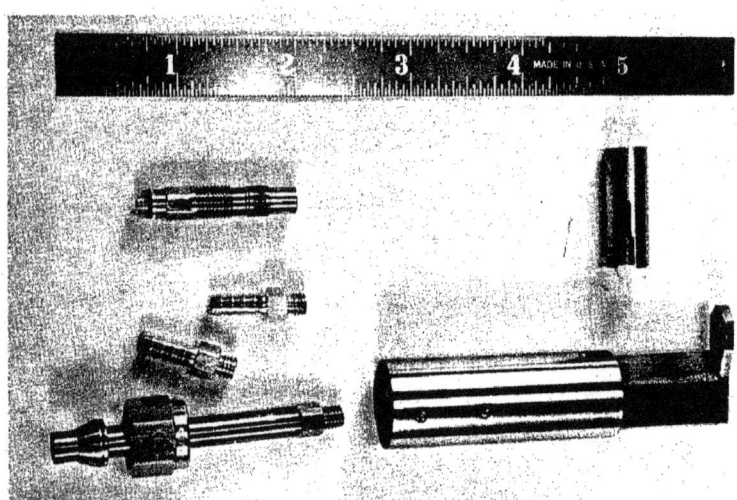
High Temperature Probe C, Assembled and Disassembled

18

Lake Aircraft

The Lake LA-4-200 exhibited some interesting aerodynamic problems.

* * *

When asked to document the building of the first Hush house, we moved to San Antonio for about six months. This was a fortuitous event because several contacts I made during the latter days of the Hush House activity evolved into Texas. Before our move to Texas, I did some consulting work for Lake Aircraft in New Hampshire and at their facility at David Hooks Airport near Houston, Texas. I did the flight test work at Hooks through an easy commute from San Antonio. Sometimes things just work out well.

My involvement with Lake was almost accidental. On one of my trips to Houston I had the occasion to stop at the David Hooks Airport near a town called Tomball, Texas. It's an unusual airport because it has a large ditch filled with water alongside one of the runways. Out of curiosity I began to explore the side of the airport near the water and was surprised to find several small amphibian airplanes parked near an adjacent hangar. I wandered into one of the buildings in the small complex and encountered Laurin Darrell, the manager of a 'completion' operation for Lake Aircraft, a manufacturer of small amphibians. At Hooks, the electronics and other fitments were installed into basic air frames in accordance with customer specifications.

The conversation wandered into the engineering vein as Darrell explained the airplane had a deficiency in its rate of climb he would like to address. I explained my background in aerodynamics, and he said he would explore the matter with the President of the company, who lived in New Hampshire. I thought no more about it and didn't expect to hear any more, so I was surprised to get a telephone call several weeks later asking me to come to Tomball for further discussions. Darrell flew one of the small amphibians to San Antonio take me to Tomball for a quick visit.

Defining the problem

The following day we tufted the airplane with woolen yarn and flew some exploratory flights to visualize the flow in the vicinity of the junction between the wing and the fuselage. As the picture, left, shows, the flow pattern in this region is confused and multi-directional not smooth, and streamlined. In the region of the wing root, the flow is reversed, flowing upstream from the trailing edge of the wing to a point somewhere near the minimum pressure point at about 25% of chord from the leading edge. Based on these preliminary observations, we decided to make further measurements to determine detailed performance of the airplane over a range of flight speeds. These and further visualization data

Wing Root Flow

were taken at the company's facility at Laconia, New Hampshire.

The arrows in the photo below show the chaotic nature of the flow in the wing intersection. It correlates well with the power required to fly the airplane in level flight.

Intersection Flow

Below is a plot of the power required to fly the airplane in level flight as a function of airspeed. The flight region in the vicinity of the tangent of a line drawn from the 0-0 point to the curve – the lower arrow – shows the approximate speed for the best rate of climb. The region around 70 to 80 miles per hour is of most interest. Although the best rate of climb for this airplane should be in the speed range around 80 mph, the airplane the could not be flown without flap deflection at speeds below about 90 mph.

Ordinarily, takeoff is done with flaps deployed and not retracted until 90 mph is exceeded. The higher drag of the flaps greatly reduces the rate of climb. If approached from higher speeds i.e. top downward in the plot, there is a sudden departure from the orderly data exhibited at the higher speeds. This event is accompanied by an un-

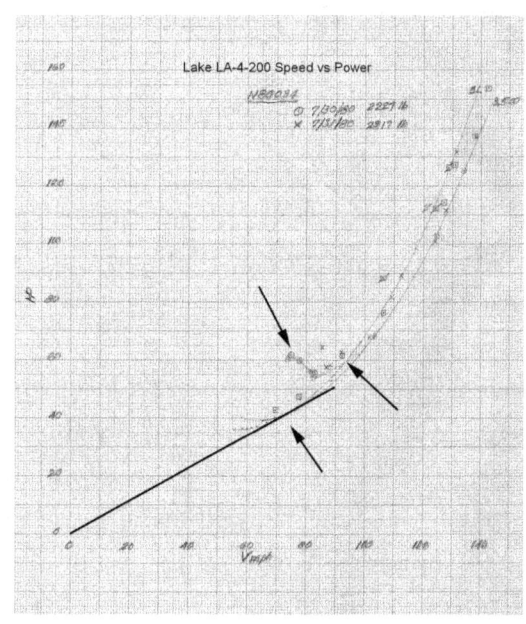
Power vs Speed

controllable nose-down pitch, and control is recovered by relaxing back-pressure on the controls and accelerating to 90 mph or greater. On an atmospherically quiet day and *very* carefully flown, the airplane could be teased down the speed-power curve (two data points in the 70-80 mph region). With any disturbance, the pitch-down and the move to the upper curve occurred (center arrow). In this flight regime it appeared the entire chaotic region in the wing intersection separates from the wing and passes through the tail plane, stalling it and causing the pitch-down as the tail trimming force is momentarily lost. In this region, relaxing back-pressure on the elevator allows the airplane to recover to level flight at a lower altitude and a higher speed, at about 85-90 mph, the highlighted data point in the plot, far right arrow.

If back-pressure is not relaxed, the nose will rise again and the pitching motion is repeated at a rate of about three or four seconds for each oscillation, a rather wild ride. The performance of the airplane is extremely sensitive at speeds below 90 mph and the flaps are deflected to avoid this anomaly.

The deflected flap compromises the airplane's rate of climb because the flap system has only two positions: up, aligned with the wing, or down, the higher drag, landing position.

The fix

The the propeller's position relative to the minimum pressure point on the wing induces the forward flow of the boundary layer in the wing/fuselage junction. The lower pressure in the propeller's in-flow region enhances the normal, lower pressure over the wing. Initially, we took the course of blocking the inward cross flow of the boundary layer from outboard toward the wing root. A simple vertical fence attached to the top of the wing near the trailing edge worked nicely and allowed the airplane to be accelerated through the 60-90 mph regime without the use of flaps. It also made a significant difference in the rate of climb, bringing it from 600 ft./min. to about

850 – 900 ft./min. While this was a relatively large increase, it was disappointing for Lake, because it didn't allow advertising the airplane's performance improvements and only aligned advertising data with the airplane's demonstrated performance.

About this time, Lake changed the gasoline-fired cabin heater mounted at the base of the engine pylon. Changing the heater enclosure required redoing a small part of the Federal Aviation Administration's certification tests. During these tests it was discovered the wing could not be held level in a stall using rudder control alone: a certification requirement. Further investigation revealed the wing, as fabricated, did not have the correct shape at the extreme leading edge. The FAA mandated inspection of all LA-4-200s in service at the time, and many more airplanes were found with somewhat flattened leading edges. The problem blossomed into a true emergency.

Lake was a relatively small manufacturer. The airplanes were built in Sanford, Maine, flown to Florida for painting, then fitted out to a new owner's specification for electronics and accessories at the facility in Texas. The paint shop people in Florida were aware of the flat leading edge problem and attempted to correct the wing contours before painting. They used a common, kitchen rolling-pin to hand roll the 'corners' (a slightly sharper leading edge radius top and bottom) of the slightly flattened region at the extreme leading edge, in an attempt to restore an acceptable contour. This ad hoc technique produced a variable result that was not easily rectified for all the airplanes then in service. A resolution of the leading edge problem was reached sometime after I completed my work.

In the ensuing effort to resolve the wing problem, the pitch/rate of climb problem was lost. Shortly after the wing problem was resolved, the company increased the engine horsepower from 200 in the LA-4 to 250 horsepower and renamed it the Renegade. The Renegade also had a longer fuselage to accommodate additional seats and the lengthened fuselage changed the relative position of the propeller and the wing. As a result, the pitching problem in the 80 - 90 mph operating regime disappeared.

In summary, we solved an interesting problem, but the commercial results came to naught. The operation was a success, but the patient died.

19

Tsunami

Racing against the crowd.
* * *

For many years, the Unlimited Class air races at Reno, Nevada was almost exclusively for airplanes derived from World War II fighters: North American Mustangs, and Grumman Bearcats, with a sprinkling of British Hawker Sea Furies and ex-Russian fighters. Tsunami was different, however. Feeling this path was at a technological end, John Sandberg commissioned the design of a purpose-built racing airplane built around the Rolls Royce Merlin engine that was the heart of the Spitfire, the North American Mustang and a number of the other top-tier fighters of WW II.

Tsunami, designed by Bruce Boland of Lockheed's super-secret 'Skunk Works,' was the smallest airplane ever built around the Merlin engine and was intended to dominate the 'Unlimited' Class Races, held each Labor Day weekend at Stead Field near Reno, Nevada. When not racing, Tsunami lived in a hangar directly across the taxiway from my hangar at Crystal Airport, in a suburb of North Minneapolis.

Jack Sandberg, the owner of Tsunami, spent much of each summer working on Tsunami's engine and making small improvements on the airplane. Jack and I had many conversations regarding the aerodynamics of going fast; in the process, Jack told me he was having trouble with engine cooling.

There was no way I couldn't get involved. Thermodynamics and air inlets had been graduate school focuses for me; I volunteered to analyze his problem. He loaded me with data on the Merlin, and I went to work.

Tsunami

Cooling the Merlin for racing is a complex problem since the engine, when tuned for racing, developed nearly twice the designed power level attained in normal production installations. The engine is liquid cooled; heat is transferred to a glycol mixture pumped through the engine to cool it and subsequently through an aft radiator, where air is used to cool the glycol. For a production design, the radiator is sized to provide sufficient air cooling at maximum speed and power level.

Tsunami Airborne

For normal air cooling at racing power, the radiator would need to be nearly doubled in size to adequately cool the engine, greatly increasing the overall drag of the airplane. Cooling for racing power levels requires spraying water onto the surface of the radiator, where it flashes to steam. The latent heat of vaporization of water is large, compared to normal air cooling of the radiator. Thus, its cooling capacity is greatly increased for a time limited by the small amount of water that can be carried.

New Cooling Inlet

Several design trade-offs are involved to give a balanced cooling system. The resulting inlet, shown here, is unremarkable except to say it is correctly sized, has a proper offset from the bottom of the airplane to bypass the low energy, boundary layer flow and a rounded lip, which results in good pressure recovery over a range of speeds. The original inlet was smaller, half round, lacked an adequate boundary layer gutter and had a relatively sharp lip that was optimal at only one speed. Jack maintained the new inlet added 15 mph to his maximum speed. He and Tsunami achieved 557 mph during a test flight at Wendover, Utah in preparation for an attempt to break the world's speed record for a propeller-driven airplane. The attempt was cut short by an unfortunate accident, when a critical pin in the landing gear failed, and one leg collapsed on touchdown. After rebuilding, the airplane was raced at Reno that year, but no all-out record attempt was ever made again.

Tsunami's days at Reno were breathtaking pylon chases with 'Rare Bear,' a modification of a Grumman Bearcat fighter, which appeared at the end of

Grumman Bearcat

WWII but never saw military action. Most of the other airplanes were left behind as Tsunami and Rare Bear dueled for 'the Gold.' Flown at various times by Steve Hinton and Skip Holm, Tsunami came close to beating 'the Bear,' losing by less than half a second.

Sandberg died while landing Tsunami at Rapid City, South Dakota in a high wind, while returning from the Reno Races in 1991. The airplane had a fatal flaw: The landing flaps were independently actuated and not linked, as is common design practice. Jack likely flew the landing approach at a much higher speed than usual due to the gusty, 50 knot wind. As a result, when he deployed the flaps, one of the actuators failed. The resulting differential flap deflection created a strong rolling moment and the aircraft struck the ground after rolling inverted.

Sadly, Jack never bested 'Rare Bear,' but he always derived pleasure in flying Tsunami home to Minnesota after each race, while Rare Bear often required an engine change.

20

Grumman X-29

A very brief exposure into research airplanes:
Sometimes vital information gets lost.

* * *

My brush with the X-29 was scarcely even a brush. I was involved in a thrust measuring program with Computing Devices of Canada. We were calibrating the thrust of 10 engines installed in Northrop T-38 trainers, using the Air Force Universal Horizontal Thrust Stand, located at Edwards Air Force Base in the California desert. At the same time, NASA's Dryden Research Center, co-located at Edwards, was doing the final fitment for flight testing of the Grumman X-29, and for unknown reasons I was invited to attend a project meeting on the X-29.

The X-29 was a true research airplane for exploring the stability and other performance idiosyncrasies of sweeping aircraft wings forward rather than aft, the accepted design practice following the first straight-winged, supersonic airplanes. Cost is often a major factor in any research program. Except for the wings and flying surfaces, the X-29 was an assemblage of parts from existing airframes: the landing gear and General Electric F-404 engine came from a General Dynamics F-16, the forward fuselage and cockpit from a Northrop F-5 fighter etc.

At the project meeting, several facets of the X-29 program were addressed, including, the engine installation. Someone noted Computing Devices of Canada was on the field, working with the Horizontal Thrust Stand to determine the factors affecting installed engine thrust, and perhaps they could contribute information regarding the X-29's engine installation. The program manager, seeking to avoid further complication, responded with a wry smile and pointed out the forward fuselage was from a Northrop F-5 fighter, it included the engine air inlets, and millions of hours of operational data were readily available; there was no shortage of inlet data.

Grumman X29

Northrop F5

Having designed the inlet geometry of the F-5 more than 30 years before and exposed to the X-29 earlier in the day, I knew the X-29's inlets bore no resemblance to those of the F-5. I struggled with whether I should point that out or let the matter drop.

As the meeting began breaking-up I approached the program manager, introduced myself as the designer of the inlets for the F-5, while working for Northrop in 1956, and during our earlier walk-around I noticed the great increase in X-29's inlet size: the two J-85 engines in the F-5 ingested about 90

Grumman X-29   247

lbs. of air per second while the single F-404 needed about 150 lbs. In the photographs on the prior page, it is apparent the X-29's inlet is larger and has a rectangular shape, while the F-5's inlet is smaller and incorporates some external and internal geometry necessary for its modestly supersonic operations. The available performance data on the F-5 inlet would obviously not apply to the X-29.

The program manager thanked me for my information. Later, my client, Canadian client received a small contract (less than $100,000) from NASA to modify its thrust algorithm for application to the X-29. During another visit to NASA Dryden some months later, I was invited to participate in a crew photograph.

X29 Engineering Group

X-29A Program. NASA Dryden, Edwards AFB California, 25 Feb. 1986, Left to right: Lt. Jan Kania & Jim Walton, USAF/NASA Dryden Graeme Dimock, Govt of Canada, Russ Alexander & Dick Reilly, Computing Devices, John Hicks, NASA Dryden, Mike Hamer, Computing Devices, Ron Ray, NASA Dryden

21

Seabird Aviation Australia

A nip and a tuck, here and there.
*   *   *

Through several more strange intersections that are stories in themselves, I was on a stage in the Sheraton Hotel in Brisbane, Australia. I prefaced my talk with mention of Sir Charles Kingsford-Smith, an Australian, who was the first to fly an airplane across the Pacific: San Francisco to Brisbane in 1928. Upon completing my talk, I returned to my seat next to the Queensland Minister Of Trade who remarked,

"If you're interested in airplanes you must see 'our' airplane" and explained that the Ministry has been assisting a small airplane development project in a town about 150 miles north. The following morning I received a call from the Trade Minister: He arranged for a pilot and an airplane to take me to Hervey Bay, where I met the owner of Seabird Aviation Australia, Donald Adams. Don introduced me to the Seabird Sentinel, a small observation airplane powered by a Wankel engine. After a walk-around inspection and conversation, Don inquired,

"Would you like to fly it?"

Sentinel Original Inlets

"Certainly," I responded, and we were off.

After climbing to a safe altitude for some maneuvering, the company test pilot turned the controls to me and I began some lazy departures from straight and level to get the feel of the airplane. This went well, so I began to expand my exploration to more interesting regions of the flight envelope. I nibbled at the approach to a stall and this went well too, and I decided to fully stall the airplane see how it recovered. This didn't seem unusual, but the controls felt somewhat soft and uncertain after recovery to level flight. We flew level for a relatively long time, perhaps five seconds or more. Then, without warning, the left wing dropped and the nose pitched over downward into a spin that I caught in about half a turn.

"Nice catch," said the company pilot, "that's a problem we have to fix. You have to push the nose down and accelerate to fully unstall it." It wasn't the sort of response to be expected from a finished airplane.

Back on the ground, there was some conversation with Don that revealed several common interests and some other problems with the airplane. While I didn't foresee it at the time, it was the beginning of a consulting relation ship was to last more than 15 years.

I flew back to Brisbane and returned home.

Several months later, with Seabird just a memory, I received a call from Don Adams asking me to return to Australia and look at some additional problems they had discovered with the Sentinel and its evolution, the Seeker, that had an enlarged cockpit pod for better crew comfort on long patrols. The Wankel engine did not have enough power to adequately propel the larger airplane and was replaced by a flat, four-cylinder Lycoming that was initially tested in the Sentinel prototype.

Back in Hervey Bay I found the new Seeker, like the Sentinel, was originally configured with under-wing air inlets for engine cooling and displayed severe cooling problems; it was difficult to complete a circuit of the field without overheating. The wing was positioned on a short pedestal with a somewhat channeled intersection between the wing and the crew pod, leading to low energy, secondary flow into the cooling inlets. Therefore, the first order of business was to

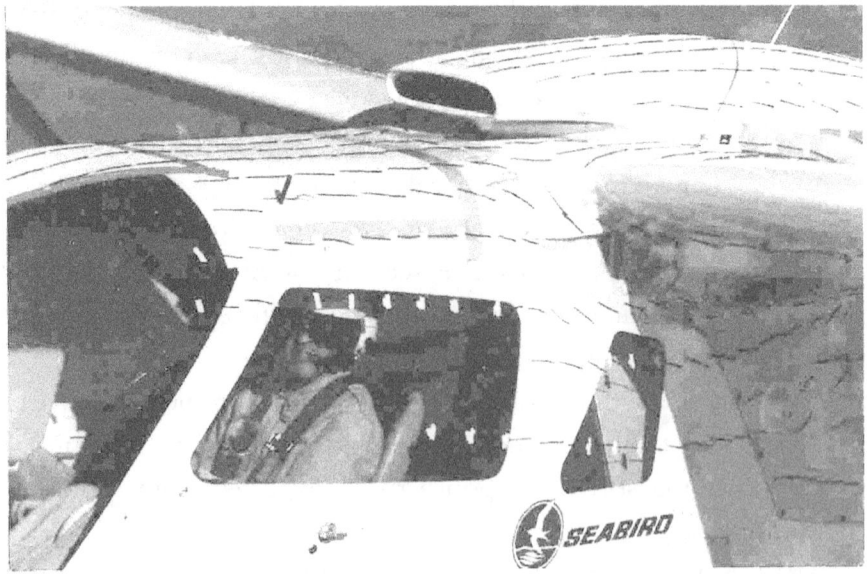

Tuft Testing

improve the engine cooling sufficiently to allow flying long enough to analyze the airplane's problems.

The original engine fairing above the wing offered an ideal opportunity to incorporate an effective diffuser section for maximum pressure recovery. This long run for a diffuser is a luxury never available with a forward engine configuration. The top inlet appeared to solve the cooling problem, and later work confirmed the solution.

Once the cooling problems were solved, there followed many hours of flight work using wool tufts for flow visualization from a second airplane, flying in close formation. The use of short lengths of yarn, attached with tape, is a classical method of determining flow direction and turbulence state for both models and full-scale aircraft. The tufts just forward and below the leading edge of the wing show high angularity with respect to the expected flow pattern and confirmed the poor flow configuration into the original inlet downstream.

On a low-speed airplane, we were able to make many quick

New Wing / Pod Fairing

modifications using Bristol board, tape and modeling clay. Beyond cooling, we undertook to clean up the flow in and around the intersection of the wing and fuselage.

The picture on the prior page shows the resulting fairing, which improved the flow in wing-fuselage junction. The aft-end of the fairing flares outward to form the exit for the engine cooling air. The total drag of the airplane was reduced by about 19% with the fairing in place and the relocated inlet.

Below is a photograph of the finished product and demonstrates

With A Little Paint

what can be accomplished with paint and skillful graphic design. The Bristol board, tape and modeling clay are gone, replaced by structural materials. The airplane is dressed up with a paint format that alters the somewhat ungainly appearance of the geometry, which is the result of 'form-follows-function' necessity.

The picture, opposite page, shows the Seeker at work inspecting a power line at low-level in New South Wales. It performs these tasks at a cost 1/5 to 1/10 the cost of doing the same job with a helicopter.

Seeker At Work

Despite the almost magic rescue work we see on television newscasts, many helicopters seldom use the vertical takeoff and landing capability; insurance for off-airport operations is often prohibitively expensive.

I must not forget to acknowledge the skill and cooperative demeanor of David Eyre, Seabird's company test pilot, picture next page. David flew beautifully executed test runs, repeated through the same altitude bands in opposite directions, to minimize the effects of atmospheric variations. Many would scoff at this boring job of flight testing, but it produced data that earned respectful comments from NASA Dryden engineers, despite the fact that we produced the data using only rudimentary instrumentation: altimeter, temperature and airspeed measurements, plus a stopwatch.

The Seeker went on to certification under U.S. Federal Aviation Administration Part 23 regulations and a checkered financial future involving a regional sale of manufacturing rights to a Malaysian company. There followed the collapse of the East Asian economy and the return of the $2 million Malaysian check.

Shortly after this financial failure, a representative of the King of Jordan appeared and revealed that the King decreed that Jordan

David Eyre (right) And The Author

would develop an aircraft industry. After a long, difficult negotiation, regional manufacturing rights for the European and Middle Eastern markets were acquired by a Jordanian firm founded for the purpose.

After completing this agreement, another snag appeared: The King wanted to acquire two airplanes immediately. The only airplane available was the flight test airplane, Australian registered as VHZIG and known affectionately as 'ZIG.' A second airplane, repurchased from an electric utility and in use for power line patrol, satisfied the King's request. Dismantled, both were shipped to Jordan. Upon arrival, one of the airplanes, fitted with reconnaissance equipment, was given to the then-forming new government of Iraq, as a gift from the King to his new neighbor. Its intended purpose was to serve as the starting point of a new Iraqi Air Force as described in a page from CISR Journal on the opposite page.

Ultimately, the Seabird – Jordanian relationship collapsed for a variety of reasons. An unintended premonition of the future occurred during a telephone call with Peter Adams, who traveled to Jordan to supervise the assembly of the shipped airplanes.. I asked him how things were progressing with the assembly. He replied, in a tired hesitant voice,

"Well, ... we got two tires inflated this morning, but it took until noon and required many people running about frantically, and shouting at one another. We're going tackle another tire this afternoon."

New Iraqi Air Force

I was a bit saddened to see ZIG leave, having spent many hours of flight test time in it. There was compensating satisfaction when the revised cooling system I designed allowed the airplanes to perform well in 130 degree ground temperatures, encountered during desert operations, with only a change to a larger oil cooler.

Finally, the Seabird technology and market rights were acquired by a U.S. Firm, Seabird Aviation America, formed to address Western Hemisphere markets, while manufacturing remained in Australia.

Recently, I found that my old friend, ZIG, injured in an accident some time ago, was successfully repaired and continues to ply the skies of Jordan.

22

Installed Thrust Measurement

e 'Engine Mafia' has pretty much free rein in the aircraft engine business. Enter from outside the fold at yur own risk, and be prepared for war. There was occasional help from the Inner Sanctum: Documents from inside the pale arrived at home addresses in plain envelopes bearing strange postmarks,

* * *

As I near the end of my story, I must deal with an effort for a Canadian Client that occupied a major part of my efforts over nine years of my professional life. It involved measurement of the thrust of jet engines while they were installed in aircraft. Over several years, I have struggled unsuccessfully with how to present this era in an understandable way, without resorting to statistical methods that were the basis of this engine instrumentation. While the *standard distributions, sigmas, and 'R'-values* of statistics are at the heart of the story, an attempt to dig deeply into statistics would not only challenge my statistical knowledge, but would be dull fare for a casual reader. I have elected to concentrate on the technical and political umbrella that shadowed this program with ethical issues.

A Canadian Beginning

As the Hush House program came to a close, Major Capps, the technical monitor in the Pentagon, and I, mutually lamented the end of our technical camaraderie developed over the prior, intense four years. Then he diverted to a different tack. He said,

"You know, it doesn't have to end. There is a company in Canada I've been working with that badly needs your help." He scribbled a phone number on a scrap of paper and said,

"Here, give 'em a call." I did so the following day and gave the gentleman that answered a very brief description of the Hush House program that had been my focus for the prior four years. The reaction was immediate:

"We have to talk. I'll buy you a ticket." It was the beginning of a nine-year Odyssey.

On arrival in Ottawa, I met Julian Romeski, Computing Devices' Marketing Manager for 'Thrust,' the shorthand for activities related to jet engine controls. It was an effort then stirring a contentious pot in the U.S. and Canadian Air Forces and surreptitiously within aircraft engine manufacturers, for more than five years. Julian took me to his office, moved a chair in front of a four-drawer file and said,

"All four drawers are full; read, and tell me what you think." After two days of reading, it was evident Computing Devices (ComDev) was in a difficult position, technically and politically. Their situation had elements of the Hush House program I had just completed, but it was somewhat worse. I had a fortuitous fit with ComDev problems: My recent political experience in the Washington government arena and my participation in the design of the Northrop F-5 fighter. The F-5 was a supersonic evolution of the T-38 trainer, the test bed for ComDev's recent development work with the U.S. Air Force.

Aircraft Engine Politics

When initially engaged by Computing Devices to assist with seeking meaningful U.S government support for *'trimming to thrust installed'*

(Thrust Computing System, TCS), I learned early-on that any related contractual activity would likely pass through the San Antonio Air Logistic Center (SAALC), and procurement of hardware would also be done through SAALC. After four years of Hush House activity I was already well acquainted with SAALC. Tentative explorations with acquaintances there revealed that not only were these events likely, the procurement community at SAALC was already riven with controversy over 'trimming to thrust.' Just how the positive part of the view originated wasn't yet clear, but the aircraft engine industry, ever watchful of its 'catbird seat' in the military business, had 30 – 35 people on their payrolls permanently deployed in residence within SAALC, to assure their interests would always prevail. There would be no working discretely to promote ComDev's interests.

In addition to engineering work, I spent significant effort on countering engine company forces, who were working to undercut this threat to their hallowed replacement engine and parts business. In this process I spoke with many people close to the military aircraft engine business and found opinions ranging from guardedly positive to spirited reluctance to engage in the relationship between engine manufacturers and military users of their product. While memory fails at the task of direct quotation, it might be useful to paraphrase some responses we received.

The Deputy Chief of Staff for Logistics Operations at Headquarters Air Force Logistics Command, Wright-Patterson Air Force Base, Ohio told us:

"The Air Force made a decision back in the 1950s that the turbine business was too complex for a government laboratory presence, so we just monitor what they do, and that's not going to change. The Air Force's interest in the Thrust Computing Program is General Garrison's interest in the Thrust Computing Program, nothing more." More about General Garrison, a key figure, later.

'Mr. Propulsion' at the Naval Air Systems Command, U.S. Navy, Department of Defense, Washington, D.C. Provided a similar response:

"We don't attempt to guide engine development, we just shovel them a bunch of money every year and hope something comes out of it."

Admiral Tom Connolly, now deceased, who worked closely with General Electric to help bring the supersonic Grumman F-14 fighter into the Navy's aeronautical inventory, thought well of the installed thrust computing concept and volunteered to take up the matter with longtime GE friends and supporters. Disappointedly he reported:

"They wouldn't even discuss it."

In a meeting that lasted several hours, the then Controller General of the Air Force – Mr. Money in street parlance – diagnosed the problem as he saw it:

"Your problem is clear; you're stepping on somebody's post-retirement job. I've seen it many times in my 40 years on this job. They retire from Civil Service at age 50 and slip into a high-level job in the industrial sector. It's known as double-dipping."

These comments set the table for my next nine years.

The Engine Business

The economics of the engine business bears some resemblance to the men's razor business: Gillette almost gives you the razor and a few blades. Then you buy more blades forever, at premium cost and they fit only their razor. While the parallels aren't precise, the major source of profit in the engine business is the parts business rather than in the initial sale of the engine. The engine manufacturer's first line of defense of their business model was: The use of any nonstandard part on an engine voids all warranties. Fortunately, the Air Training Command's T-38s, with their General Electric J-85 engines, ComDev's focus, were well beyond warranties. Despite the expired warranties, having an outsider's thrust measurement system installed and field tested on these engines was an unacceptable risk to the entire industry, and they responded forcibly if not visibly.

The primary arrows in our quiver was NASA's enthusiastic support due to successful use of the TCS on a number of experimental flight test programs at its Dryden Flight Test Facility in the California desert.

A Little Background

Trimming to Thrust is fundamentally a problem of statistics and a very brief exposure thereto is essential to understanding the Thrust program. I promise only one diagram and I'll not get into statistics beyond a few superficial examples.

Measure the heights of people in a crowded auditorium or in an entire state or country and plot the sums of people at each height increment against the height will show the individual heights tend to group around a central value. The same might be said of the weights of individual apples in a bag from the grocery. Most of the remainder will spread around this dominant value in a curved pattern termed a 'normal distribution' by statisticians. There will be a few values that don't fit the pattern, often called 'outliers.' The tall distribution in the diagram, following page, while specific to aircraft engines, is typical of a 'normal distribution' and with different numbers could represent any random collection of similar items or devices.

Mass-produced items, while often regarded as 'identical,' will vary slightly from one another depending on the nature of both the process used to manufacture the object and the means of measuring the characteristic of interest: size, weight etc. If we attempt to measure the size of two mass-produced, allegedly identical parts we find them to be slightly different by an amount that depends on both the machine that produced the part and the accuracy of the measuring instrument. If we make the same measurement with a similar but different instrument we will get yet another result: close but different. Expanding the number of parts and/or using different measuring devices, eventually produces a band of measurements, similar to the normal distribution of people described above. The numbers will be very different but will center around some nominal value with a scattering of sizes around that value; yet another normal distribution. Combining many such parts into similar jet engines will yield a varying thrust grouped around a central value and a band of variations around that value, also another 'normal' distribution.

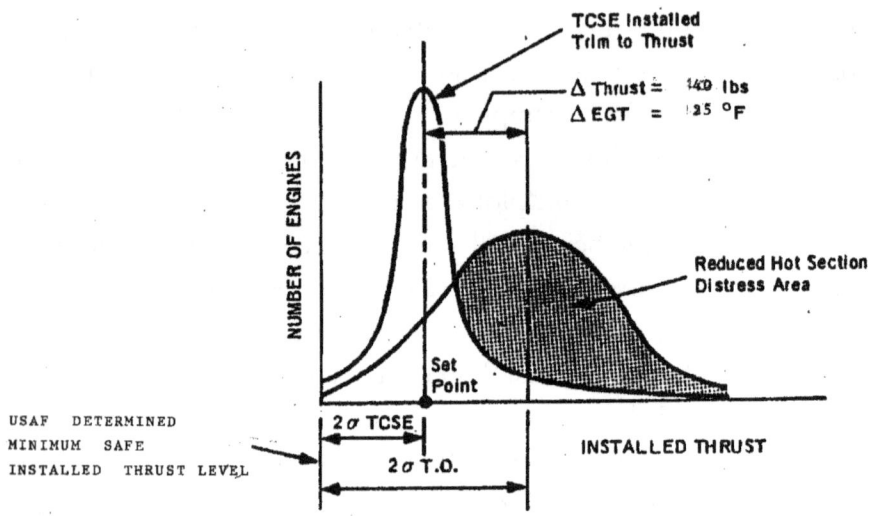

Statistical 'Normal' Thrust Distributions

The tall center plot in the figure above represents a *conceptual sample* of a group of engines with thrust determined by a Trim-to-Thrust computer with the engines installed in an aircraft. At the time of the subject program, the second curve to the right had never been constructed because data for the plot were never recorded – and perhaps never will be – in sufficient numbers for constructing a statistically valid normal distribution. Both curves must meet the USAF Technical Order for minimum installed thrust, the left limit of the plot. Both plots are aligned to their bottom 2 sigma values.

The broader normal distribution on the right, conceptually presents a thrust sample resulting when a bare engine, tested in a remote thrust stand, is installed in an aircraft and its thrust is affected by the airframe's detailed anomalies. While new or overhauled engines are evaluated in thrust stands, the force to drive the airplane must include the losses resulting from the aircraft's inlet and duct system. The installation effects for the T-38 Trainers that were the subjects of Computing Devices' focus, were limited to measurements by the airplane's manufacturer on a single airplane and two new engines some 30 years before. To my knowledge, airframe-to-airframe variations were never addressed by the Air Force.

The plot is presented to support the following discussion and to convey a concept; it does not represent actual data.

Economics of Installed Thrust

In turbine engines, the turbine stages operate very near the metallurgical limits of the materials employed in their construction. Generally, for a given engine, the higher the turbine temperature the greater the thrust; in a sense, temperature is thrust. At these levels, a few degrees temperature reduction can correspondingly reduce the operational cost of purchasing new 'hot parts,' the labor cost of replacing them and testing of the repaired engine. This was the initial driving force behind 'Trimming to Thrust.'

Trimming

A new or newly-overhauled engine is mounted in a test stand and 'trimmed.' To simplify a somewhat complex process, trimming sets the engine fuel control so when the pilot advances the throttle to 100% power, the engine produces the USAF minimum thrust in the above plot and does not exceed the critical temperature of hot section parts. If the figure were to present valid statistical measurements it would consist of data from tens if not hundreds of engines.

At this point life gets complicated. The temperature of exhaust gases passing through the critical turbine blades also exceeds the survivable temperature of sensors to measure temperature. Typically, the sensor is located downstream of the turbine and measures values that are only a related proxy for the higher temperature of interest.

Beyond allowing for installation effects, setting the minimum acceptable thrust is a matter of deciding on the degree of risk involved in at a particular point in flight, usually a takeoff related condition. The USAF minimum acceptable thrust is based on 95% (statistical value approximately 2-sigma in the diagram) of the engines in the population of engines meeting the minimum thrust specification. Once that determination is made, all other engines in the fleet are operating at higher thrust levels and temperatures higher than required, victims of the 'normal distribution. The incentive is to squeeze the more-spreaded distribution of the population (lower curve, right) toward the more compact grouping at the left. Since we have no knowledge of the airframe uncertainties, trimming with thrust measured across the entire flow system is a practical method of removing the airframe uncertainties, squeezing the population to the left and increasing the size of the hatched area in the plot.

The lower curve in the plot must also include the deterioration of the engine population with time in service. The magnitude of this allowance for deterioration rate is linked with the selected time between engine removals and re-trimming to maintain the minimum acceptable thrust levels. Re-trim with installed instrumentation and a small computer in an outdoor parking area could drastically reduce the allowance needed to assure safe thrust levels across the fleet while also reducing the hot-section stress on the fleet's engines.

Trimming to thrust installed, is based on measuring pressures across the propulsion system, from inlet to exit, and eliminates several inherent uncertainties:

- The use of proxy temperature measurement for critical parts
- Airframe-to-airframe difference in inlet performance
- Measurement anomalies between test cells located at different geographical sites.
- Uncertain compensation for engine aging variables.
- In addition, pressure-based measurement can be more compatible with high temperatures

The diagram illustrates how trimming to thrust installed has the potential to reduce the hot-section temperatures of the engines.

At the time of the Thrust program the characteristics of the T-38's duct system was enigmatic. The aircraft manufacturer said the engine inlet performance for its airplanes varies by no more than ½ percent. The Navy's Flight Test Center at Patuxent River, MD told us they "can't even repeat its aerodynamic performance measurements on the same airplane to better than about three or four percent," which is of the same order as my personal experience with aerodynamic measurements. Thus, the entire operational milieu has an element of certainty similar to the tables in a Las Vegas casino. Trimming to thrust with the engine installed in the aircraft eliminates many of these installation uncertainties as the final thrust is rolled-up into a single measurement.

How large is the uncertainty? I asked that question of the U.S. NAVY'S flight test people; here are some answers:

"I had an F-14-D on the stand and only read about 17,000 pounds when I know it should be about 23,000." Another added,

"Some airplanes are sure better than others. There's an F-14-A out there that will almost keep up with the "D"[model] that's powered with the F-110 (a more powerful engine version)."

"I had a couple of F-18s in the ATEF (thrust stand) and the measured thrust wasn't even close."

Deterioration

All engines deteriorate in service and inspection intervals should be coordinated with deterioration rate to meet the acceptable risk level. Trimming installed enables more frequent trimming and enhances flight safety without the cost of removing engines from the aircraft, moving them to a test cell environment, returning and reinstalling. All uncertainties cause all the engines in the sample to be moved rightward and some run at temperatures higher temperatures than needed. The ability to measure thrust of individual engines while installed in the airframe has the potential to have many engines in the sample running at cooler temperatures, with less expenditure of hot parts ... and lowering the engine industry's guarded profits.

Other Imperatives

Currently, engines must be removed and installed in a stationery test cell for trimming. Major downtime and expense is involved in complying with 'the book,' which specifies engines shall be re-trimmed with every 30 degree change in outside air temperature. This is somewhat impractical at the training bases in the U.S. Southwest during winter, where daytime temperature swings often exceed that value. It is unclear just how or whether this requirement is met in normal Training Command operations. Some alleviation may be achieved by concentrating training activity in early morning and late afternoon/evening, but under the best of circumstances some of these 'requirements' push operations to the edges of practical limits.

Improved flight safety could be achieved and much inconvenience avoided by installing the TCS system on the entire engine fleet. Quick re-trim using a portable computer evaluation at the parking ramp would minimize the entire spectrum of variables listed earlier

Flight Safety Issues

The T-38 design dates to the mid 1950s, and its J-85 engine was originally intended for use in a one-flight missile. As a result, early versions used in the Northrop N-156 design were not noted for their durability and were still 'evolving' during the time of early Trim to Thrust/ComDev endeavors. Even with a properly performing engine, the airplane could not accelerate out of ground effect – a lower drag region of flight at an altitude of about half the wing span or less) – after the failure of one engine. If an engine failure occurred just after liftoff (about 110 knots) and before the aircraft reached 180 knots, the airplane could never accelerate and was, in a word trapped in ground effect and would fly on in ground effect until it encountered some durable object.

As of the time of the 'Thrust' program, Computing Devices had developed a working relationship with the U.S. Air Force Training Command at Laughlin Air Force Base using T-38 aircraft. Laughlin was commanded by Gen. Lawrence Garrison, who encouraged the Trim to Thrust explorations by ComDev, likely because of flight safety issues. Later he moved to Air Training Command Headquarters at Randolph AFB, near San Antonio, Texas, where his support of trimming to thrust continued.

This became important because the engine manufacturer's defense against intruders, the warranty shadow, had expired since the T-38 and its engines had been in service for more than 20 years at that time. The airframe manufacturer's claim that the airframe variations 'might be as much as a half of one percent' was somewhat undermined by the Navy's test data. Further, and the current method of thrust setting was based on a single flight-test airplane with two new engines during the late 1950s, hardly valid for a fleet of several hundred airplanes with aging engines overhauled many times since new.

Intermediate Summary

Trimming engines in while installed in aircraft has many potential benefits, all of which could be grouped generally as reducing thrust uncertainty and operational inconveniences. The ComDev group concentrated on refining the statistical algorithms while I worked on political problems.

The statistical work needed more historical trim data, which was denied, perhaps at the behest of the resident engine influence living within the SAALC. As an American citizen I filed a 'Freedom of Information Act' request for the needed data. It was 'slow-walked' through the system and when delivered after some months, was heavily redacted. Some pages were entirely black, save the page numbers, which demonstrated only continuity of pages. The downside, after several years of my involvement was that, despite the positives, we were discovering data that a number of powerful entities didn't want disclosed or discussed.

A Contract

The slow progress turned into frustration. After a swing through Washington political sources, Julian Romeski and I stopped, late in a day, at the office of General Garrison, who had moved into Air Force Headquarters in the Pentagon. The conversation ranged widely; it was after 19:00 and everyone was getting hungry, when Genral Garrison cut to the chase:

"What would it cost to do a Training Command fleet test of 'Thrust?'" Romeski replied,

"Not over $10 million dollars, for a guess." Garrison responded,

"Lets do it; we spill more than that." Although General Garrison was an enthusiastic supporter over many years, he wasn't at the front of a budget battle.

After some work back in Ottawa, it was decided Julian's off-the-cuff estimate was reasonably close, and it was time to visit the people I'd previously worked with in the basement of the Rayburn House of Representatives office building in Washington. We also conducted discussions with the General Accounting Office that were key to getting the Thrust program into the 1982 Budget Bill. While $9-million is a lot of money to most of us, it is 'noise' in the U.S. Budget and we managed to get Thrust 'adjusted' into the 1982 budget.

The following two pages were abstracted from the 1982 House of Representatives budget bill and contains the descriptive language justifying the budget 'adjustment.' The Senate bill simply lists the Thrust programs as a $9-million line item in a summary table.

97TH CONGRESS } HOUSE OF REPRESENTATIVES { REPORT
1st Session No. 97-333

DEPARTMENT OF DEFENSE APPROPRIATION BILL, 1982

NOVEMBER 16, 1981.—Committed to the Committee of the Whole House on the State of the Union and ordered to be printed

Mr. ADDABBO, from the Committee on Appropriations, submitted the following

REPORT

together with

ADDITIONAL VIEWS

[To accompany H.R. 4995]

The Committee on Appropriations submits the following report in explanation of the accompanying bill making appropriations for the Department of Defense, and for other purposes, for the fiscal year ending September 30, 1982.

APPROPRIATIONS AND ESTIMATES

Appropriations for most military functions of the Department of Defense are provided for in the accompanying bill for the fiscal year 1982. This bill does not provide for military assistance, military construction, military family housing, or civil defense, which requirements are considered in connection with other appropriation bills.

The new budget (obligational) authority enacted for the fiscal year 1981, the President's budget estimates, as amended by House Documents 97-29, 97-61, 97-94, 97-101 and Senate Document 97-8, and amounts recommended by the Committee for the fiscal year 1982 appear in summary form in the following table beginning on page 2.

JCS Exercises

The Reagan Administration Budget contained major increases for Joint Chiefs of Staff directed and coordinated exercises. The original budget proposal was to increase the program from the $180 million level in fiscal year 1980 to $483.3 million in fiscal year 1982. The Committee's review of this estimate determined that it would be exceedingly difficult to conduct an exercise program of this size in fiscal year 1982 in lieu of the major increases in other non-JCS directed and coordinated exercises also scheduled. In fact, the original plan was so large that the Military Airlift Command could not fly the entire program and still conduct necessary training and support of the overseas air logistics system. The original plan called for 62,000 C-141 equivalent flying hours of which the MAC was programmed to fly 45,000 with the balance being flown by commercial aviation. Because of the capability problem and the problem of finding suitable host nations in which to conduct some of these exercises, the administration recommended a reduction in September. The Committee has increased $79.4 million reduction in the bill as reported by the Committee transfers the trans-addition and $15.0 million in the Air Force appropriation. In appropriation related funds from the individual military service appropriations to the JCS (Defense Agency) appropriation where they can be managed, supported, and defended by the Joint Chief of Staff.

Thrust Management/Thrust Computing

In January 1981, the Committee asked the General Accounting Office to follow-up on previous efforts by the Defense Audit Service on the use of thrust/power management for jet aircraft. A preliminary report from the General Accounting Office dated October 27, 1981 (B-204813) dealt primarily with one particular system for measuring installed engine thrust. The analysis shows, that accurate measurement in setting of thrust for installed jet engines is of vital importance not only for aircraft readiness and safety, but also for operation and maintenance cost reductions. The Air Force has conducted extensive tests that will measure thrust of installed J85-5 engines but has not implemented a program to do so. The Navy has not performed any test to determine whether its aircraft jet engines might benefit from a similar system. Engines trimmed to minimum required installed thrusts operate at lower temperatures, which increases engine life and improves operational readiness. Also, safety of flight can be enhanced, particularly on take-off, when a mechanic has the ability to readily check and set installed engines to required thrusts.

The Air Force has recently experienced major problems in attempting to deal with the thrust management problem on its highest technology aircraft engine (the F-100) installed in F-15 aircraft. Engine durability has been much lower than expected and the Air Force responded by making a parts-saving, decision to down-rate the F-100 that would produce 96 percent, plus or minus 2 percent of rated thrust. Unfortunately, the Air Force has no simple way to measure the thrust of installed engines and the procedures are difficult. Because of the inability to measure installed thrust, it has been estimated by the Air Force that as many as 15 percent of the F-15 aircraft are operating below the detuned performance levels with some aircraft 15 percent below these levels. At this point, aircraft safety could become a factor.

Based upon extensive testing of the system designed for the J85-5 engine, the Air Force estimates that it could save about $4.7 million annually in hot section parts and probably an equal amount in fuel savings. In addition safety can be enhanced by insuring that no aircraft are operating significantly below performance standards.

Although the Air Force has decided to implement the thrust computing system for its J85-5 engines no funds for this effort were requested in the fiscal year 1982 budget. If funds are not made available soon, the system may never be implemented because the contractor has already waited two years while the Air Force made up its mind on the system. The GAO states that if funding is not provided, "the Air Force will lose millions of dollars already invested in the program in addition to the millions in projected savings, but more importantly, failure to implement the system may reduce aircraft readiness." In view of this situation the Committee has added $9 million to the aircraft modification program to complete the J-85-5 thrust computing work.

The GAO will continue its work in reviewing thrust management, thrust computing and engine monitoring systems for the Committee.

Civilian Personnel

The budget for the Department of Defense proposes a moderate increase in civilian personnel end strength numbers. This is in contrast to a steady decline throughout the decade of the 1970's. The Committee believes that the civilian personnel ceilings have served as a deterrent to the effective and economical execution of the Defense budget. Because of the ceilings, the Department has had to depend on consultant contractors to perform technical engineering and management support services. Efforts in shipyards, depots, and repair facilities appear to be adequately funded but undermanned because of the personnel ceiling.

The responsibility for lower than adequate Defense personnel levels rests with the Administration. The two percent latitude in civilian personnel hiring provided by the Congress would easily allow the Defense Department to man all of its requirements. The Administration, through the OMB, continues to impose artificial ceiling constraints on programs that the Congress has fully funded. An increase of from ten to twenty thousand (10,000-20,000) spaces would allow the Department to perform its mission with no increase in funding and with a corresponding decrease in consulting contracts.

Keeping in mind the Administration's policy of increased Defense readiness, the Committee urges that civilian personnel ceilings for the Department of Defense be eliminated. Otherwise the logic of major funding increases for defense provided in this bill make little sense. Obviously, the amounts requested by the Admin-

The End Of The Road

Like the old song you hear on your way to work in the morning and then persists daylong in your head, the Thrust program continued to haunt me after funding in the U.S. Budget. Embedded engine industry forces began to introduce complications into the application of the hardware ComDev was then building. Setting the thrust line in the figure described earlier became an unbeatable football kicked around by the engine industry.

In an attempt to settle the thrust value to be used in the overall program, five T-38 aircraft were flown to NASA Dryden's thrust stand, located at Edwards Air Force Base in California, to determine the installed thrust of the ten engines. Tests showed the thrusts of their engines varied around an unexpected 10% band and much hand wringing ensued without resolution.

ComDev delivered 400 engine instrumentation kits and 40 computers on time and at the bid price, but they were never installed in aircraft pending a thrust setting, whose numerical value was never settled. After pursuing this product for 15 years, ComDev reluctantly closed this area of business.

Decades Later

After demise of the program, our foreign contacts with Turkey, Greece and Portugal expressed interest in purchasing the Air Force systems for their T-38 fleets. They were rebuffed. Later, some 20 plus years after the program ended, I received a call from a man in Indiana, who said he had just purchased a numbered-lot of 'surplus' at SAALC containing the 40 computers. He wondered whether there was anything valuable in the computers and was told that I would know. I told him there were some Rosemount temperature sensors in each computer worth about $1000 each. However, – with the foreign interest in mind – the real value, perhaps orders of magnitude greater, could be realized only if the engine kits were also included in his purchase. He replied:

"I asked about whether there were any additional parts to the system that might make the computers more valuable. I was told that San Antonio ALC scattered associated engine hardware in a field and drove over them several times with a bulldozer."

It would seem that The Engine Mafia wanted to assure that 'Installed Thrust Measurement' never found a home on a military engine.

23

Kavouras Inc.

An eighteen-year consulting job with many diverse objectives.

* * *

My eighteen year relationship with Kavouras Incorporated was a broad, interesting experience ranging from technical product development in Minnesota to political and physical mining in the subterranean annals of the Federal Government in Washington, DC. This unusual milieu evolved via an attorney I met through another client. He scarcely topped five feet and perhaps didn't. A diminutive figure sitting in an executive chair, his feet swinging as those of a small child, he emphatically told me,

"You have to contact this little outfit out at the airport." Our micro attorney, as we referred to him, dug in his pocket and came up with a scrap of paper he handed to me saying,

"Here's a phone number for their Chief Financial Officer; they're trying to bid for a government contract and they're lost. They need your help; it's called Kavouras Inc." A little background research turned up some basic information.

The company carries the surname of Steven Kavouras, its founder. Its major business activity involves the collection of meteorological data and processing it into visual products for distribution to airlines and television stations across the United States. They are exploring expansion into government markets.

* * *

A Little History

Sitting on his back porch one stormy summer day, Steve Kavouras watched the lightning show of a threatening thunderstorm and thought, 'Wouldn't it be great if people could see this on TV, or even view it as a severe weather warning service?' He sought out the local head of the National Weather Service (NWS) and proposed to design a piece of electronic equipment that would make the NWS data stream available to television stations.

The idea was one of those right-concept-at-the-right-time intersections. The gentleman from the NWS took Steve under his wing and helped him with access to a source of current weather data and related factors involved in working with the government data stream. RADAC was the result, the company's first hardware product. It was sold to television stations and changed the format of television weather presentations from hand-drawn, chalk board drawings, by a father-daughter team, to the live radar presentations we take for granted today.

While RADC appeared in the early years of the personal computer and depended on software Steve developed, the company ultimately shunned the software business and developed software only for use in its own hardware. Steve's business philosophy, simple:

"I want to do hard stuff, both hardware and difficult system integration. Sell software alone and you'll wake up one morning to find some 12 year-old kid, with an Apple, has blown you out of the water." A second principle he espoused was: "You have to make stuff people want, put it in boxes, ship it to them and they'll send you checks."

* * *

In the Beginning

The following day I called the number; Dennis Sanford, the company's CFO, answered immediately. Using the micro attorney as a reference, I explored the issue of their upcoming technical proposal.

"Have you constructed a 'shall-list'?" I asked.

"What's a shall-list?" he replied. I explained to him the word *shall* has a legal meaning in government solicitations and the evolving contracts.

"*Shalls* denote issues a company *must* address in its proposal responding to the solicitation. In fact, there is a Military Specification defining the words *shall, will, should* and *may*."

"When can you come out here? We have to talk," was his response.

It was the beginning of a consulting relationship that lasted 18 years and ranged far beyond meteorology. Dennis and I hit it off well; we worked day and night for several weeks to develop a proposal answering the government's solicitation and resulted in the company's first government contract.

A sporadic series of small jobs developed in the beginning years of consulting activity with Kavouras. I never met the company's founder and President, Steve Kavouras, during this time. Steve was somewhat reclusive, spending much of his time in his windowless office quietly hatching new-product ideas. When he appeared, he was an imposing figure. Six feet four or five inches tall and broad-shouldered, he sported a shock of black hair and a neatly-trimmed, black beard. When annoyed, his dark eyes were often indicators of his current demeanor and flashed a warning.

He was a prolific producer of ideas and had a small clique of trusted employees who seemed to compose an informal advisory board that passed judgment on his latest brainstorm. To these people he was a close friend; to other employees he was an enigma, feared by some, but not without good reason. Steve worked incessantly; the eight-hour day was a rare occasion. I worked with his staff or technical people and was not concerned with his idiosyncrasies.

For several years I received the occasional call to develop some computer software or work on a political problem in Washington; it was interesting work, near home and filled-in between jobs in Washington, Canada, Europe and the Middle East.

As I passed her desk one day, Steve's secretary stopped me and said,

"Steve wants to see you in his office as soon as possible." As I walked toward the secluded office, I reviewed recent events attempting to recall what might be the reason for this unusual summons. Termination of my consulting activities crossed my mind as a possibility as I knocked on his office door.

"Come in," came the response.

I entered; Steve extended his hand and offered me a chair. We faced one another for a few awkward moments.

"I understand your wife has a health problem," he began. I acknowledged that she did.

"What kind of health insurance do you have?"

"I have the best Blue Cross policy I can buy as an individual," I replied, "but with health insurance you never know what you have until you use it."

Steve waved away my response and took a different tack.

"Look," he said, "I'm putting you on staff here with a salary of $1000 per month, effective today. I don't want you to change anything you do; bill us for your time in excess of the salary, as you always have. I want to be sure you're well covered, and the salary will put you on our insurance program." I was speechless but managed to mutter a weak 'thank-you,' a miserable response for such a magnificent gesture. Steve continued,

"Don't alter your activities; I know you're always running around the world, and I want you to continue to do those other things as long long as you can find some time for us along the way." We shook hands on that basis.

As I walked away from his office, my thoughts turned to Dennis. He likely had a hand in my change of status. As Chief Financial Officer of the company, he had a reputation for wise frugality that kept the ship of state both successful and solvent. Further, only Dennis knew me well at the time. Upon reflection, it occurred to me this welcome and expensive gesture probably involved both men.

Bag Man

VP Government Programs

VP Business Development

Our working relationship blossomed and broadened in many directions. I became a sort of 'Jack-of All-Trades,' taking on tasks others couldn't or didn't want to do. Eventually, I acquired a private office with telephone answering services that provided a base for all my business activities. I accumulated stacks of business cards depicting me as 'Vice President' of whatever the immediate impending assignment required. In general terms, the work was technical at the outset, but it expanded in the direction of the Washington political scene from time to time.

Politics and Such

The National Weather Service was the major source of meteorological data, the Federal Communications Commission controlled the communication frequency spectrum the company used to deliver its radar products, the Federal Aviation Agency controlled the operating world of many of its customers, and the Department of Defense was the umbrella for weather-users in the Army, Navy and Air Forces. In short, there was plenty to do in Washington.

Historically, this was 'Clinton time' and a difficult period for Steve, whose political instincts were very conservative. A particular thorn was his local Congressional Representative, Martin Sabo, who was a liberal Democrat. Since I was often in Washington for other reasons, I began to stop-by Sabo's office to make Kavouras Inc. known to Sabo. Eventually, I struck up an amiable relationship with Sabo's Legislative Assistant that was useful in ways other than Kavouras business. It enabled me to get a Congressional signature on anything needed a high level push. I wrote many 'poison pen' letters for Kavouras, and Sabo 'signed' them. Most political offices in Washington have 'signing machines,' a pantograph-like device that holds a pen and 'remembers' hand motions for duplication. Many of my missives were so treated.

Bag Man

To get any real attention in the halls of Congress requires – you guessed it – money, and this created a problem for Steve: He just couldn't go to some political soiree and hand a check to his Democrat Congressman. As a result, this became one of my occasional chores. Some of these fundraisers occurred in downtown Minneapolis hotels, while for reasons unknown – a mailed solicitation perhaps – I would sometimes carry a check to Washington to deliver in-hand to the Congressman's Legislative Assistant.

This manner of contribution was effective for me because I needed general political contacts for many reasons. Handing a check to a

Congressman's high-level staffer somehow left the impression that the Congressman was but one of Kavouras' many benefactors. The relationship was effective and was sustained by a short luncheon meeting and a bit of political conversation now and then.

Technical Work

When I arrived on the scene, Dennis Sanford was struggling with the company's first attempt to tailor the RADAC to meet a government solicitation. After winning this contract, airline interest heightened in having continuous weather displays available for flight planning and crew insight into the weather expected on a pending flight. This, in turn, led to a flight planning division, which catered to smaller airlines and operators of corporate aircraft.

Flight planning combined the company's copious weather data with aircraft performance as a function of load, speed, temperature, pressure-altitude and fuel burn-rate. Aircraft manufacturers presented these data in the form of books and tables organized along lines of flight parameters. I saw all this tabular data in a different light.

Having spent some time in the flight test business, I knew a bit about how this tabular data was created. By applying regression analysis techniques, I reduced the tabular data to a few mathematical equations that described each airplane's performance. An additional benefit was that data from the describing equations sorted out errors in the tabular data. The occasional erroneous values in the tables appeared as individual statistical outliers when we plotted the data to check its validity.

Radar

The flight planning business was interesting but was 'selling data' and conflicted with Steve's interest in 'doing the hard things.'

Portable X-band Radar

The company's focus naturally turned toward controlling the source of the radar data the company received from the Weather Service: Steve wanted his own radar. The beginning was modest. Kavouras pur-chased small, X-band radars and packaged them onto trailer-borne systems using extensible arm supports that allowed rapid deployment in a variety of field operations. Proposed to various military organizations they elicited some interest, but the desire for better performance led to the design of a family of radars of varying dish sizes, deployed in several overseas military locations such as Iraq, Jordan and China, for weather observation and prediction. The Jordanian facility supported cloud seeding operations with the aim of enhancing rainfall prediction for improved agricultural production in a dry climate.

Portability requirements led to the design of a six-foot dish-support yoke, light in weight while retaining the stiffness required for unsheltered operation. The arms of the yoke were shell struc-

Six-foot Portable (Iraq)

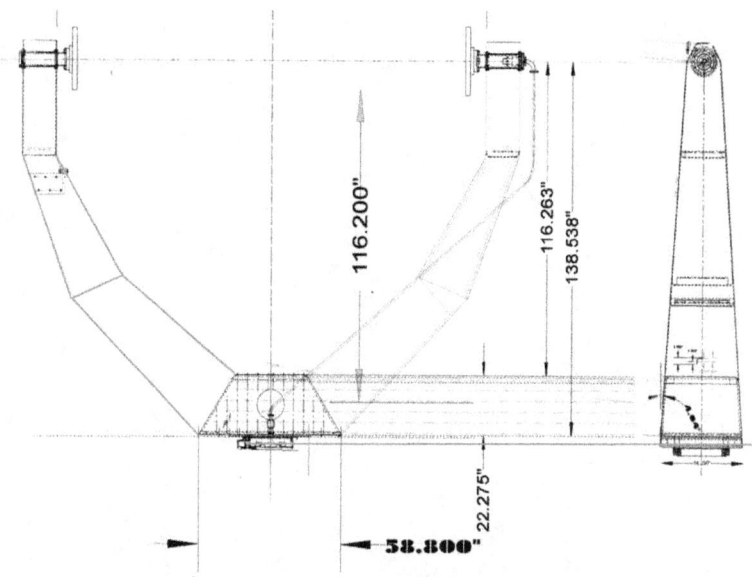

14' Radar Yoke Design

tures that carried loads at the outer extremities with minimal internal supporting components. Bolted to a center section, the arms could be disassembled for compact air shipment.

After completing the design of the six-foot dish support frame, I explored a variety military agencies for potential applications. While the concept of a small, quickly deployable radar was well received, the need for better sensitivity was evident from these contacts. This led to duplication of the dish support yoke in 10' and 14' sizes.

Then, the need for increasing the radiated power became evident – not a simple electronic problem. An experienced radar designer was necessary because the company couldn't afford to build an entire supporting radar division; He/she had to 'do it all:' without training; the ability to produce from the first day was essential.

Consulting professional society journals I identified a possible candidate working at a small electronic firm in a rural Alabama town. To avoid possible legal complications related to 'stealing' employees, I ran a descriptive ad for a

Ten and Fourteen Foot Radar Dishes

radar designer in a small, rural, weekly newspaper and waited. The ad had everything but this man's name on it. Within a week an envelope arrived with the proper return address. Despite some personal idiosyncrasies, we hired Paul Croft. It worked out well: the right man for the time.

A Million Watts

Applying his extensive radar design experience interwoven with Steve's business objectives, Paul proposed several designs. With more study and discussions, we settled on a difficult objective. In accordance with Steve's business philosophy of 'doing hard things:' a million watt transmitter became the objective.

The prototype modulator appears opposite. To dissipate heat, the electronic package cooled in a circulating oil bath approximately 2-1/2 ft. x 6 ft. x 2-1/2 ft. deep. The red

Kavouras Incorporated

Experimental Power Supply

frame around the oil bath is support for a winch arrangement to raise and lower the experimental electronic components into the oil bath.

With the power supply under way, the company had all the major components of its own radar, either in manufacture or in laboratory testing, but it lacked a field testing site. Experimental convenience led to a decision to build a tower for the antenna dish and its mechanisms, adjacent to the corporate headquarters building in a South Minneapolis suburb.

The Tower

The proposed tower height (about 100 ft.), when combined with Minnesota winter weather and winds, presented problems of safety and personal comfort. Climbing and frequent access, essential for research activity, via an open tower structure, was almost inconceivable. To explore other options I went back to my old client, Brown-Minneapolis Tank.

Radar Tower Placement

BMT built the tower in two major sections using automated welding equipment that produces cylindrical tank sections. Open cylinders, rolled from flat steel stock, rotated past a stationery arc-welding sta-- tion to join the segments. This allowed constructing a 100 ft. tower for about the same same cost as the open-structure towers often seen in power line and communication industries. In addition to the obvious comfort and safety factors over open structures, BMT added an interior, circular stairway with a railing, wind-ing helically along the interior walls of the tower for easy access to the work area.

Tower Assembly

The cylindrical section was capped by a work room, an exterior catwalk, the radar dish and a radome. A buried, multi-ton concrete ballast supported the entire assembly and resisted overturning wind forces. The assembly of major sub-components is shown opposite and on following pages.

Setting On Base

Catwalk Placement

Radar Dish In Place

Radome Placement

The completed tower is shown on the following page.

Completed Radar Tower

A Final Task

While smaller, day-by-day tasks persisted for 18 years, the last memorable job I did for Kavouras involved a major sea voyage: RIMPAC 96. RIMPAC (Rim of the Pacific) is a cooperative military exercise held biennially during summer months. The first such drill was held in 1971 with Australia, Canada, New Zealand, the United Kingdom (U.K.) and the United States (U.S.) participating. In later years, the list has expanded to include forces from Central and South America, Europe, some Scandinavian countries and in 2016, China. The objective of the exercise is improve the interoperability of the forces of countries located on the shores of Pacific Ocean. Now held biennially on even-numbered years, RIMPAC 96 was conducted in June of 1996. It is traditionally hosted by the United States Navy operating out of Pearl Harbor, Hawaii. Kavouras, with its worldwide meteorological capability, was invited to provide weather forecasting for the 1996 operation. Steve seized the opportunity for a bit of public relations activity and asked me to join the Command Ship of the U.S. Third Fleet, the USS Coronado, on its return voyage from Pearl Harbor. Several experiments conducted during the nine-day trip, required close coordination with Kavouras' meteorological staff in Minneapolis.

While our operations went well, RIMPAC 96 had an ignominious distinction in the RIMPAC series. A Japanese cruiser shot down a U.S. aircraft, when the ship's gunners focused on the tow-plane rather than the towed target. Fortunately, both crew members of the aircraft ejected and survived.

For me, the voyage was both a technical exercise and a pleasure trip. Due to the time differences between Minneapolis and the moving position of the ship, I had some very late night work coordinating the transfer of meteorological data. However, I had a private cabin that allowed a nap now and then.

The weather office on the top deck had a porthole, one of two on the entire ship – the admiral had the other – that provided a view of miles and miles and little else, as the sea was calm during the entire, nine-day voyage.

Although there were three separate mess halls on the ship, serving a crew of more than 700, I was invited to eat in the admiral's mess, adjacent to his cabin. The evening meal was special and formal: fresh flowers on the tables, place cards and a seating chart that changed every day. The dynamic seating allocation assured the ship's officers and guests had an opportunity to expand acquaintances and to engage in a semi-private conversation with the admiral at least once on the voyage.

Always punctual, the admiral stepped out of his cabin at 18:00 – don't be late – and set the tone for the meal with a beginning note that always began with:

"Another fine day at sea," and then called on one of the ship's officers for a prayer, which always included a request to God for a safe passage.

The exquisite cuisine was prepared by the admiral's personal chef, working in a kitchen about six by eight feet in size. Working alone, he began with an early-morning offering of freshly prepared rolls or other pastries and the good food continued to flow from the miniature kitchen all day.

The Admiral presented the cook's Philippine origin as a universal tradition at his rank, an object of pride and a not-so-friendly competition among flag officers. When I commented on his wonderful culinary endeavors, the admiral launched into a lengthy tirade about how hard he struggled to get this man on his staff, and how difficult it is was to retain him.

The cook's Philippine origin was traditional, almost a given, and inserted rarity into the competition at the outset. With the enlisted man's rank and salary topped-out by regulation, the Admiral gave much time and thought to what unique, but legal 'perks' he could offer to make the cook's service-life interesting.

The length of our nine-day voyage to San Diego was the result of the failure of one of the ship's main, steam-driven turbines. Not to worry; the ship contained a fully equipped machine shop. The crew dismantled the turbine down to the individual parts, diagnosed the problem, then rebuilt it while we proceeded on course, albeit at reduced speed. I spent some interesting times marveling at the competence of these young crew members as they machined the required repair parts from raw materials carried aboard.

* * *

Epilogue

In writing this segment of the foregoing narrative, I sought some pictures that were difficult to locate and asked Steve if he could find the photos I needed. He spent several days searching his files to provide them. I am indebted to him for his dedicated assistance.

Upon receiving the photos, I sent him a note of thanks. He responded with the most heartening professional communication I've ever received. It read:

"Thanks Back To You Dick,

Thanks for:
- being a mentor (*he is about 25 years younger than I am*)
- knowing what made me tick
- always watching my back
- being someone I could always trust
- maintaining the humor during bad stuff
- handling the sticky stuff

Steve."

* * *

What better way to finish a career.

About The Author

Richard J. (Dick) Reilly grew up in 'Hokah,' a small, Southern Minnesota, rural town named after a Sioux Indian Chief. After primary and secondary education in local schools, under the tutelage of the School Sisters of Notre Dame, he enrolled in the Aeronautical Engineering program at the University Minnesota, receiving a Bachelor of Science degree in 1951. After two years of postgraduate work, he began a professional career that spanned the aeronautical sciences, including basic research in boundary layer flow, high altitude research using free-flying balloons and engineering flight test work on general aviation airplanes, supersonic military aircraft and instrumentation for the U.S.'s first manned space flight.

After 18 years working within corporate structures, he began a 30-year consulting career reaching across 16 countries on five continents. Project work focused primarily on the aeronautical sciences and basic physics. He worked with a variety of corporate, international and government organizations, including the Advisory Group for Aerospace Research and Development (NATO), NASA and as guest lecturer at MIT, Penn State, Stanford University, Middle East Technical University, the University of Minnesota and universities in most of the NATO countries.

Reilly holds 16 patents in the general areas of aerodynamics, fluid power, control systems and computing devices.

www.ingramcontent.com/pod-product-compliance
Lightning Source LLC
Chambersburg PA
CBHW061434180526
45170CB00004B/1411